# ONLIFE CRIMINOLOGY

# New Horizons in Criminology series

Series Editor: **Andrew Millie**, The Open University, UK

---

*New Horizons in Criminology* provides concise, authoritative texts which reflect cutting-edge thought and theoretical development with an international scope. Written by leading authors in their fields, the series has become essential reading for all academics and students interested in where criminology is heading.

## Out now in the series:

*Island Criminology*
**John Scott and Zoe Staines**

*Visual Criminology*
**Bill McClanahan**

*Redemptive Criminology*
**Aaron Pycroft** and **Clemens Bartollas**

*A Criminology Of Narrative Fiction*
**Rafe McGregor**

*Transnational Criminology*
**Simon Mackenzie**

*Wildlife Criminology*
**Angus Nurse** and **Tanya Wyatt**

*Imaginative Criminology*
**Lizzie Seal** and **Maggie O'Neill**

*A Criminology of War?*
**Ross McGarry** and **Sandra Walklate**

Find out more at
**bristoluniversitypress.co.uk/new-horizons-in-criminology**

NEW HORIZONS IN CRIMINOLOGY

# ONLIFE CRIMINOLOGY

## Virtual Crimes and Real Harms

Janos Mark Szakolczai

BRISTOL
UNIVERSITY
PRESS

First published in Great Britain in 2025 by

Bristol University Press
University of Bristol
1–9 Old Park Hill
Bristol
BS2 8BB
UK
t: +44 (0)117 374 6645
e: bup-info@bristol.ac.uk

Details of international sales and distribution partners are available at bristoluniversitypress.co.uk



British Library Cataloguing in Publication Data
A catalogue record for this book is available from the British Library

ISBN 978-1-5292-3590-6 hardcover
ISBN 978-1-5292-3592-0 ePub
ISBN 978-1-5292-3593-7 ePdf



Cover design: Bristol University Press
Front cover image: Alamy/Jochen Tack
Bristol University Press uses environmentally responsible print partners.
Printed and bound in Great Britain by CPI Group (UK) Ltd, Croydon, CR0 4YY

Bristol University Press' authorised representative in the European Union is:
Easy Access System Europe, Mustamäe tee 50, 10621 Tallinn, Estonia,
Email: gpsr.requests@easproject.com

FSC
www.fsc.org
MIX
Paper | Supporting responsible forestry
FSC® C013604

To Effe
And our children,
Who sang while I typed,
Who suggested when I asked,
Who laughed in communal despair,
May I return this time for the effort of thee.

# Contents

# Series Editor Preface

*Professor Andrew Millie, Department of Social Policy and Criminology, The Open University, UK*

Recent years have witnessed a blurring between our day-to-day real-world existence and our online presence. We live our lives both online and offline, switching between the two and often interacting with both at the same time. Talk of a metaverse and an Internet of things further blurs these boundaries. In this way it makes less sense to have a neat divide between what is real and what is virtual. Instead, by drawing on Luciano Floridi and colleagues (2015), we can think in terms of an 'Onlife' existence, both online and real life, one impacting the other in a hyperconnected reality. In this important book Janos Mark Szakolczai develops this idea and applies it to criminology. While there have been books on cybercriminology, Janos takes this further by considering the harms and/or crimes that are possible in an Onlife world, in those blurred spaces between real world and online world.

Books in the New Horizons in Criminology series provide concise authoritative texts that reflect cutting-edge thought and theoretical developments in criminology and are international in scope. The aim is for them to be written so that the non-specialist academic, student, or practitioner can understand them by explaining ideas clearly before going deeper into the subject. This is the approach Janos has taken with this book. It starts by looking at the evolution of the internet in Chapter 1, from a utopian space to one where there is control, harm, and criminality. The second chapter introduces us to the concept of the 'captaverse', where the capturing of others' data is all important, despite the possibility that this may be harmful, or even criminal. The discussion is taken further in Chapter 3 by looking at surveillance, privacy, and security.

For many of us, our day-to-day lives are impacted by our interactions with social media. At the time of writing, the ownership and control of social media companies is a major concern for many, as are the use and misuse of data, the algorithms that expose users to unpleasant content, the general toxicity of platforms in terms of language and misinformation, and the risk of stalking, trolling, and generally harmful discourse. Much of what we experience on social media is therefore of criminological interest and Janos explores this in depth in Chapter 4. For Chapter 5 the focus is corporate-level harm and criminality, from the in-built obsolescence of tech, through to the control and abuse of staff in a gig economy with harms straddling both our online and offline existence.

Chapter 6 explores the misinformation and conspiracy theories that populate the Onlife, including the alt-right and QAnon. The focus is the content-based harms fsed by trolling, doxxing, and stalking. For Chapter 7 the discussion moves to the use of AI, deepfakes, and the 'perpetual threat to the distinction between reality and the digital world'. It is tempting to see our Onlife future as dystopian as there is increased blurring between what is real and imagined, between what is factual and fake. Yet, Janos concludes by considering 'some small, albeit significant, proactive and resilient means to improve the Onlife', including our right to be ignored and promoting the Onlife as art, not merely as a somewhere we must survive or escape.

This is a very timely book. It is a new horizon for criminology, but also one that is applicable to the daily lives of so many of us. It is theoretically sophisticated and provocative, yet also highly readable. It is highly recommended reading for criminologists, but also for anyone interested in our contemporary and future social problems, including those in sociology, anthropology, digital humanities, or elsewhere.

# Acknowledgements

This book is the conclusion of my doctoral thesis and the realization that something is missing and needs to be added to the understanding of contemporary criminology – especially from a cultural angle. As such, I need to thank yet again (and over and over) my doctoral supervisors Maggie O'Neill and Tom Boland for their support and my external examiner Majid Yar for making so much effort to make sense of my lifetime dedication.

Writing, however, would have not been possible without the endless prompts of my series editor, Andrew Millie, and of my Criminology colleagues at the University of Glasgow and the welcoming 'Ivy Lodge' encounters with other Scottish Centre for Crime & Justice Research (SCCJR) members, doctoral researchers, and aficionados (including Ryan Casey, William Webster, Mike Nellis, Steve Kirkwood, Ben Collier, Richard Jones, and many others).

Broadly, within the University of Glasgow, I am grateful for the stimulating collegial support, and exchange of ideas, comments, and sources with Les Back, Bridgette Wessels, Andrew Hoskins, Bridget Fowler, Lluis de Nadal Alsina, Mark McGill, Stephen Brewster, Matt Dawson, Alessandro Vinciarelli, and Catherine Happer.

Even more broadly, I am truly grateful for the email exchanges and note-filling conversations over the years with Geert Lovink, Katja Franko, Keith Hayward, Anita Lavorgna, Dario Melossi, Alan Levinovitz, Marco Antônio Sousa Alves, Giovanni Ziccardi, and, finally, to close the circle, Luciano Floridi, who kindly allowed me to borrow and play around with his personally and professionally (on)life-changing term.

1

# Introduction: Terms for Unprecedented Consent

## Criminology of the hyperconnected life

The ambiguity of contemporary life constantly tackles the existence of 'reality' and the multiple dimensions of its 'essence'. Our Globalized technocracies are fundamentally shared within an online, internet-induced, digital, and, especially 'virtual' world, combined with concrete, 'in real life' (IRL), away-from-keyboard (AFK), and 'meatspace' existence. Mireille Hildebrandt's work emphasizes that our real lives are neither solely online nor offline, highlighting a blended existence that we are still in the process of understanding (Hildebrandt, 2015: 42). Hildebrandt asserts that we are transitioning from an information society to a data-driven society, which has significant implications for the world we rely on, underscoring the extensive use of machine-learning technologies that drive data-driven agency, posing threats to privacy, identity, autonomy, non-discrimination, due process, and the presumption of innocence. For Luciano Floridi, hyperconnected human societies are becoming more and more similar to 'mangroves growing in brackish water' (Floridi, 2020: 1). This is the fundamental basis of the *Onlife Manifesto*, edited by Floridi in 2015, and is a central reference of this book. As coined by Floridi, the term 'Onlife' is a blending of the words 'online' and 'life', implying 'the new experience of a hyperconnected reality within which it is no longer sensible to ask whether one may be online or offline' (Floridi, 2015: 1). Floridi and his colleagues drew inspiration from Hannah Arendt's *The Human Condition* (1958) to explore how information and communication technologies (ICTs) interact with public spaces and contemporary life (Simon and Ess, 2015). To go 'offline', users may no longer unplug their devices or leave them at home, as was already observed in 2014 by the magazine *The New Yorker* (Cep, 2014); rather, our existences are loaded regardless in webpages, pictures taken of us and shared among endless groups, and content produced, replicated, modified, and regenerated.

Similarly, crime and criminality impact everyday life in ways that fall within the spectrum of both cyber-related crimes and traditional in-person offences. Founding cybercrime scholar Karuppannan Jaishankar defined cybercriminology as 'the study of causation of crimes that occur in the cyberspace and its impact in the physical space' (2007, para 1), and this powerful force is increasingly central when defining the hyperconnected existence of the contemporary age.

In 2015, the *Onlife Manifesto* was already discussing the sociological, ethical, and legalistic implications of what this hyperconnected age means and what its legacy will be. A decade later, the impact of crimes and the recurrence of harms, focusing on the tools, means, and rhetoric behind the systems and platforms Onlife users interact with daily as part of their very existence, will be discussed in this book. This existence experiences greater and greater subjectification, surveillance, and control, but also the escalation of toxic discourse, hate speech, armed responses, and the overall systematic, endemic, endless exploitation of the diminishing resources of our world and what is 'real'.

This work offers promising research, observing not only the criminal elements that characterize the Onlife scenario, where the cyber impacts the physical, but approaches these from a zemiological perspective, proposing a specific scenario for studying digital or Onlife harms. Digital harm has been theorized in the work, among others, of Mark A. Wood (2022), recognizing 'the need to go beyond cybercrime' necessity. This work wishes to combine the elements of cyber harm with a novel conceptualization of the culture surrounding the causation of harm.

## The context of this study

The essence of Onlife's hyperconnected existence lies in the multi-layered interaction of users across various platforms. However, these layers initially appear one-dimensional. Users directly interact with peers, purchase goods globally, consult public reviews, stream live debates, and engage with instant content. These are straightforward, often public forms of interaction. Nonetheless, a significant amount of 'background' activity supports these everyday instances. This 'behind the scenes' aspect of Onlife is inherently multi-dimensional. This book explores these background elements, specifically focusing on the cryptic workings, consequential harms, and crimes that occur without users' knowledge. These harms are primarily corporate, embedded (sometimes intentionally, sometimes incidentally) within platform designs, and they directly and indirectly impact individuals' daily lives.

Much of the focus of the book is the decade between 2014 and 2024, which entailed a fundamental change in our relation to technology, particularly digital and smart media. Indeed, since the publication of the *Onlife Manifesto,* this is the age characterized by the aftermath of the 2014 Snowden Revelations, the 2016 Brexit referendum, Donald Trump's 2016 election, the Cambridge Analytica scandal (2015), the Hong Kong Umbrella protests (2014), the COVID-19 pandemic, the effects of the highly (social-medialized) war in Ukraine, especially from 2022 onwards, and the advent of mass-use, generative artificial intelligence (AI) since 2023. In particular, the effect of the COVID-19 pandemic on hyperconnectivity, digital citizenship, and smart-working has fostered the conditions for the 'Onlife', turning it into a matter not simply of the Global North but embracing the globe in general. This has altered our relation to crime, deviance, its control, and the related harms. But here is the twist of my interpretation: much of what I highlight is not specifically harmful or criminal, and thus it has turned elusive so far from most tribunals. It has also hindered all major forms of stop, boycott, and closure. Serious response has been complex and difficult for so long, I argue, because the design of the apps, the structure of the platforms, the sense of their influence and the nature of their investments, development, and experience are ambiguous and, in many ways, cryptic. As Mireille Hildebrand argues in the *Onlife Manifesto* (2015), hyperconnectivity may act as a 'pharmakon', depending on the quantities, it cures or poisons. Within criminology, I would argue it acts more like a 'nocebo': the opposite of a placebo, a substance of reality, a new reality that is doing nothing bad – until it is.

## Summary of the book's themes

The Onlife, as such, is a complex yet holistic structure: information and users are channelled, metrics calculated, and environments controlled. The information highways conceived by Bill Gates in the mid-1990s have become increasingly inclusive and overarching within a system not simply of information but one influencing users' existence (1995).

The 1993 notorious *New Yorker* comic strip of a dog sitting by a computer and claiming 'On the internet, nobody knows you're a dog' was, twenty years later, re-edited with a more delusional 'Remember when, on the internet, nobody knew who you were?' What would be a fitting joke today? Perhaps nothing too funny. With Apple commercials for the 2024 Olympics depicting anachronistic bird-like closed-circuit television (CCTV) cameras gazing menacingly into users' phones – and thus replicating the eternal trope of potential 'privacy-breaches luring users everywhere' – the Onlife recreates a channel of interaction where external influence and imposition are frighteningly applicable. Of course, internet connection is far from being a functioning apparatus across every part of the globe. However, cheaper microchips and increasing satellite connections bring such a reality closer. More than that, depending on the government and regime, the spread of Onlife interactions within an individual's everyday life takes control of one's ideology, finances, interests, whereabouts, and, ultimately, moods and perhaps even thoughts. The claim of everything now being vulnerable as argued by Nicole Perlroth (2021) is more and more evident by the apparent ease with which Russian hackers may access nuclear plants, aeroplane black boxes, and presidential elections at any given time, with zero-day menaces (previously unknown software vulnerabilities) compiled into the flawed operating systems we so much rely on.

Corporations seem aware of the influential implications of the Onlife as well. Take another Apple advertisement, the 2024 iPad Pro 'crush'. With scary confidence, we are presented with a giant press that 'crushes' material objects of human engagement, from saxophones to LPs, arcade games, paints, newspapers, scripts, and a guitar, compacting it all into a new, shiny, smart device. In that tool, all this new set of information can be stored – from our music to our thoughts (I *am* writing an early draft of this text on my iPad Pro's Notes app), as well as our memories, our biometric data, our screen time habits – putting into practice, day by day, what Naomi Klein, writing for *The Intercept* in 2020, cautioned as the 'Screen New Deal', where 'every move, our every word, our every relationship is trackable, traceable, and data-mineable by unprecedented collaborations between government and tech giants' (2020). But surely we have all sorts of privacy rules that offer confidence in the protection of the realm of the human mind that is now stored in apps, and thus on remote cloud systems, on offshore servers, to which no company has actual knowledge as to where all the information is and how it is stored.

On the other hand, Nayib Bukele, the controversial head of state of El Salvador since 2019, is pushing cryptocurrency into the transactional mindset of Global South citizens, proposing digitalization as an effective model to free oneself from imperialist domination – which sounds all fair and good until the complexities of such a highly experimental world strike back with another form of tech-based domination – similar to the new panoptic means of colonialism and the caste system in India as highlighted in the ongoing research of lawyer and scholar Nikita Sonavane (2023).

In a further combination of these scenarios, Bhalla and Harrisberg of Context.News (part of the Reuters Foundation) reported in 2022 that citizens in the Global South have been granted increased security through covert surveillance. This monitoring often involves facial recognition cameras provided as goodwill gifts by Chinese and Taiwanese manufacturers. These surveillance systems, deployed widely across continents (Bhalla and Harrisberg, 2023; Langa, 2024) may subtly serve an additional purpose: refining AI algorithms to address the well-documented racial biases in biometric systems (Sumsion et al, 2024). But the problematic techno-bias works just as surreptitiously in the Global North, worryingly merging humans with machines. For example, in the US, a Michigan resident, Robert Julian-Borchak Williams, was wrongfully detained in Detroit after facial recognition technology misidentified him as a suspect in a theft case (Hill, 2020), while, in the UK, the Surveillance Camera and Biometrics Commissioner, Fraser Sampson, noted in 2021 how an unknowing citizen had the logo on her jumper misread as a licence plate by an ANPR (Automatic Number Plate Recognition) camera and sent a fine to a driver hundreds of kilometres away (BBC News, 2021), confirming the long debate that 'having done nothing wrong' is far from being (if it ever was) a justification from the endless assemblage of surveillance (Sampson, 2021).

As such, the 'Onlife' does appear as a new, polished, and shiny titanium cage (the preferred material top end smart devices) as opposed to the rational iron box/cage envisioned by Max Weber, to which there seems to be little alternative. Of course, there are modes of action, resistance, and liberation, but these are interestingly considered as deviant perspectives – through so-called 'dark-web' navigation, hacker forums, Tor and Pirate Bay enthusiasts (Collier, 2024) – underlying significant criminological angles that are just on the verge of study. As such, to be part of the Onlife, one becomes a subject; to resist one becomes a deviant: in between, there may be space for discussion.

In detail, Chapter 1 explores the contemporary Onlife scenario, tracing the internet's evolution from a utopian space to a controlling institution and defining key terms such as crime, harm, cybercriminality, and digital harm. Chapter 2 proposes a novel epistemological analysis of data and harm, examining the concept of the 'captaverse', that is, considering the abusive means of surveillance and data profiling and how such dynamics have been tackled and considered within a neutralizing dynamic. Chapter 3 examines modern Onlife surveillance systems, their impact on privacy and security, and the replication of gendered and domestic harm in the digital realm. The chapter also addresses issues like nanny cams, hidden cameras, and the broader implications of Onlife surveillance and control – emphasizing both the macro (urban) landscape of these dynamics and the micro (domestic) equivalent. Chapter 4 reflects on the misuse of social media, addressing issues like stalking, trolling, and data misuse that are designed within an overall flawed system that 'leaks' the dynamics of harm in the everyday lives of individuals. It discusses the criminological aspects of social media, the dangers of data misuse, and the role of Big Data misconduct and surveillance capitalism in perpetuating harm, focusing on issues like gender-based violence, toxic language, systematic racism, and misinformation. Chapter 5 analyses corporate-level harm and criminality, focusing on Big Tech misconduct and its effects on users, consumers, and producers. It examines issues such as Amazon's control over consumers and staff, gig economy abuse (for example, by Uber), technologically planned obsolescence, and environmental harm. The chapter also discusses the malpractices and criminogenic offences committed during the COVID-19 pandemic, including data colonialism, surveillance in the Global South, and algorithmic racism. Chapter 6 explores toxic talk and conspiracy theories in Onlife info-wars, discussing the spread of alt-right and QAnon theories, 'Plandemic' delusions, and other web-based cultural phenomena. It analyses the cultural and criminological implications of online trolling, doxxing, and stalking and considers global perspectives on content-based harm and crime. Chapter 7 considers the impact of AI and its effects on reality, discussing the impact of deepfake software, the dark web, and the perpetual threat to the distinction between reality and the digital world. It examines the social and criminological implications of false information and new technologies, highlighting the responsibility of altering the Onlife dimension. Chapter 8 concludes the book by summarizing the theories and perspectives presented, discussing the elements of Onlife friction, the 'right to be ignored' and the potential for obfuscating tools and 'offlife' alternatives for sustainable internet use.

## From cybercrime to digital harms and beyond

Following the path markers placed by the *Onlife Manifesto*, I will continue the discussion to highlight how, since COVID-19, the effects of abusive hyperconnectivity are becoming more and more evident and require a rigorous empirical study from a criminogenic perspective. This aligns with Australian criminologist Mark A. Wood's (2022: 509) theories proposing a stratigraphy of harm that examines human–technology and technology–harm relations to 'delineate the socio-technicality of harmful events'. He distinguishes four technology–harm relations: (1) instrumental utility harms, (2) generative utility harms, (3) instrumental technicity harms, and (4) generative technicity harms. This creates a covert environment where abuse, deviance, and harm can be systematically directed toward vulnerable members of society (Wood, 2022: 509). Consequently, integrating smart devices into the Onlife experience introduces new complexities in the power dynamics and responsibilities within the network under discussion.

The aforementioned technologically induced harm dynamics that involve easy access to capturing information practices are crucial not only from a social perspective (Pemberton, 2015) but also – expanding on Wood's framework – from a rhizomatic viewpoint on the 'accidentality' of harm. Adopting a rhizomatic approach means moving away from the traditional belief in the individual as the centre of the world (Deleuze and Guattari, 1987). Instead, it highlights the intrinsic value of the intricate network of relations – both human and non-human – that collectively shape our reality (Van Brakel and Govaerts, 2025: 15) and, paraphrasing the 1912 article by Georg Simmel, the experience of the *fragmentary character* of 'Onlife'. As Henry et al (2020a: 1847) synthesize, technology in the digital era is 'not merely a tool of abuse, coercion, and harassment, but also often integral to the perpetuation of harm, suffering, and stigma of victims'. Therefore, this book aims to make a significant contribution to digital criminological theory by proposing a rhizomatic perspective that can enhance our understanding of the complexities surrounding current issues related to the Onlife captaverse – a focal problem and occurrence in our everyday lives.

In agreement with Floridi's considerations on the neutrality of technology, I agree and consider as paramount the idea that:

> no technology is ever 'at rest' in the 'neutral' sense, not least because every technology is always designed according to some implicit or explicit values, by some people for some people, within a culture and with a culture in mind, for some uses rather than others, with affordances and constraints, and so forth. (Floridi, 2023: 60)

This point is important, as the book positions itself as a follow-up to the zemiologic perspective outlined in *Beyond Criminology* (Hillyard et al, 2004). Its new harm-focus approach seeks to chart a fresh horizon by focusing on 'labelling and sanctioning these extensive forms of harm' (2004: 4). In the current scenario, the technologically able, the parental and hegemonic 'strong' are evidently in power over the technologically, economically, subjugated weak. Yes, the harm involved is digital and extracorporeal: oftentimes hidden and unperceived. Onlife becomes an ideal and unique way to engage with the elements of crime that are otherwise vaguely perceived as problematic, such as monitoring children remotely, observing partners' online activity, and distributing harmful content.

## *Cyber-necro-utopia*

William Gibson famously coined the term 'cyberspace' in the dystopian science fiction novel *Necromancer*, published fittingly in 1984. The novel describes a 'consensual hallucination' formed by the hegemonic power of multinational corporations that resembles Bentham's original vision of the Panopticon yet expands it into a 'private, profit-making institution' (Melossi, 2008: 18). Gibson's view was strictly in opposition to those expressed in the later 'Declaration of the Independence of Cyberspace', published 'worldwide' in 1996 but signed at the World Economic Forum of that year in Davos by John Perry Barlow (1996). Barlow made it clear to 'governments of the industrial world' that the internet, or what was extravagantly called 'cyberspace, the new home of mind', was intended to be a perfectly free environment, where no foreign authority was welcome: 'You have no sovereignty where we gather', Barlow notoriously claimed. Gibson rather saw only abuse and 'a constant subliminal hum, and death the accepted punishment for laziness, carelessness, lack of grace, the failure to heed the demands of an intricate protocol' (2016 [1984]: 9). In this perspective, cyberspace itself represents the ultimate environment of deviance and harm, limitless and unregulated, and held in the hands of a few who are in control of all. Perhaps incidentally, while Gibson's novel was published in a year that recalls Orwell's 1984, Barlow's declarations came shortly before one of the first major surveillance state leaks, the 1998 public disclosure of the ECHELON scheme, anticipating the Assange and Snowden scandals of the 2010s (Ziccardi, 2015). The ECHELON scheme, operational, allegedly, since the 1960s, consisted of an effective surveillance apparatus between the United Kingdom and the United States that allowed indiscriminate interception of unimaginable quantities of communication crossing any medium or transmission line (Ziccardi, 2015: 166). Free flow of information, connected to the inevitable utopia of free-thinking medium, has long, if not always, allowed the precise and ever-growing invasive apparatus of surveillance and control over the information in a pure Foucauldian interpretation (who incidentally also passed away in the year 1984).

Of course, one cannot accuse Barlow of being responsible for, nor blind to, the development of corporate surveillance. However, it is evident that for anyone looking closer at the neoliberal enterprise of laissez-faire deregulation, we struggle to find the egalitarian voice within the powers of the Big Data corporations. The evolution of information flow in the context of online digital content from the early 1990s onwards underscores a shift from passive citizens to active users who contribute to and engage with the dynamic flow of information in the cyberverse. The idealistic notion of 'rendering the internet free', thus making it more accessible for users to interact and exchange information without unnecessary constraints, highlights the changing dynamics of online engagement and the central role of users in shaping the digital landscape. In the realm of digital content production, the collection of data encompasses the very notion of information. Here, the flow of information no longer solely pertains to citizens but rather extends to users who actively engage with and contribute to this stream of data – the purified, 'quantified' everything of metrics and clicks. These users serve as the dynamic agents within the information ecosystem, interacting with and exchanging information, thus propelling the flow of 'energy', metaphorically representing the exchange and dissemination of information in digital spaces: the new frontier of being together and connecting. This idea, crucial and entirely idealistic to the 'online experience', becomes the main target of 'rendering the internet free' – with 'data', as it is known, being the subtle currency, be it digital, crypto, and so on, in any possible quantifiable, metricated scenario, both on and potentially offline, fostering assumptions about immediacy and accuracy (Marx, 2017).

When navigating the web, the aggravation of illegal activity is almost elemental – if the web itself is deviating from the norm, whatever the norm was before the web, the navigation in itself reiterates the deviant conduct. As I will discuss in this book, the structure of the Onlife scenario itself is designed in such a way that some sort of abuse, some sort of exploitation, some sort of covert monitoring, surveilling, or controlling is always taking place, and the users accepting these conditions are capable of replicating such dynamics at any given time.

The 2017 movie *Molly's Game* (Sorkin, 2017) offered a quite fitting quote that may be traced back to many discussions online: 'When doing something illegal, don't do anything illegal.' The point being, don't aggravate something that is already on the border, that is, liminal, transitional, on a threshold. Protagonist 'Molly', inspired by the real-life Molly Bloom, who organized high-stakes underground poker games, watches and takes care, controls, and monitors, allowing fun but in a controlled environment. She lets players/users live an 'ideal life' of gambling, sex, and pure hedonism. This, in many ways, is the seduction of the internet itself – and which the Onlife explicates.

The concept of liminality again is at the core of this hybrid condition. The user is no longer necessarily lingering on a bulky monitor to practice illegal activity (be it covert, be it active, be it direct). But via hyperconnected smart devices, it follows users in their pockets, and stores users in servers, and shares users via covert networked schemes, and enlists them in private agendas. This argument is closely tied to discussions regarding smart technology and surveillance discussed later. The omnipresent watchful eye has seemingly been replaced by sophisticated panoptic control (Fludernik, 2017).

As I will discuss, secrecy, opaqueness, and shadiness are among the keywords of today's internet interaction. It acts as the adhesive of the deviant conduct online, of the repercussion offline – the effect, the lingering, the recurrence.

### *Divided, mastered, and commanded*

Onlife is the ultimate liminal space, granting the hybrid states that mix the virtual with the 'real', but reality and 'unreality' also intertwine with the notion of what is life beyond being online. Crime, for that matter, is also a strictly correlated liminal term – its very etymology derives from the Proto-Indo-European root *krei, to sieve, thus 'discriminate, distinguish', which is the root of several unrelated words, very relevant for this book, such as *crime; criminal; concern; crisis; critique.*[1] In the case of its criminal-critical nature, it implies the action of dividing and thus becoming divided from society (in the case of the deviant) and from law (in the case of the criminal). The criminal deviates from the norm – the deviant that in itself changes whatever the norm is supposed to be. The internet has placed itself as a deviant establishment – changing, shaping, and shifting societies and norms with unprecedented rapidity, influence, and effect. Crime, in such an ambiguous and liminal space, only ideally propagates itself.

But what is the fundamental vantage point of doing crime online, and more specifically for this book, its hybrid elements and conditions?

The online allows a shapeshifting of the offline – and what happens online may shapeshift and have consequences offline. In this, the early contemplations (and warnings) of Sherry Turkle's *Second Self* (2005) become only more and more convincing and relevant. The individuals who use the web act differently because of it; it affects them, forming a new 'tethered self' (Turkle, 2023). The influence is palpable, and as this book describes, this exchange goes back and forth, and it is no surprise that Dr Jekyll referred to his evil double Mr Hyde as his own 'second self' (Stevenson, 2014 [1886]: 80).

When considering the dual nature of the Onlife, Marc Andreessen, the founder of the historical browser Netscape, is a pivotal figure in the narrative of techno-capitalism (2023), presenting a vision whereby the technologist becomes not just a leader of business but a custodian of social order. The techno-capital machine promotes a gospel of progress and innovation, sharing a narrative that underscores the positive impact of technology on society, producing innovations that benefit the world. This perspective aligns with Buckminster Fuller's 'ephemeralization' assertion coined in 1938, proposing that technology enables us to achieve more with less, ultimately reaching a point where we can accomplish everything with nothing (Buckminster Fuller, 1973). The reading of Marc Andreessen propels the notion that technology is indifferent to factors like ethnicity, race, religion, and other personal attributes. However, this supposed indifference is not entirely altruistic: technology's convenience in disregarding such distinctions serves the interests of its producers. In essence, technology is intricately tied to the surplus it generates and implies for its creators.

My critical viewpoint throughout the book suggests the opposite – the risk of doing nothing with everything. Everything is designed in a way we are not capable of doing anything about, affecting factors such as ethnicity, race, religion, and other personal attributes.

For now, to be fully integrated appears as the ultimate goal of the perfectly functioning Onlife engagement. Just as with our devices, everything works beautifully with the right assistance and check-up. The proper password log-ins and the cosy 'green' status bar of stable connection and full battery are natural 'relaxers'. When the cog runs smoothly, fun, entertainment, and productivity are all guaranteed and potentially unlimited. However, such a system applied to global societies as a whole is a worrying phenomenon, with a curious potential: it is exactly in these circumstances that the Onlife works best to marginalize, exclude, sort, and control.

## 'Sub'veillance

Since the 1990s, influential scholars such as David Lyon (1994) and Gary T. Marx (1998), and later Helen Nissenbaum (2009), Simone Browne (2015), and Shoshana Zuboff (2019), all noted how the digital surveillance structure surrounds the web and its content with worrying, if not unethical, implications. When users divulge and 'give away' their information, it appears as something 'out there for [anyone] to use' (Marx, 1998: 178): the idea of consent or choice within the online realm is 'disingenuous to the extreme' (Marx, 1998: 178). In the analysis of social theorist Byong-Chul Han (2015), the new means of a form of psychological power eclipses Foucault's biopower (2014): the subjectification of the self becomes a direct digitalization of the self that is ever more fragmented, with no entity exercising control over its surveillance mechanisms – data becomes the ultimate objective, the user the ultimate prey.

As such, the subjectification of the self, as discussed in the context of Michel Foucault's analysis of disciplinary practices, has undergone a profound transformation in the digital age. What was once a phenomenon mainly observed within the confines of utilitarian and colonial institutions, such as factories and slave trades (Browne, 2015), has now permeated all spheres of life. The mechanisms of control and monitoring, reminiscent of the panopticism noted in the study of the gig economy by Jamie Woodcock (2020), are no longer limited to the workplace but extend into the digital realm, where algorithms and digital incentives play a pivotal role.

This falls short of Deleuze's conceptualization of a 'surveillance assemblage' (1992), a prison-like yet discrete system where we are granted access to places and spaces only by constantly showing some electronic identification. 'Individuals have become "dividuals" and masses, samples, data, markets, or "banks"' (Deleuze, 1992: 5); non-abidance only leads to further marginalization and exclusion. Such a 'dividual' becomes a single entity in the gender-neutrality of the Onlife – to which no specific gender nor race is attached. It does not matter before the machine, as the user is intended as an ideal metrical machine. Users turn into passwords which protect them (with endless privacy-washing manoeuvres), yet perpetually define them; they sort us, enlist us (Lovink, 2019), fostering technical anonymity (Bancroft, 2020; Collier, 2024) as well as social anonymity – in the constant fear of social stigma, that the 'real' self becomes 'leaked', revealed, 'doxxed'. In this scenario, the 'sovereignty' (Barlow, 1996) of what is being gathered appears stoically unregulated and limitless (Yar, 2014). The 'black box' society conceptualized by Frank Pasquale back in 2015 and the prison-like digital scenario described by Brunton and Nissenbaum (also 2015) envision how users are entrapped by their very data, the use of their data, the definition defined by the very data that follows them everywhere, both on- and offline (Floridi, 2015). While offered consent forms when navigating the web, at least according to various European regulations and the European Union Data Act 2023, what really goes on in the background is out of reach or knowledge – with data wallets (Dataverse, 2023) and the like fostering a means of full data agency that is, to date, still (forever?) at the twilight stage.

Crypticism acts in strict correlation to what is known as a 'blowback' effect in an advertisement (that is, an unexpected negative response) – it acts in unknown dimensions and un-transparent facets. It can be scattered and fragmented, a jump into the unknown of the effect and meaning. To be 'cryptic' is the core of effective criminal control within a liminal environment – especially if the system is aided by a dark platform design aiding filter bubbles/echo chambers, fostering personalized online environments that expose users solely to a targeted content of existing beliefs and interests (Pasquale, 2015). As Ben Collier noted in a 2023 article, the trivial scenario of two academics travelling together in a foreign country may encounter contrasting content on their browsers: tailored, liberal, and welcoming messages from one government agency, while simultaneously receiving aggressive and xenophobic discourse from an overseas source (Collier, 2023). The terms of inclusion and exclusion are ever more cryptic and the influence ever more covert. Biometrics have now become an everyday means for the 'purposes of identification, verification, automation, and convenience' (Browne, 2015: 120), with security, as noted in a captivating article by Lianos and Douglas, 'a major consideration at all levels' (2000: 16) even before 9/11. From the carpark ticket to the automated cash machine the individual is constantly identified, with immediate and objective means to control and exclude whoever does not abide by the system. The novelty of this is the lack of tolerance or, in general, the possibility to apply, with the aid of technology, a command to all members of society at an unprecedented scale: one does not have to look 'dangerous', 'suspicious', 'aggressive', 'threatening', or 'dodgy'. One does not even need to break rules to be excluded: rather, one needs to be associated with an 'avoidable threat' – one defined by 'automatic indicators of dangerousness' (2000: 26).

The Onlife user is subject to all, an active and passive participant of an ongoing sociological and criminological experience – and this condition's biopolitics are becoming increasingly complex. While Shoshana Zuboff has defined the market workings and profit to be made from our data in her book *The Age of Surveillance Capitalism* (2019), in Siva Vaidhyanathan's *Antisocial Media* (2018) we see a variation of this theme in understanding the use of social networks and media not only in controlling us but in our controlling each other (Trottier, 2015). If everyone is potentially watching, they will also be 'hungry' to see what is not 'shown'. Vaidhyanathan (2018) notices the everyday life dangers of surveillance: not simply being observed by a remotely controlled CCTV camera, but filmed, recorded, and observed through high-definition lenses of smartphones, available virtually everywhere and always at hand, whereby 'anyone of us who carries a camera attached to a mobile phone is an agent of surveillance' (Vaidhyanathan, 2018: 53). Data as such becomes the justification of control, and the object of control – to which all users participate, extrapolate, and reciprocate whether they are aware of it or not. We can see examples of this in the public shaming of highly popular 'influencers' (Forestal, 2023), but also through the global COVID-19 lockdown, with cases of filming and monitoring, and subsequent commenting and shaming, of other citizens not 'conforming' to the norms and putting others 'at risk' of contagion (Hess, 2020).

### *Data-caption*

In 1998, Gary T. Marx recognized that data collection implies some form of surveillance, arguing for a fixed set of etiquettes, thus preventing 'immoral' or harmful conditions. From a scholarly viewpoint, this translates into a sort of necessary 'prudence' on behalf of the collector and the need for 'consent' from the collected. This is all fair and good when academic work is carried out, ethics forms are filled out, and the information gathered is protected and harmless. When we look at what is commonly known as Big Data, we refer to the 'information' 'aggregation, analytics, and predictive modelling' (Brunton and Nissenbaum, 2015: 51) and consider how the collecting of data implies the 'taking' of information 'we have willingly shared, or have been compelled to provide, [in order to] produce knowledge from inferences' (Brunton and Nissenbaum, 2015: 51). When this takes place through virtual and digital means within (but not limited to) a web-based/online interface, the concepts of consent, morality, and harm change their perspective.

This paradigm differs from Deleuze's conceptualization of a 'surveillance assemblage' (Haggerty and Ericson, 2000), which presents a prison-like yet discrete system. In this construct, access to places and spaces is granted only through the continuous display of electronic identification. Non-compliance leads to further marginalization and exclusion, a perspective that is of particular concern to internet critic Geert Lovink (2019) and scholars such as David Lyon (2018, 2022). They observe how the devices we carry continuously define, categorize, and enrol us, sometimes through demeaning means. Building upon Foucault's theories on the centrality of discipline in the context of blind surveillance, Deleuze posits that 'societies of control' are integrated into an automated system – an assemblage where surveillance unfolds in a truly rhizomatic structure, as envisioned by his collaborator Guattari, one characterized by 'variation, expansion, conquest, capture, offshoots' (Deleuze and Guattari, 1987: 21).

The word 'data' is ubiquitous and ambivalent – though it shouldn't be. It has long suffered from an epistemological fallacy, one we can no longer afford to ignore. Very straightforwardly, 'data' originates from Latin: it is a *datum*, something given, handed out. When this takes place, we notice implied action of consent, a *do ut des,* 'I give, so that you may give' dynamic. Nevertheless, when something is given out and later used, sold, targeted, and processed beyond the original purpose, such an event should reasonably raise concerns. While many of these have been raised repeatedly, there is still a lack of precision in addressing the problem. This is perhaps because the very wording of what appeared problematic has not been addressed properly. When scholars, corporation, governments, and platform creators talk of 'data', they tend to suggest it is rightful to consider it something handed out voluntarily – rather than something 'taken'. It is the basic difference between something 'gifted' and something 'stolen'. One is an action of care, the other an offence. When we talk of 'data', we must be more precise. Indeed, most of the time the 'information' is not 'handed-out', there is some enticement taking place. A trick of some sort. Thus, it implies not a 'datum', but a 'captum'. It leaves users with a bad taste in their mouths, and the feeling that they have been somewhat tricked into accepting all the unprecedented terms.

## Disclaimer of (and against) a bestiary

Let me offer some final housekeeping so as to shed a light on any ambivalence concerning the interconnectedness of social and criminal life. The structure of this book follows a (soft) rhizomatic approach, assembling the argument in a non-hierarchical manner. As online users, we are objects and subjects of crime in an interchanging manner – part of an ever-shifting, hybrid and liquid ecology that this book's chapter subdivisions try to grasp comprehensively. While the individual chapters might appear to be structurally unstructured, but nonetheless a reasonable form of joy ride, I do not particularly vouch for a single chapter read alone, as the entire book gathers together and refers to various aspects of a whole issue.

Regardless of the reader's preferred format, I made a conscious effort to prevent this book from becoming a bestiary filled with fantastical devices and the human depravity that can be found in the Onlife – where the images and uses, gimmicks and news, no matter how entertaining now, appear medieval and awkward in the year (months) to come, if not by the time of publication.

As such, the ambition of this book is not like Nicole Perlroth's haunting yet alarming work *This Is How They Tell Me The World Ends* (2022), aiming to ring by criminological means the warning bell and confirm on top of an already long list of ongoing disasters and global threats (no reference necessary, I assume) that 'the world is on the precipice of a cyber catastrophe' (2022: 391). Instead, in agreement with the efforts of authors such as Naomi Klein, I aim not to foster an otherwise 'righteous rage or fury at injustice' (Klein, 2023: 226) via the means of *Shock Doctrine* (Klein, 2008), but of one of setting out the 'precondition for focus, for the capacity to prioritize' (Klein, 2023: 226). Klein refers to this as the need to write to instil 'calmness' in readers. Indeed, instead of petrifying (and thus subjugating) readers to the dangers and horrors that develop in the Onlife world – similar to how many conspiracy discourses are developed – this book attempts, with unforeseeable success, to touch upon, discuss, comment, and critique the crime and harms of the Onlife by standing back and trying to visualize the whole of the mosaic. It seeks to stoically examine the various, complex, intricate, and even rhizomatic ways in which harms and crimes are incidentally and insignificantly produced within the very systems we use every day – systems that are progressing globally, embraced by governments, supported by politicians, and enforced by police authorities (Van Brakel and Govaerts, 2025). As such, to paraphrase philosopher Andrew North Whitehead's conceptions on the 'art of life' (1929), what are today's means to promote the 'reasonable' existence Onlife, and thus to be Onlife in a satisfactory way, so as to further acquire an increase in satisfaction of our Onlife existence, free from harm, subjugation, criminality, and danger?

2

# Enter the Captaverse: An Epistemological Analysis of Data and Harm

With the corporate conceptualization of the 'metaverse' (Beer, 2022), and the exponential 'Onlife' digital existence brought forward by the pandemic, a whole new frontier of 'meta-crime' (Lloyd, 2021) has unfolded with the profiling of, and profiteering from, European and global users' information. This chapter attempts to sketch the connection between data and harm (Redden, 2018) by addressing the issue as an epistemological problem: when considering the word 'data' (Latin, datum), it translates into something 'given'. However, a much better definition is something taken, a *captum*. The data versus capta dichotomy is not novel in the social sciences (Lanigan, 1994; Chippendale, 2000), however, it lacks sufficient information in this high-tech age, particularly in the field of criminology. By addressing and denouncing the elementary zemiology of the capta dynamics, the information mining and coaxing out of Onlife users' data turns from the digital world's tolerated currency of 'no-free-lunch' into a semantically abusive and controversial tool of harm and deviance. This chapter looks at the precedents and implications of this different wording and considers the modes in which capta analysis may be considered and addressed, not only in forming a specific and novel interpretation of meta-crime within a captaverse but as a new way of doing research altogether.

## Terms of data collection

A central dilemma posed by this book concerns the method by which data are gathered, and how the word 'data' has, in the context of this work, become almost a misnomer – implying something that is not given, but taken. The very notion of 'data' is thus a central element of criticism within this work: the influence of data on users, the manoeuvres and conditions under which data are gathered, and the social harm involved in monitoring, filming, and recording individuals, especially when there is no awareness or consent. Such considerations necessitate an alternative 'tool' to study the 'tools' that surround us.

Data today has become an umbrella term of ambiguous implications. With data, we underline the information flow and make sense of the virtual, digital, and cyber exchange of personal, targeted recollections of our internet activity.

In the last decades, scholars have advanced the concept of 'dataveillance' (van Dijck, 2014), emphasizing the power and pervasive implications of automated systems for collecting data through clicks, searches, and purchases (Beer, 2016). The emphasis has been placed on problematizing the dynamics of corporate surveillance, digital tracking, Big Data, and privacy (Christl and Spiekermann, 2016) within a 'dragnet' system of restless monitoring systems (Angwin, 2014). These activities are often subject to hidden and covert designs implemented by corporations, state agencies, governments – even insurance companies, as explored in Pasquale's *Black Box Society* (2015). In *The Quantified Self* (2016), Deborah Lupton discusses the agency aspects of digital surveillance as the means for self-knowledge through numbers, investigating the quantified collection of data on individuals, framed from a social good perspective, such as improved health and fitness tracking (for more on this, see Chapter 5). This proved particularly significant during the COVID-19 health crisis (Liang, 2020; Maras et al, 2023). However, the normalization of digital surveillance still faces opposition today due to concerns about the 'colonizing' (Mejias and Couldry, 2024) and gazing or 'data grabbing' (Fraser, 2019) manoeuvres of Big Tech corporations.

## Disingenuous consent

Gary T. Marx published his examination of data and surveillance in 1998, soon after 1996's 'Declaration of the Independence of Cyberspace', published 'worldwide' by John Perry Barlow. Barlow made it clear to the 'governments of the industrial world' that cyberspace was to be intended a perfectly free environment, where no foreign authority was welcome: 'You have no sovereignty where we gather'. Yet, such a broad request would only find an echo in the contested military and government-financed programmes of surveillance being set up between the United Kingdom and the United States, foreshadowed by the mysterious ECHELON programme that had already been operational since the 1960s but only coming to public attention in 1998 (Ziccardi, 2015: 166).

Indeed, in October 1999 Harvard Professor Lawrence Lessig addressed the forthcoming dangers of cyberspace as a tool for control (at a distance) (Lessig, 1999). For Lessing, Adams Smith's 'invisible hand' was about to shape the market – virtually and physically – as a precursor of the Onlife ecology, transforming privacy from a right to a commodity. These years are crucial in the formation of a sort of 'lukewarm' realization of the 'mass surveillance' of web users, one formed by a global 'pan-optimized' society, where Lyon and Bauman notice a recurring 'adiaphorization' (that is, a morally neutral or indifferent attitude) towards control and surveillance, 'in which systems and processes become split off from any consideration of morality' (Lyon and Bauman, 2013: 13). Interestingly, the term is used in the evaluation of surveillance practices, proving the problematics of online devices' potential for harm, one that is not taken with due care by consumers – quality checks are not only unchallenged, but often the consumers themselves contribute to the quality assessment through their usage and data (Witley, 2023).

That 'privacy is dead' was suggested as a fact already in 1999 by Sun Microsystems' (now Oracle) CEO Scott McNealy, and his statement to reporters to 'get over it' (Sprenger, 1999). The fatality of such a reality has been emphasized to us repeatedly by, among others, entrepreneur Mark Zuckerberg, who underlined how privacy is 'no longer a social norm' (Johnson, 2010). It is thus somewhat surprising we are still trying to act normatively or are surprised by the breaches and misuses of our data. The common notion of privacy, as discussed in *The New York Times* by Andrew Burt and Dan Geer, refers again to the basic definition of privacy as 'the right to be left alone', describing the perpetual monitoring of our offline and online activities in the following way: at every moment of our lives, we no longer have a place to hide (Greenwald, 2014), both in our private and public activities (Burt and Geer, 2017).

In this perspective, and as noted by Marx (1998), it appears evident that the idea of consent or choice within the online realm is 'disingenuous to the extreme' (Marx, 1998: 178). Let us briefly consider this: still by 2025, we are indeed offered consent forms when navigating the web. We are given a right to divulge our data, or not. We are also offered some idea of to whom eventually our data will be sold. This is all good (and somewhat anachronistic, as, yet again, Gary T. Marx talked about this in 1998), until it is not. Some websites, apps, and devices restrict full access to their platforms unless you agree to their terms – a practice that is inherently self-limiting. Most of these tools and platforms are essential for your work or life in general, and consent and terms of acceptance are a pseudo-lapalissade. Either you are content to fully consent or you are, at least partially, excluded.

## Epistemological dilemma

In a joint offline and online technological 'system' of control, users are observed both while walking the streets and while surfing the net, with a fundamental common denominator: users are somewhat conscious of this, and yet, for most of us, this form of 'indirect' surveillance involves us without our ever actually seeming to 'touch' them (Giglioli, 2019). Users are aware that they are being recorded, but these recordings typically do not result in any obvious harm to them. As a result, we often feel 'left alone' by surveillance, or even reassured by it, particularly when it helps in preventing or solving crimes. This sense of reassurance holds as long as we adhere to the security standards and laws of our society (more on this in the next chapter).

There are means to actively resist the conditions of surveillance, in particular through 'obfuscation', which consists of 'the deliberate addition of ambiguous, confusing, or misleading information to interfere with surveillance and data collection' (Brunton and Nissenbaum, 2015: 1).

It is, in other words, a means 'to put some sand in the gears, to buy time, and to hide in the crowd of signals' (2015: 2) so as to resist the means to be, yet again, 'on a list'. What is particularly problematic is the ease in which populations are sorted under the umbrella of anti-terroristic acts and the like across the world. Helen Nissenbaum has developed some practical plug-ins such as the AdNauseam browser extension that can click all ads on a page to scramble the real interests of a user or TrackMeNot that generates automated random searches that scramble the 'sensitive … patterns recorded over time [which] are potentially a window into our lives, interests, and ambitions' (Howe and Nissenbaum, 2009: 20).

Obfuscation techniques show the problematics around data collection but offer a means to limit their precision (but not their invasiveness) – an increase in the scale of indexing and sorting of individuals' choices, appearance, and existences. Be it scrambled, the information, however, is still collected unchallenged, and here I wish to argue that it is the intrinsic approach that needs re-thinking.

## Capta-vaillance

As discussed, the notion of digital data is commonly perceived as the exchange we offer, almost reciprocally, for 'free navigation' of the general internet experience. However, this sense of gratuity becomes somewhat paradoxical within the context of our neoliberal milieu, transforming into a form of 'no-free-gift' compromise (Douglas, 1990 [1950]) that society has grown accustomed to. With its problematics and controversies of what is taken, stolen, pasted, plagiarized, and exploited, the internet is effectively built upon a collective effort to produce content. Such content is quintessentially represented by Wikipedia, where any user may contribute to editing and producing articles. The mentality, as noted by Jaron Lanier (2010) – who is highly critical of the platform – is one of 'so-called' wisdom-of-the-crowd (Surowiecki, 2004): the greater the involvement, the closer we reach the truth of things. Such an idea of global involvement to collectively produce content is a recurring aspect, one that partly justifies the capta dynamics that corporations engage in. Any visitor to a particular website may contribute to making it function. It is, in a farfetched manner (or is it wishful thinking?), a perspective of 'reciprocity' – hands-free (oftentimes worthless) content – and speculates on it.

Back in 1994, Philip Agre explored the nature and challenges of 'captivating surveillance', centred on the critical issue of tracking. In Agre's perspective, tracking is closely linked to automation and the scientific work on efficiency associated with Taylorism (Agre, 1994: 117), which effectively subjectify users to 'detailed digital measurements and statistical analysis of individual worker performance' (Wood et al, 2018: 62). Both automation and Taylorism address the imperatives of efficiency and control by pre-determining precise action sequences (Agre, 1994). Agre genealogically associates the surveillance model with secret police organizations and 'their networks of listening devices and informers, most prominently in the totalitarian states of Nazi Germany and the Soviet Union' (1994: 106). Contemporary 'captivating' practices evoke parallels with a different form of Nazi-induced control – cold, automated, and remote analysis using powerful IBM machines to relentlessly gather vast amounts of data from unknowing citizens (Black, 2001).

Such occurrences are, sadly, not exclusive to the 'Old World' nor to global conflicts. A recurring anecdote, both used by surveillance critiques as well as conspiracy theorists (Klein, 2023), is the one concerning the creeping distribution of IBM computers to identify and censor population. Specific 'electronic tabulators' were also significant in the oppression of people living under apartheid in South Africa – along with other powerful new technologies for metrical analysis, including 'x-ray machines to check personal possessions, passbook fingerprinting equipment and communications logging' (Chokshi et al, 1995) which were all available to police forces to use on civilians.

We may at this stage briefly mention the famous argument highlighted in the 1977 article 'Would you sell a computer to Hitler?' by Laurie Nadel and Hesh Wiener. The two journalists raised particular concerns about IBM's sale of computers to repressive governments in Latin America, which used the technology to enable repression and extrajudicial killings. More recently, sociologist Gavin Smith (2015) has proven that no form of surveillance is entirely neutral – it entails something, and its purposes, in the long term, have a significant effect on users and their peers – whatever the original purpose of the analysis.

Data are not merely information: they serve as the very substance used to measure, quantify, and lubricate the engagement, advertising, personalization, or digital experiences (Pasquale, 2015; Beer, 2016; Lupton, 2016). In the realm of Big Data, information is taken from users, analysed, collected, and stored on a regular and escalating basis. For the much-cited Frank Pasquale

(2015), there exists an infrastructure designed to personalize the online user and digital experience as much as possible, tailoring content based on individual searches, preferences, and tastes, resulting in exponentially increased data value. Other researchers have approached the issue, for example, by using the term 'data grab' (Mejias and Couldry, 2024), highlighting the colonial dynamics of data use, abuse, and ideology (Táíwò, 2022). However, even here, the term 'data' carries significant weight as it illuminates the nature, operations, and purpose of this process. Data, especially in the context of Big Data, are not given but taken – transforming the perspective from 'datum' to 'capta' – and thus creating a direct 'capta-veillance' scenario.

This reconceptualization is not unique to the field of information technology; it also occurs in other disciplines, such as archaeology (Chippindale, 2000) and social sciences (Lanigan, 1994). This discussion, though not new, has taken on a somewhat anachronistic character, emphasizing that capta is not only a currency but also a powerful tool embedded in the systems that surround us. It represents a form of surveillance that captures without bounds, establishing a dynamic of capta-veillance. It is not centred on a specific political agenda but on the surreptitious and constant accumulation of information. While the approach may not aim to maximize control through transparency, it does assemble an expansive repository of latent potential, a phenomenon further magnified by the internet and the extensive engagement it affords in the Onlife.

## Zemiology of the (captivating) Onlife

As discussed earlier, the concept of capta-veillance encapsulates the sense of the control apparatus we are entangled in, one that keeps us perpetually at risk. The capture of information operates in a constant state of vigilance, continuously expanding. It gathers increasingly precise details about our lives, tracking us in many ways from womb to tomb.

Capta collection becomes the unwary and incidental cyber-tool for spying, controlling, and manipulating – and doing so, and wanting to do so, with endless means, an aspect that has seriously troubled the ethical consideration of this book and other aspects of my research. As such, the Onlife has become an element of the everyday life that I have tried to describe, gathering a decade-long of on and offline impressions, sensations, and intuitions that have been delivered to me, handed out, found, and shared.

As in Hillyard and Tombs's (2004) analysis of harms, my considerations lie in the idea that the harm caused by capta-veillance is a product of neoliberal globalization. This involves the reckless advancement of technologies in the name of highly specialized profit, with very limited concern for the social implications of these advancements. The neoliberal paradigm is evident in the way in which smart devices were launched into the market and flooded everyday interactions through platforms that also invaded the lives of users/consumers. Much of the technological advancement occurred with a reasonable amount of hype and caution in its use, ultimately leading to a rapid increase in acceptance and widespread enjoyment (Latour, 1990; Virilio, 1998). Many corporations have taken full advantage of unsanctioned data collection practices, as evidenced by the seemingly endless free flow of data enabled by the hyperconnected, new technological paradigm.

Therefore, prioritizing capta within the context of the Onlife presents an ideal and distinct approach to address harms that are often perceived vaguely as problematic. These include remotely monitoring users, observing others' online activities, distributing harmful content, and even engaging in practices like 'sharenting' – sharing personal and confidential information that is later accessed and exploited. These behaviours trivialize the dissemination of information, which increasingly becomes entangled in the abusive habits prevalent in online environments.

## Caring for data

Despite the presence of consent forms, as mandated by various Western regulations, the actual processes transpiring in the background remain beyond our reach and understanding. The exchange of data epitomizes the structure of today's web-based society, where cyber and virtual realms frequently intertwine, blurring boundaries and complicating the concept of user interaction as an ongoing and freely given process. This vision, once idealized as borderless by Barlow in 1996, has since evolved. M. Douglas's 'No-free-lunch' analogy (Douglas, 1990 [1950]) and Gary T. Marx's (1998) considerations on the disingenious development and acceptance of cookies (tiny text files stored on your device that remember preferences, login information, or preferences) underscore that data exchange comes with a cost. However, the implementation of the UK's General Data Protection Regulation (GDPR) and EU-based data Acts across websites, devices, and platforms has somewhat undermined this system's efficacy, requiring users to spend time providing data rather than simply consenting to its collection.

Yet, cookies represent just a fragment of the broader issue of data distribution. When we download applications onto our smart devices and accept their terms, we unknowingly grant access to cameras, pictures, locations, and other personal details, sparking an ongoing debate.

What, then, do we mean by 'giving away' information? As noted, in coding, as in society, language shapes understanding. 'Data' implies a reciprocal exchange, akin to borrowing a pen to a colleague during a meeting. However, it becomes problematic when the pen borrower starts cataloguing its make, measuring its liquid, asking for personal details, and analysing it for fingerprints. This shift – from giving and receiving to taking and keeping – reflects the core of internet navigation today: data are not simply given but captured, stored, monitored, and analysed in an ongoing cycle.

This normalization of data capture contrasts sharply with the benign connotations of the term 'data' itself. I claim a more accurate term might be 'capta' – something taken rather than given – an idea discussed by Lanigan in 1994 and increasingly relevant today.

This perspective challenges us to view the internet not merely as a realm of information exchange but as a digital frontier where personal data are continually mined and exploited. Obfuscation efforts like Ad Nauseam[1] aim to disrupt this cycle, creating friction in data collection practices. However, addressing this issue requires more than technological countermeasures: it demands a societal shift toward recognizing meta-criminality – where responsibility extends beyond data providers to include designers and promoters who manipulate and profit from personal information.

As we navigate this meta-reality and respond to its challenges, it becomes urgent for citizens and users not only to protect their data for privacy and property reasons but also for the dignity it represents, especially when new forms of biometrics and age-verification data collection is being implemented in the US, Australia, and the UK as reported by Ofcom (2024). Ongoing scandals involving big data underscore the need for proactive measures and accountability, urging us to safeguard ourselves and demand protection from those who exploit our information for unclear purposes.

# 3

# The Smart Surveillance of All

## Culture of observation

In the so-called age of Big Data, all aspects of the everyday become significant elements for monetization. The issue of privacy breaches is still an ongoing concern, but the criminology of this matter can shed light on the secret ways in which the digital world can be utilized to quietly examine and analyse the everyday aspects of individuals.

Already in 2002, Andrejevic defined the concept of 'lateral surveillance', involving a unilateral aspect of peer-to-peer monitoring to gain information about friends, family members, and prospective love interests. Andrejevic's work on peer-to-peer surveillance introduced the concept of 'DIY' surveillance, where individuals actively engage in monitoring others, often facilitated by online resources. This practice has become especially prevalent in investigating current, potential, or past partners, using spyware integrated into various overt and covert activities. With the false presumption of privacy, the distribution of images and content is universal and ubiquitous, as in Anita Lavorgna et al's study on the criminological harms involved in 'sharenting' practices (2022), where parents share and distribute images of their children online, be it on social media or via instant messaging chats. On the one side, we have the menace of 'paedophilistic' prey, who may unknowingly collect and share pictures and information about minors. But from the perspective of the 'black box', discussed by Pasquale (2015), the harms and risks associated with the digitalization of parenting issues are reflected in the underlying analysis of children's medical, mental, and social conditions. This is central to the over-distribution of 'sharenting' practices, where yet again captivating the data (Agre, 1994; Szakolczai, 2023) of everyday users become the consumeristic capitalistic gold mine of the Big Data age (Zuboff, 2015).

In this chapter, I highlight the systematic progression of surveillance and control, touching upon the biopolitical, invasive, pervasive, and harmful but also insignificant and incidental elements that the Onlife surveillance (and the surveillance of the Onlife) entails. Central to this potential scenario is the means to expose oneself within the Onlife combined with the fundamental real-time application of surveillance technologies. The Onlife user may be, at any given time, zoomed in upon and not only identified but potentially 'subjectified'. Their means are excluded from space and places for a variety of reasons, influencing biopolitically the body (virtually and physically) with efficiency and immediacy (this theme is developed further in the following chapters).

As such, I highlight the micro and macro means by which surveillance enters our homes and follows us outside, with the augmented ability to observe and monitor not only biometrics but also the expressions and essences of individuals.

Overall, the chapter considers the warning signs of these tools, taking into consideration the nonchalance of surveilling, controlling, and harming elements that have in many ways quietly, inevitably crept into our everyday lives. The Onlife in this scenario represents the quintessential space of coercive control: what goes on in the everyday is recorded, and what is recorded is captured, only to be further used and replicated.

## Products to be harvested

At the turn of the millennium, internet entrepreneur Josh Harris orchestrated a 'social experiment' work of art called *Quiet: We Live in Public*. The project commenced at a Millennium Eve party and lasted for an entire month until interrupted by the police. Taking place in a New York City basement, the six-storey Broadway warehouse housed an ad-hoc community living in wired pods, functioning as individual TV channels streamed live to the web (Salkin, 2009).

Harris, often dubbed 'the greatest Internet pioneer you've never heard of' (Waite, 2020), envisioned a future shaped by the internet and media technology, one characterized by perfect 'publicness'. In order to finance the project, around 100 participants joined together to bring Andy Warhol's notorious vision of everyone enjoying '15 minutes of fame' to a perpetual excessiveness. For Harris, this meant people demanding 15 minutes of fame every day, a future he believed was inevitable whether embraced or not. Before the camera, as quoted in *The New York Times* in 2009, he felt he was nothing more than 'a product to be harvested' (Carr, 2009).

These dynamics echo Michel Foucault's discussions in the lectures he gave at the Collège de France, published in the volume *On the Government of the Living* (Foucault, 2014), where he examines the monastic practices of early Christianity and identifies two key imperatives: that one must fully disclose the truth about oneself and adhere completely to the rules (demonstrating absolute transparency and obedience).

Indeed, following the project's forced closure, Harris continued experimenting with internet publicness by setting up 24/7 live stream webcams in his home, streaming his personal life online under the project 'We Live in Public'. Eventually, this endeavour ended in Harris's relationship breakup, bankruptcy, and a nervous breakdown (Carr, 2009).

While Harris's vision may be compared to an Orwellian environment of complete surveillance, it also resembles the lesser-known novel *We* by Russian writer Yevgeny Zamyatin, published in 1924. Zamyatin's dystopic universe is one of total openness and transparency, where all actions and every instrument are synchronized: all functions and feelings are fully visible.

Zamyatin described his novel as a warning against the dangers of the hypertrophic power of machines and the state (McCarthy, 1984: 123). The protagonist, D-503, struggles to contain his free thoughts in a society heading towards the perfect mechanization of movements and thoughts, abolishing privacy completely – to the point that the sole concept is disgusting and outrageous.

To be 'public' and perpetually connected becomes the quintessential element of the Onlife, one that nevertheless replicates a systematic epistemological and political 'problem' with how the world surrounding us is developing. As such, the prevalent, if not dominant, 'structure of feeling' today is what Paul Virilio (2000) termed 'polar inertia'. The German translation, 'rasender stillstand' ('frenetic standstill'), more accurately captures this contradictory experience of the present where everything happens without the need to go anywhere (Virilio, 2000). Visibility is ubiquitous and imposed on users in the increasingly accelerated pace of life in the Onlife – another important concept for Virilio. He emphasizes the 'dromosphere', an accelerated techno-communications culture (Virilio, 1998), and highlights the risks associated with 'hyperconnectivity' (Hoskins and Tulloch, 2016). I will in this chapter explain and describe the various dimensions in which such surveillance is developing, highlighting, possibly, the future direction of such an overarching scenario.

## Surveillance as life

Digital devices have had an immense influence on the 'dromospheric' rapidity with which the 'problem' has escalated – and how it is dealt with. As discussed by Haggerty in 2005, the speed has escalated further means of military security, with surveillance contributing to an 'information overload' and transforming 'military command into a version of the man with the hammer who approaches every problem as a form of nail' (2005: 264).

The Onlife elements of surveillance go far beyond the simple and active surveillance potential, especially considering the quantified and self-tracking elements that have rapidly evolved within Onlife gimmicks.

Smartwatches, with their highly personalized monitoring via sensors and fitness-statistical self-tracking, offered a new dimension of quantified data: either given or taken. As pointed out in another classic work, Deborah Lupton's *Quantified Self*, self-tracking offers some perspectives on sense-making and identity formation that have broader relevance (2016). Information becomes in this reality a benign apparatus, an asset that needs constant investment both by the user and producer. Data are not only collected, they are produced and shared for the greater good of the so-called data philanthropy (Kirkpatrick, 2019). Such a perspective is clear in the integration of technology and social welfare concerning the potential of e-health in the monitoring, study, and treatment of health conditions, particularly heart rates (Ajana, 2017). There is nothing new in noticing how easily the processes and features have been sold to users of the Onlife. Health and fitness are not simply a further asset, but an evident source of pride – augmented and endorsed by fitness brands and sports tech companies. However, the record of one's personal information comes at a higher and higher price, as noted by Pasquale (2015). But the very record carries a heavy load. What if they reveal more than we want others to know? From a basic criminological standpoint, smartwatches and the like act as luxurious electronic bracelets that justify compliance (Nellis, 2013). Their functioning, especially with the use of more sport and fitness-based devices, acts and prompts us into action: they push the users into more training and more movement. They 'know' the person and suggest improvements, be it standing up, drinking water, or practising exercise. The self, via smart bracelets, acts as a mini-corporation of self-improvement, but within a docile environment. Not only is all action scaled to a medium level – such as the widely recommended 10,000 daily steps suggested by the World Health Organization (WHO) – but the device also has the potential to provide insights into the user's stress triggers, whether at work or at home. It allows one to know 'who' the problem in their life is and offers insights on who the user actually loves and or hates within the (dis)topia of a 'Quantified Us' (Jordan and Pfarr, 2014).

But caring for the self and 'gazing' constantly at our data (Beer, 2019a) is only part of the observing aspect. Coercive forms of observation fulfil parental anxiety and control and go hand-in-hand with hard-profit solutions (Marx and Steeves, 2010). Indeed, these elements have a direct effect on the way families may engage with the data produced. The subjection of children to surveillance is a recurring theme in the work of Valerie Steeves (Steeves and Jones, 2010), and the discussion extends to different aspects of the Onlife. Not only surveillance by governments and corporations but also in the form of convenient, even 'friendly' social media surveillance in which parents across the world seem to engage (Hjorth et al, 2020). Collecting data, in this case, appears again in a caring perspective: it is done for the common good, and it prevents unwanted scenarios. Nevertheless, such a system of 'caring' control not only takes place within the boundaries of parenthood, it may involve any family member, and at any age, in any sphere – from the most formal to the most intimate. In this reality, kin watches over the other to know if 'everything is OK' – they comment on, participate, and even request further proof of wellbeing. As revealed in a study by Hjorth et al (2020), the monitored often enjoy these elements of surveillance. They appreciate the feeling of being watched over and taken care of. When looking at the monitoring side, the control aspect may go beyond simple 'online', software monitoring and become hardware elements of control, even 'fancy' and 'normative' ones such as the Apple AirTag device that enriched by Hermes protective leather became a luxurious tool that can generate 'more fun'[1] by being available in different colours or engraved with emojis. It is a small device, capable of doing nothing but keeping control – of things, people, or indeed both – as in subsequent cases of stalking (Snyder, 2022). Smart technology is allowing not simply a cheap and immediate form of response and protection, but also a trivialized, if not infantilized, use of the highly detailed and well-hidden potential of control. This appears central when we recall that before turning users into controlling agents, the real agents of control are the devices themselves. These evolving smart-home tools are not simply 'robots' to answer commands, they are intended to help us out, offering us useful skills – filling the loneliness of our lives; minding our business in the best possible sense of the term – they 'watch over' our groceries, our bills, our temperature – they care for the home, and they are part of it: invest energy in technology and help save time and money.

But, if we take the must-cited (alleged) quote by Konrad Zuse literarily, 'The danger of computers becoming like humans is not as great as the danger of humans becoming like computers'.[2] What does the progression of surveillance entail? What are specifically the grounds for and the possibility of resisting and refusing specific measurements?

As noted earlier, Jordan and Pfarr (2014) highlighted the 'Quantified Us' as a significant evolution of personal data tracking. Its central purpose is one of enhancing our capability to predict, control, analyse risk, and improve decision making, among other things, in important bio-sociability trends such as patient–doctor relations. But one can easily see how this may well develop, and already has, in bio-criminality trends. This is evident in the monitoring opportunities to prevent calamities, inducing other 'states of emergency', and aiding the policing involved (more on this later). Again, we come across the basic element of controlling and comparing *Small Data* versus *Big Data*. And again, we consider the basic, almost intrinsic elements of freedom versus security in our democracies (Gearty, 2013). Health statistics become ideally correlated with geographical whereabouts, footfall control, and even cataclysmic alerts. By sharing *everything, everywhere and all at once* (alluding to the 2022 film), users and governments may potentially act together to assist one another – especially in times of crisis.

This concept of 'data philanthropy' (George et al, 2020) highlights how social media has become a valuable source of data for tracking everything from earthquake impacts to disease outbreaks and the misuse of prescription drugs.[3] However, this idea of donating or sharing data for a good cause aligns with technocentric propaganda within Anthropocene visions. It promotes a perspective that emphasizes the role of technology in shaping our world, echoing elements of Marc Andreessen's much-criticized 'techno-optimism manifesto' published in 2023 (Lopatto, 2024).

The basic principles of privacy, in the current consumeristic agenda of data philanthropy, act almost as deviant elements – in opposition to the public good of what data can and may achieve. Figures like Edward Snowden, the former National Security Agency (NSA) contractor who became a whistleblower in 2012 (Greenwald, 2014), may, under such rhetoric, be viewed as significant obstacles to truth and progress. After all, data collection and the systematic monitoring of spaces and places have come to aid climate change itself. The more information is collected and gathered the greater understanding we have in preventing calamities (be it fire, wind, water, or earth). And while satellites roam our skies monitoring all the 'normal' functioning of these elements – combining geological data with forest erosion, wild fires, and tsunamis – climate change activists are also monitored by anti-terrorist programmes such as Prevent in the UK (Nevett, 2023).

Such a paranoid stance seems only to confirm the pre-9/11 warnings highlighted by Michaelis Lianos and Mary Douglas in their discussion of the new forms of security based on invasive, automated means of control. For the two authors, '"Security" is now a major consideration at all levels, from choosing a neighbourhood to live in, to driving the children to their school, from following specific preventive strategies when walking home to not using underground transport after a certain hour or in specific areas' (Lianos and Douglas, 2000: 16). With everything and everyone scanned, all is potentially within the realm of a threat:

> That suspicion and danger are the contemporary vehicles of this social axiom, shows precisely the shift towards a new sociality which is not based on dominant values but on avoidable threats. It follows that visible qualities which can be associated with the lower classes – such as race or subcultural attitudes – become automatic indicators of dangerousness. (Lianos and Douglas, 2000: 26)

In the work of Ajana (2020), security and border control become central elements concerning how such precise means of surveillance may evolve. The individual's subjection, encompassing practices such as biometric identification of bodily 'passwords', border scanning, workplace health assessments, and dietary regulations, intersects with the ethos of the 'Quantified Self' movement. From a biopower perspective, the Onlife world with its invasive devices becomes an even more central element of subjectification. The health data collected on individuals is not only vast but also encompasses an unprecedented variety of contexts and instances. What does the smartwatch heart rate monitoring tell us (them?) when combined with visiting specific websites? And what evidence does the geolocation of individuals offer regarding potential breaches of quarantine during a significant virus transmission crisis? Within this framework lies the notion of 'control' as a biopolitical mechanism, echoing ideas from philosophers like Michel Foucault. It encapsulates the governance and regulation of life itself, including health and bodily aspects. The normalization of control is, yet again, in the guise of freedom (Agamben, 2004). For Agamben, concepts scrutinize how modern states wield power, employing security measures and biometric identification purportedly in defence of freedom, yet paradoxically enhancing control and surveillance. The amalgamation of truth-seeking and self-improvement within these practices underscores a complex interplay between personal enlightenment through data and its potential impact on individual autonomy and societal control. Biometrics in this sense becomes the baseline for active citizenship, something that touches upon Paul Rabinow's concept of bio-sociality (1996). For Rabinow, the intersection of biology and sociality takes over from Foucauldian understanding via individual organization, new communities formed by shared experiences related to biomedicine, genetics, or specific medical conditions (Rabinow, 2017). These e-health predispositions become thus the baseline for new boundaries and societal connections, but also intersect with Foucauldian notions of biopower and subjectification of the body. Data gathered on patients becomes the central element of e-health surveillance via digital devices (Adams et al, 2017: 165) – especially in order to profile anomalies (Adams et al, 2017) and potential 'risks' (Rabinow, 1996; Rose, 2000). Biopolitically, an individual becomes a specific string of knowledge that not only distinguishes the person by their specific DNA but all aspects of them can be recollected and monitored in an environment of perpetual and invasive 'dataveillance', mixing and altering concepts of 'norms' and subsequent social norms (Adams et al, 2017: 61).

Surveillance in such a scenario is aided by the presence of the smartphone in everyday existence and constitutes something that Alan Levinovitz (2024) defines as 'grassroots' surveillance, made up of political activism mixed with the immediacy of filming environments. Siva Vaidhyanathan (2018) has noted the dangers of surveillance in everyday life: not simply by being observed by a remotely controlled closed-circuit television (CCTV) camera, but filmed, recorded, and observed through the high-definition lenses of smartphones, available virtually everywhere and always at hand, whereas 'anyone of us who carries a camera attached to a mobile phone is an agent of surveillance' (Vaidhyanathan, 2018: 53). Social media acts as the quintessential tool to mediate such reality: shifting content, of whatever validity, to the global view at any given time.

Other than the moral entrepreneurs filming bystanders and thus subjecting themselves to further moral crusades online, the pivotal experience in mid-2020 of the US-based Latin American worker Emmanuel Cafferty (Redstone, 2020) not only highlighted the problem of being filmed and thus 'shit-famed' online, but also of one not being able to effectively trust what takes place in the Onlife dimension. For context, Cafferty was photographed while driving next to a Black Lives Matter rally, and the ambiguous positioning of his hand hanging out of the car's window was perceived by later Twitter users as resembling the 'OK' sign that is associated with white supremacists. The outcry of his apparent action led to his identification (or doxxing) and the immediate termination of his employment. Other than evident controversies around the incident – which have been eventually and painstakingly proven as a misunderstanding – subjectification of media over the lives of unaware individuals is central. Users of the Onlife are not simply filmed at a given time and place, their existences may be shaped and concretely affected without their being aware. As such, the assemblage of surveillance that takes over 'englobes' everything, judges it all out of context and misinterprets it, with very little if no agency to control and rectify things, hinting yet again at the fractured mirrored world Klein refers to in her book *Doppelganger* (Klein, 2023).

If we have ventured into the general aspects of surveillance, I will now focus on highlighting the more practical means of smart surveillance in the Onlife scenario: the micro and macro milieu. For the micro, I will concentrate on the infiltration of surveillance technology into intimate spaces, in which a symbiotic relationship is created between smart devices and their users, where luxurious, fun, and essential blurs the lines between protection and abuse, making surveillance an almost unquestioned part of modern family life.

For the macro, I will further analyse the realm and implication of future Onlife cities, highlighting the covert integration of surveillance into existing urban spaces.

## Gazing (into) the intimate environment

Surveillance per se is an object of intimacy. It involves some sort of hidden space that allows listeners to hear, and observers to watch. The dynamics of surveillance as a specific culture has been forwarded by Foucault (1978) and discussed in detail by David Lyon's lifelong work (see full relevant list in References). In their arguments, what is seen and controlled replicates elements of social engineering, which, derived from military dynamics, replicate in the biopolitical structure of modernity (Foucault, 1978; Melossi, 2008). In this scenario, such military and hegemonistic dynamics replicate very well in the parental role over children and siblings (Livingstone, 2002). In families, the intimate lives of their members are very frequently, and very easily, placed under scrutiny (Nelson and Garey, 2009; Steeves and Jones, 2010). However, modern technologies and Onlife scenarios have rendered surveillance not only possible on a whole different level, but have increased its features, as well as its strategies of covert control/observation, as well as engendering negotiation and resistance.

Within a global trend of 'domestic surveillance' (Maalsen and Sadowski, 2019), surveillance technologies infiltrate our intimate spaces, creating a symbiotic relationship with other smart devices and their users, who use them to control themselves and each other (Maalsen, 2024). Siblings and partners all become subjects of surveillance practices, reflecting a growing trend that extends beyond domestic walls, with smart devices as the common denominator.

This central theme was fully explored in the work of Caron Margareth Barron (2014), who shows the dynamics whereby the tools of surveillance, such as smartphones, become themselves tools to 'scramble' parental control. Children not only gain and earn devices with the 'excuse' of safety and 'emergency', but develop specific languages and elements of secret coding through texting as forms of 'escaping' surveillance (Kaufmann, 2021). This perspective of an alternative language is not limited to the smartphone but has been related to short message service (SMS) texting (Livingstone, 2002), and can be easily detected earlier that. Children, returning to Barron, are not 'passive, powerless recipients of surveillance, rather they tell us of the forms of negotiation and resistance to monitoring after play spaces'. (Barron, 2014: 411). The remote aspect of these devices is central: they can observe, control, 'record, store, collate, relay and replay data' about their child indefinitely and with practically infinite means (Rooney, 2010: 344). Indeed, Rooney discusses the central point of trust and the lack of it, fed by the replete scenario of consumeristic tools available on the market, one that, as discussed by Marx and Steeves (2010), has created a gold mine for those producing gadgets, baby monitoring tools, kits, and devices, out of a 'crisis of trust' within society. Indeed, this mistrust is not only limited to parents not trusting their own children or the children of others – but is embedded into a specific culture of suspicion, fear, and anxiety (Kennedy and Madelaine, 2022). This extends to the other's parents, teachers, institutions, politicians, and strangers, in fact, to any 'other'. To track, monitor, and control appears as the only solution for a increasingly mediated and scandal-seeking reality – another apparent feature of the online scenario. Also, a central aspect is that this form of control and surveillance, especially through the post-COVID-19 dynamics, has become ever more 'biological' in its scope and aim. It attempts to 'catch' under its gaze all aspects of those observed, again, especially within the intimate/domestic sphere – not only his or her whereabouts but the interaction, the contacts, the moods, and dynamics. Thanks to the normalizations of parental control apps (such as Google Family Link), and covert domestic CCTV installations (Maalsen, 2024), all this has become a recurring element of the Onlife reality.

Equally important to Lupton's work is her study on the 'ludification' of parenting by devices (Lupton and Thomas, 2015). The actual pleasure of doing surveillance as a parent – and most of all the normative aspect – strikes one as opening a variety of new scenarios for the power and integration of these tools – the playful element that involves control – and the successful limitation of potential deviance and disobedience. The dynamics and boundaries of what is protective and what is abusive are harder than ever to pinpoint due to the easy availability of the software, the 'fashionable' commercialization of its features, and the safe-keeping perspective in an ever-growing web anxiety. The ludic and rewarding elements of 'doing good' mix and potentially confuse with elements of 'doing harm'.

But the potential of these smart technologies is not simply that of controlling, but of controlling without letting others know. They act in secret, with covert features and hidden potential. Special gizmos like those seen in James Bond films are purchasable with a click. They are also apparently very effective and well-produced, at least according to the reviews visible online. Their availability sets a new condition of being monitored, observed, and even controlled: if jokes, from *South Park* to *The Simpsons*, are created around the invasion of some bulky, expensive gizmo into the home, their presence has become within the Onlife not only integrated but extremely hard to spot.

These tools come in different sizes and prices, with items like a baby monitor that resembles a standard webcam displaying cheerful images of children on a small smartphone screen. Additionally, there are micro-cameras, often labelled as nanny cams or spy cams, some showing hypothetical scenes such as a masked figure mimicking a thief or a miniature figure that suggests live Wi-Fi viewing on a smartphone.

These devices often appear in search results together, potentially influenced by search algorithms and shared item descriptions. Further exploration presents an array of micro-cameras concealed within everyday objects such as watches, speakers, USB plugs, clocks, and power banks.

As I have discussed in previous research (2021), these items offer discreet monitoring capabilities, accompanied by various features like motion sensors, video and audio recording, and night vision. What unites all these devices is the hidden camera feature – underlined by the 'cam' suffix – thus apparently fulfilling the desire to see, which is very central to the work of Foucault (1978). Such a camera function appears as the fundamental, yet disguised, feature: we find it concealed in the face of fully functioning alarm clocks, hidden in the numbers of wall clocks, hidden in the frame of watches, pens, the buttons of a loudspeaker, or in clothes hooks (BBC News, 2023).

How much of this is purely creepy? What might be considered, effectively, dangerous and criminal? The threshold, as in all Onlife implications, is very subtle, and in terms of legislation it changes from country to country. The Onlife allows triviality of actions, as certain purchases can take place without question and be installed undetected within households. Episodes of abuse are, in such a context, a growing concern (Maalsen and Sadowski, 2019; Marganski and Melander, 2021; Tanczer, 2023).

## Anti-cities unbounded

Surveillance influences and alters our choices and the ways we are perceived. This is what Lyon considered to be the growing issue of 'social sorting' (Lyon, 2003): with the tools becoming more and more remote, effortless and cheap, the individuals being watched are immediately categorized and easily differentiated, that is, indexed.

Beyond such devices, which are invisible and yet somewhat 'impersonal', for Lyon there is the 'everyday practice [of surveillance] in which human beings engage routinely often unthinkingly. Parents watch over children, employers watch over workers, police watch over neighbourhoods, guards watch over prisoners and so on' (Lyon, 2009: 107). With the trivialization and normalization of monitoring technologies such as the Amazon Ring doorbell video cams accessed by US police officers (Belanger, 2022; Morrisons, 2022), the embracing and connecting of digital personas with their Onlife equivalent represent the haunting visions of the CCTV invasion, prominent in UK cities since the early 1990s – a time when, according to David Lyon, citizens: 'seldom [knew] that they [were] subjects of surveillance, or, if they [did] know, [were] unaware how comprehensive others' knowledge of them actually [was]' (Lyon, 1994: 5). However rudimentary, the 1990s wholesale implementation of CCTV footage represented the first step of the trivialized 'medialization' of public citizens within a closed system, that is, subject to reverse, forwarding, zooming, and scaling within and by some form of highly pervasive media. The use of these technologies has long produced a mixed response, from security and crime reduction enthusiasts to those concerned about privacy issues (Smith, 2015). Nonetheless, the discussion of the pros and cons of the use of CCTV never actually managed to halt the phenomena. Instead, in the words of Scottish CCTV scholar Gavin Smith, they continued to legitimate the role of CCTV in the public imagination (Smith, 2015).

What is the equivalent of this normalization deep into the second decade of the millennia? For criminologists such as Keith Hayward, the collection of data via new smart technologies becomes the prime focus of urban design (Hayward, 2020). 'Urban intelligence' becomes central to both managing the city and controlling its bodies, that is, those who commute and engage with its fabric. Citizens, in perfect Onlife conditions, become the ideal users. Their existence leaves trails in the urban fabric just as web navigation feeds cookies and 'hotjars' (web analytics and feedback tool on user interaction). Their existence is a sensitive and sensible asset, whereby all sorts of information may aid social, commercial, and urban management to augment the commuter experience and maximize functionality. The focal objective of this mega investment across the world represents utopian agendas for green technologies, better waste management, more fluid traffic control, and, of course, better security (including emergency response) (Schuilenburg and Peeters, 2018; Gassmann et al, 2019: i–xx; Cugurullo, 2023). Such an approach is the recurring utopia of crime control and traffic management with invasive and covert measures. Already in 2013, the City of London boasted the use of smartphone tracking bins that picked up users' Bluetooth signals as they passed by (BBC News, 2013). Today, cities across the globe make use of footfall technology, 'heatmaps' (colour coding spatial data), and smart energy metrics. Notorious are examples in the Asian urban context where street and traffic lights may be remotely altered to create direct freeways for emergency services, as reported enthusiastically by various news outlets. As such, the individuals may be remotely channelled and halted, either via traffic lights or, potentially, smartphone notifications. Examples of such Internet of Things integration are also being trialled and implemented in urban spaces across Europe, with traffic lights, CCTV, digital signs, air quality monitoring, lighting, and parking bays all connected through a communications network. As noted by Hayward (2020), city management has become very closely associated with crime management, enriched by security protocols regulating buildings, spaces, and actors. The smartness of the city space is one of ultimate control. Everything in this futuristic environment, which has equivalents across the globe, is dedicated to the concept of monitoring: be it the air quality, the energy level in the EV chargers, the traffic flow, or the gait of a hesitant subway stroller, even sleep data (Belcher, 2022). Everything in this environment is captured, and anything can be functionally perfected. One may wonder, who would want to live in a city like this?

The South Korean city of Songdo, built from scratch near the suffocating megalopolis of Seoul (which has a population density of 17,288 per square metre), has been repeatedly used as a parable of the smart cities' concept failure. The city is conceived as the ultimate international business district, no matter it being one of the costliest urban investments ever made (US$40 billion, according to Gassmann et al, 2019), but has proved to be a phantom estate, with less than 200,000 permanent residents.[4] An even more disastrous example is the US$100 billion ghost town known as 'Forest City' in Malaysia (Descalsota, 2022).

However, these failures by no means prove that there is a lack of investment interest in the 'concepts' of such assets. Technology appears as the prime reason for expense, and so is the development of securitizing, controlling, and surveilling technology. Another example highlights this picture: the futuristic urban project 'The Line', conceived of as a 170-mile-long city developed on a straight line across Saudi Arabia. The Line project presents an alluring vision of the future city, which completely changes our traditional understanding of cities as a collection of people and places to live on a human scale. And, of course, much of the argument is connected to a long history of class divide, formed by exclusion and control, especially for the Global South's 'new rich' (Davis and Monk, 2007). However, it fails to address important issues such as environmental impact, destruction of natural habitats, disruption of migratory paths, and displacement of indigenous populations. Despite these concerns, The Line project still appears attractive due to its simplicity and ease of implementation, though recent reports seem to suggest that its implementation is being scaled back (Jones and Brown, 2024).

The more concrete potential of smart cities is thus not in the sophisticated 'ex-novo' investment or its highly privileged gated 'Eden' infrastructures but in the creeping implementation of smart functions in the public space of our cities. When using various browsers to search the web for 'smartest cities in the world', one may unequivocally notice mention of major European capitals, with London at the top of the list, along with New York, Taipei, and Lima. Monitoring technologies and crime control measures are thus not built into the urban fabric but merged into it, covertly developed within its spaces, blending with the otherwise latent functionalities, as with the previously mentioned data collecting bins in the early 2010s in London, or with soft 'nudges' (Schuilenburg and Peeters, 2018) knitted into the urban fabric of Eindhoven, with its 'cooling' effect smart projections that discourage episodes of 'aggression, excessive noise, public drunkenness, vandalism and violence' (Pali and Schuilenburg, 2020: 780).

The use of surveillance, as such, is becoming a systematic means of controlling, monitoring, and calculating both micro and macro spaces of interaction, where technologies are, on the one hand, voluntarily purchased and integrated within domestic environments, and, on the other, are projected into the urban fabric, with a mixture of planning development, luxury estate investment, and general hype around the potential of Internet of Things technology.

Such a reality becomes even more problematic if we consider how precisely technologies can be used today to track animals of all sorts. In their highly engaging conversation, Simone Browne, Francisco Klauser, and David Wood (2022) further discuss the implication of an all-controlling, all-limiting scenario. They mention the work of Roger Søraa, who analysed 'CyborGoats', referring to the digitized geofencing systems used in Norway (as elsewhere) for keeping goats within a predefined geographical area without physical fences (Søraa and Vik, 2021). As Klauser asks, 'What if the same happens, via smart devices, to citizens navigating the "city limits"?' (Browne et al, 2022).

## Cybergoaters

Among the most insignificant tools that have crept into the fabric of everyday devices is the progressive use of face-recognition technology. While promoted to enhance security, especially within smart device technology, much of its uses, however, are actually misleading, and in many ways useless. The face recognition that current smartphones use is incredibly limited. Like the use of FaceID, TouchID, OpticID, and so on, the amount of information used to identify one person from another is quite superficial. Regardless of marketing names, to remotely identify individuals and objects is another matter.

The use of software to understand human patterns again very much resembles the various algorithms and plug-ins that websites use on a superficial basis for daily navigation. From cookies to hotjar heatmaps monitoring not only clicks and scrolls but also visuals and sensory elements across the page, the use of the mouse, the pressure on the screen, and the existence of the Onlife user is fully calculated and quantified.

Face recognition is a powerful tool in identification – a technology that can be used on humans, as well as vehicles and even animals, with such deep learning technologies as BearID,[5] which monitors wild bears (Odgen, 2020). These advancements and research trends demonstrate the surreptitious and invasive potential of improving technologies with anthropocentric means. The hindrance of anthropic flaws in their use, however, is evident, and their functionalities have become ever more a problem of unexpected harm and disruption.

On the problematics of human face recognition, examples of misuse and abuse have been debated in the media and academic discourse for the last decade. Particularly significant has been the use of live technology in the

UK to monitor the crowds at the coronation of King Charles in early 2023 (Dodd, 2023), or as a systematic tool to oppress dissidents in Putin's Moscow (Masri, 2023). The use was highly discriminatory and problematic when set against the right to protest, especially when questions are raised on the deletion of images recorded and what sorts of cross-checks are made after the protests have ended.

Moreover, these considerations are based on the idea that the technology works. It is something of a known fact that, up to the early 2020s, face recognition was only efficient on the faces of middle-aged White men. Racial bias was prominent (Najibi, 2020),[6] especially in multicultural environments. Simone Browne already in 2015 noted in her book *Dark Matters* how face-recognition technology was based on 'pseudo-scientific racist and sexist discourse that sought to define racial and gendered categories and linearly order humans to regulate those artificial boundaries that could never be fully maintained' (Browne, 2015: 111). Perhaps, as noted by the Home Office during the Conservative administration in late 2023, gender or ethnicity identification is improving (Home Office news team, 2023). But this improvement is also problematic when enhancing the accuracy of ethnic disparities, such as with the Uyghur population in China (Bhuiyan, 2022) or the pseudo-colonialist practice of abusive Brahmanism hyper-surveillant policing in India (Sonavane, 2023), which is exactly the target of this Onlife technology (this will be discussed further).

Live recognition of licence plates and other objects is another prominent technology, particularly, again, in the UK and the rest of continental Europe, for processing fines relating to speeding and unlicensed or untaxed vehicles. While allegedly recognizing licence plates is more straightforward than recognizing faces, the system also creates significant mayhem when one considers the rapid potential of its 'fine' producing process.

A notorious case is that of a woman from Surrey wearing a knitted jumper who was mistaken by an automatic number plate recognition (ANPR) camera for a vehicle.[7] Indeed, when such a mistake is multiplied by the thousands it has a detrimental effect on a significant number of citizens who need to prove themselves innocent. Again, one must not be unreasonably luddite about a technology that makes mistakes and is most probably improving with every new upgrade. However, it is important to highlight the harms and miscarriages of justice that, albeit in a small number of cases, create a problematic condition for the unknowing receiver of a fine who must prove their innocence via a notoriously difficult and time-consuming system. Moreover, small numbers overall should by no means hinder the significance of a faulty system – especially if the system provides collateral harms and victimhood.

Has surveillance taken over all aspects of the Onlife? Perhaps not, but it is disingenuous to claim one may simply find a cabin in the woods to be free from it. Not simply through the use of drones, as proven during COVID-19 (Jackman et al, 2024), or satellite imaging (since the 1990s), the ubiquitous means of Onlife surveillance utilize face-recognition technology on all living beings. Indeed, the Onlife establishment, as mentioned before, is well entrenched in the wilderness and natural habitats. Non-human animals have long been subject to technological surveillance of sorts (Søraa and Vik, 2021). The precise identification of endangered grizzly bears through face recognition may very well improve research and help protect them.[8] However, it is important to highlight the collateral victims of yet another use of technology. In the Piedmont border region of Italy, disguised 'photo-cages' were installed in strategic spots by the local authorities. The excuse was that it provided the best way of monitoring the migration of animals. However, it soon became evident that the 'photo-cages' were being used to catch human trespassers, 'crimmigrants' (Franko, 2020), who, according to local activists, regularly try to reach France through the woods.[9] The use of more advanced surveillance technology and face recognition united with night visions and motion sensors is evidently a very big step – and not an insignificant one, as noted earlier in the chapter.

## Conclusion: 'Moodizens'

I have in this chapter ventured upon the various aspects of surveillance today, and in particular the trivialization of its uses, be it corporate, governmental, administrative, domestic, or personal. Nevertheless, its dangers are unilateral and ubiquitous, a true assemblage to which little alternative and resistance is offered.

As we mentioned at the beginning of the chapter, Josh Harris's 'We Live in Public' project, which through voluntary actions (with glimpses of obsessive narcissism) objectifies the subject of total surveillance, shows that activists have used the means to totally surveil themselves (sousveillance) as a form of activism (Mann, 2016). Another example is the public life of media artist Hasan Elahis, who responded to his being placed on the terrorist watch list by loading every detail of his existence online – his whereabouts, meals, toilet visits, and so on.[10]

However, the tools to surveil individuals in the Onlife are progressing in further directions with the use of automation and artificial intelligence (AI), which have even more criminological implications.

Already in the early 2000s, the cyberpunk graphic novel *Transmetropolitan* envisioned surveillance cameras capable of detecting 'violent thoughts' in children, resulting in their expulsion from schools. It is unsettling to see how quickly such dystopian and previously ironically depicted technology may progress into identifying violent thoughts. After all, AI may soon be much more credible in doing the job than operators scanning the minds of children envisioned in *Transmetropolitan*. While face recognition focuses on identifying individuals based on their facial features, mood recognition operates in a more nuanced manner: powered by algorithms and powerful application programming interfaces (APIs). These systems aim to identify and classify different emotions by analysing facial features like the position of the mouth and eyebrows. Their features are specifically designed to classify emotions and moods, resembling the psychopolitical modulation of crime control and crime prevention. The data related to mood and emotion can be identified as significant as the 'mental state of a person … directly relates to his intentions or the physical efforts that he must be applying for performing tasks' (Mehta et al, 2018: 1). Such Onlife technology would ideally be most effective in mega-event security or in specific areas of large pedestrian transit, where the analysis of facial features may not simply identify but foresee individual distress and, potentially, their actual intention, with the use of augmented reality glasses – more on this later. The deployment of facial recognition technology is merely a precursor to the more insidious application of affective computing, which can be readily experimented with online and are likely to become increasingly sophisticated and invasive through the integration of artificial intelligence.

The immediacy of 'total monitoring', which may very well include 'total control' also applies to the development of new satellite technologies. If the police are still apparently resisting the use of drones from being deployed with taser weapons (Olumhense, 2023), experimental satellite technologies such as StarLink are rendering the notorious lag of satellite imaging (because of the earth's rotation) much more immediate (Reuters, 2024). One may speculate on where this is going by adding two and two. While such a 'security camera for the planet' is, according to *The New Yorker*, being deployed with apparent evidence of climate change control benefits (Brown, 2023), the potential for shifting the lenses onto people is negligible if not, potentially, a normal feature of the Onlife.

This normalization, leading to systematic 'grassroots' filming of everything and everyone, becomes not simply a resemblance of the Zamyatin 'living in public' phenomena, but it is a necessary, at times consolatory, response to the fact that everything is visible. To film each other is no longer an act to defend ourselves from something, it is an act to defend the filming of each other. The Onlife systematics is central to this perpetual selfie mode we exist in – one where to film oneself, to actively participate in surveillance, is an action of protection, from others, from ourselves, from society, and the world – that has no end. However, as I will discuss in the next chapter, this mediated approach to 'life', that as a consequence becomes mediated, comes at the price of being permanently mutable, constantly in change, and fundamentally, and deeply, unreliable.

4

# Not So Friendly

## Community and/or commotion?

Today's Onlife engagement provides unprecedented levels of communication between otherwise unconnected users. Social media has effectively provided concrete instances of moral panic that underscore the delicate balance of online discussions and their impact on everyday life. Already well-known on the anonymous image-board platform 4chan (Threadgold, 2019; Ball, 2023) hybrid forms of mass raids have gained global attention. These incidents often involve groups of youths, dressed in dark hoods, storming popular shops to steal goods in a swift, coordinated manner – a trend widely reported across the UK in recent years. Similar tactics have also been observed in the US and Brazil, where social media has played a key role in mobilizing pro-Trump supporters (Klein, 2023) and pro-Bolsonaro groups (Malleret et al, 2023), amplifying and organizing such actions. More subtly, social media platforms foster environments where toxic elements mirror traits associated with the 'Dark Tetrad' of personality – narcissism, Machiavellianism, psychopathy, and sadism (Craker and March, 2016). These traits are not only visible in the toxic gendered communities of spaces like the so-called 'manosphere' or 'femcels' but they also serve to ignite and spread harmful ideologies and behaviours that cross races, gender, and the political spectrum (Johanssen and Kay, 2024), with artificial intelligence (AI) chatbots only making the matter more complex and harder to reason with (Alegre, 2024). Despite the damaging nature of toxic communities, intervention by platform moderators often comes too late – banning content and users only after significant harm has already been done (Hoffman et al, 2020; Ball, 2023).

I begin this chapter by discussing the historical 'pros' of advocating for the use and impact of social media, highlighting how quickly the detrimental effects became evident within the lenses of the Onlife. These dynamics are apparent in how social media platforms are designed and promoted, with corporations feeling the pressure to present a unified image and uphold a carefully curated ethical stance. This push for a singular identity often results in subtle but powerful effects on users and society at large. Indirect surveillance – where individuals' actions are constantly monitored without their full awareness – becomes normalized. At the same time, social isolation increases as people are encouraged to engage primarily through online platforms, reducing face-to-face interactions.

Mimetic scapegoating also plays a role, where certain individuals or groups are blamed or targeted based on trends that emerge in the digital sphere, often amplified by algorithms that prioritize controversial content. This, in turn, leads to data subjugation, where people are not just participants in these platforms but also the source of data that is continuously harvested, analysed, and used for corporate or governmental control.

One of the more troubling trends is the emergence of 'rule-by-data' systems, such as social credit models, which are now looming on the horizon in Western countries. These systems can determine a person's access to services, opportunities, or even freedom based on data-driven evaluations of their behaviour. Through these frameworks, social media platforms can 'harmonize' information (curating or suppressing content to fit certain narratives), shift public opinion by manipulating polls, and control dissent by censoring voices remotely, silently, and instantly without visible repercussions or public outcry (Torpey, 2020). From this troubling scenario, the internet as we know it today has emerged through a series of failures marked by audacity and even bravado. It reflects a series of managerial choices and the Schumpeterian notion of 'creative destruction' – the strict necessity of breaking eggs to make an omelette – that has shaped the shiny yet flawed and dangerous reality of the Onlife world. I continue by discussing these platforms, outlining the causes of their popularity and the effectiveness of their tools, and especially their potential future, considering virtual reality (VR) and its augmented uses.

What drives the conduct, behaviour, and nuances that leak within online and offline scenarios, mixing and matching episodes that perhaps do not appear problematic by themselves, yet together constitute a whole new horizon in criminology?

## Social virtual spaces

In the now-classic *Alone Together* (2011), sociologist Sherry Turkle demonstrated how technology is viewed as a solution to the commodification of human relationships in late-capitalist society. Turkle explored how mass media trivializes social interactions and how technology intensifies the growing alienation from what is considered 'real', now perceived as a collection of experiences. Ironically, the technological solution ends up becoming part of the problem, creating new forms of solitude and isolation. Turkle's early work (2011) is particularly interesting for having foreseen the use of sociological lenses, a criminological outlook of harm and deviance that came to characterize our Onlife social interactions. While the names of platforms change, their pattern seems to be replicated, with few improvements and no new boundaries. But what constitutes the problematic core of these platforms?

The notifications we hear of X/Twitter, texts, Facebook, and so on serve to distract us and make us feel like we are at the centre of the world, yet our biopolitical subjugation to these very tools appears to be one of powerlessness.

The anti-social elements of 'social media' have long been debated by digital zemiologists (Wood, 2018) and media critics (Vaidhyanathan, 2018), and even by popular documentaries such as *The Antisocial Network* (Jones and Angelini, 2024). This becomes even more evident within the lenses of the Onlife, where it seems we do not use social media to establish contact with other human beings but to keep them at the 'right distance'. Through smart devices users may technically interact with anyone, but with a significant set of caveats that any derailment, off-tone, or incomprehension may lead to immediate banning, blocking, and reporting (Nguyen, 2021). This takes place both on social media and via reviews, comments, posts, and in groups. We are free to communicate immediately within an Onlife of immense potential but with a number of ambiguous rules of engagement that rapidly shift and further alienate users. The platforms to which we are 'stuck', in the words of Lovink (2022a), shape our interactions and the bio-sociality of engaging with one another, whereby 'We can no longer ignore the depression, anger, and despair, pretending they will be gone overnight after installing another app. Addiction is real, buried deep inside the body. Habits need to be unlearned, awareness' needs to spread' (Lovink, 2022a: 6). But the way we interact, both civilly and abusively on these tools is shaped by their very design – one with many flaws. Such considerations have become increasingly important since the outbreak of COVID-19 and the resulting social isolation it imposed. Zoom calls, webinars, and other forms of virtual meetings replaced physical gatherings with unprecedented commitment.

In a 2022 podcast with the popular American host Joe Rogan, Facebook's CEO Mark Zuckerberg criticized Zoom for turning users into isolated entities, with participants confined to small boxes that fail to create a tangible sense of dimension or meaningful space (Metz and Thorbecke, 2022). The shortcomings of Zoom and similar web conferencing software bear an unsettling resemblance to the panoptic gaze arrangement of isolated peers lined up and overseen by a central, anonymous recording lens. Zuckerberg apparently noticed the same thing, building a fresh new look for how future meetings can develop and become more efficient via the Meta platform in a multiverse establishment. I will return to this point, and the harmful implications, later on.

## Sourcing friends

In the virtual sphere, the birth of any 'social' space has always aroused great interest in a vast and growing cohort of internet users. These communities, now intended as 'social networking' sites, are still relatable to boyd and Ellison's 2007 definition: 'a web-based service that allows individuals to (1) construct a public or semi-public profile within a bounded system, (2) articulate a list of other users with whom they share a connection, and (3) view and traverse their list of connections and those made by others within the system' (boyd and Ellison, 2007: 211).

Let us take a small step back. The late 1990s set the stage for the new liquid environment (Bauman, 2000), which also describes the blurring effect of losing solidity and losing ground. Already by the 2000s, according to Rotman (2000), the sense of a borderless state allowed organized crime to 'create flexible, global networks and thus evade state regulations and cumbersome international law enforcement' (Rotman, 2000: 4). By 2001, security meant something quite different – one that can be associated with the 'insecurities' around the 9/11 attacks (Furedi, 2001). The entire Western world watched the twin towers of the World Trade Center collapse one by one on their screens and then sat in front of another screen to discuss, comment, and write about it online. A merging of intermixed realities occurred: civilization could not just watch and stare, it wanted to take part in what it was seeing, hoping to also change things, and largely unaware of how much they would soon change regardless. As noted by Lovink (2019), the Web 1.0 randomness of platforms, the vastness and hyper-personalized structure of blogs and other websites were indeed liberating, but also confusing – as evidenced by the dot.com crash that peaked in the year 2000, out of the ashes of the 'Y2K' moral panic.

One may argue that after a series of half-baked social media platforms, Facebook was the one able to consolidate the income-generating advertisement potential on the new network – particularly the aspects of data collection and fixed user interaction, which would become so predominant and popular. It came to represent a system that de facto united the world with an impressive and universal enthusiasm: a true globalization of styles and communication skills, the 'like' that said it all, the picture that described everything. If the early 1980s' scholars boasted of the 'McDonaldization' of the free market economy and society (Ritzer, 1983), claiming that no country owning such franchises ever went to war with each other, a novel revolutionary 'WebDonaldization' of everything would similarly build new identities, forge new trends, destabilize governments, and unite cultures across the world – as long as it adhered to its winning, stable, friendly model. In its extreme, as noted by Jessa Lingel (2019, 2021), it offered a 'gentrified' virtual space, where the unregulated digital world would be neatly, monetarily, and obediently channelled: 'a connected but separate set of issues in the kinds of online spaces and relationships that are increasingly encouraged or restricted online' Lingel (2019). By calling the contemporary internet gentrified, Lingel's goal 'is both to diagnose a set of problems and lay out what internet activists can do to carve out more protections and spaces of freedom' (Lingel, 2019). Facebook became an ideal example, offering a clean, safe, censured environment, where users, first in a privileged campus environment and later as a growing cohort of youths, are prevented from touching on certain topics, posting certain content, and are 'gently' invited to behave properly by 'moderators' and fellow users – thus disintegrating the replication of 'real life' subcultures and 'borderline' expressions that are not tolerated by Silicon Valley principles. Lingel compares Facebook to the 'Walmart of the Internet', winking to its invasive structure, but potentially underlining the sterilization, consensual hyper-control and securitization of its premises – similar to the panoptic considerations at Disneyland, as noted by Clifford Shearing, who was gently walked out of the theme park by 'Mickey Mouse' after his daughter happened to be accidentally shoeless (Shearing and Stenning, 1985). Whatever does not fully 'fit' the picture is 'softly' banned, blocked, and denied access – to be a maverick, to be someone thinking 'out-of-the-box' becomes the 'bug' of a system that was nevertheless built by those trying to 'break' down the wall of conventional thinking. Mark Zuckerberg, among many, was one of them.

## Digital quests

The story of Zuckerberg and his company is well known, conceived in the midst of controversy in the mind of a young Harvard student in 2003. (The 2010 major motion picture *The Social Network* (Fincher, 2010) made even the socially awkward and generally unlikable billionaire appear more human). The question, however, remains: why did such a stale platform as Facebook rise to become so powerful in comparison to other similar competitors? As noted by Angwin (2009), the simplest answer is perhaps the most convincing one. The year 2003 was also when the first digital cameras became a commercial object. With pictures suddenly becoming easy to load onto a computer, and thus to a homepage, 2003 was also notable for being the first year that digital cameras outsold film ones. Before that year, digital images were quite hard to get. One needed a digital scanner, which was even harder to obtain. The social network company Six Degrees' demanded photo IDs of all new users and received millions of them by post, which then needed to be scanned (Angwin, 2009). Of course, no start-up or big corporation had the manpower to do this. Facebook didn't need to.

Digital images, which became the central element of the 2010s' decade of surveillance, constituted the ultimate step in social media, becoming the integral tool of the Web 2.0 internet phase. Smartphones and apps, with their mobile data packages offering perpetual internet access, soon followed. By then, Facebook, like Google, was already dominating the internet scene – and managed to direct their billionaire investments accordingly.

Digital images (and digital photo identification) thus had the consolidating effect of putting the real in the internet experience – perhaps the first step towards a total Onlife interaction. One's digital expression became part of the wider internet and was shared as such. Images are no trivial matter. They can change the meaning of words – they 'expose' and 'exponentiate' their effect. When, in Roberto Calasso's interpretation, John Searle wrote that a virtual hurricane does not wet (Calasso, 2017), this was before the merging of digital experience and photography could be matched. Ever since, cyberspace has changed connotation: just as one cannot simply shut the computer to avoid participating in a harmful conversation, digital data has become associated with the real persona.[1]

## Friendly surveillance

Facebook created the quintessential platform where people could both share publicly and talk privately: this distinction is central when seeking the connection between data and harm. Facebook had access to both the voluntary exposition of everyday life as well as private, more secret interactions (Nissenbaum, 2009). Both would prove inconceivably lucrative. They also proved unprecedentedly harmful. Social media created an Onlife scenario aided by technological tools such as smart devices. They formed new all-encompassing institutions against whom users had very limited tools to protect, hide, and defend themselves. The watchful 'gaze' of corporations and peers (Beer, 2019a) became unilateral and ubiquitous. Surveillance became an essential component of the Web 2.0 development of the internet, and later Web 3.0 hyperconnected experience. Again, we have a central dichotomy between corporations and users that blur into one monitoring device. This has been described in many ways: the all-seeing Panopticon (Foucault, 1979); the branching out and fracturing of the Synopticon (Mathieson, 1997); the privileged views of the Oligopticon (Latour, 2005); the exclusion dynamics of Ban-opticon (Bigo, 2008); the invisible means of Nonopticon (Vaidhyanathan, 2008); and more recently, the negative gaze of the Malopticon (McNeill, 2019).[2] When specifically observing the essence of social media, we come across the central characteristics of observing and controlling users via public posts integrated with private messages. It is a practice that is simply becoming integral to the Onlife essence, via GPS and other mobile-led sensors. Again, as noted by Giglioli (2019), the labyrinths of digital surveillance spread without true awareness, and evidently with little concern. Whatever concern has been raised regarding these practices, Onlife social interactions have come to replicate the global village that Marshall McLuhan anticipated (Levinson, 2001).

But surveillance is not solely the domain of governments and corporations: it permeates the daily lives of all digitally, technologically, and socially connected individuals. Everything is not only visible to the corporation and one's peers but there is also no way out – or no easy one at least. It is like the recurring joke of the ease of entering a madhouse: but how to prove you are sane and leave? The desire to even do so may appear anti-social, problematic, and suspicious.

## Mimetic (dis)order

Social media, with its evolving dynamics, has proven to be a problematic environment, with its chaotic functioning being intrinsic to its very design. Returning to actual online engagement, the promotion and distribution of content are strongly manipulated – a topic that had at the time of writing almost become a 'well-known fact' to most users (Zuboff, 2019; Hari, 2023). The tendency to falsify and promote 'echo chambers' (closed social structures that reinforce users existing beliefs) is allegedly central to the early development of the platform (Pariser, 2011). Notably, an early and principal Facebook investor was Peter Thiel, a former student of sociologist René Girard at the Massachusetts Institute of Technology (MIT) in the 1980s. In his own words, Thiel found the theories of mimetic desire, whereby social individuals seek and copy each other's wishes, 'fascinating'[3] – and central to his concepts of making the 'world better via social media'. What for Girard was a powerful driving force of human nature became the inspiration for Thiel's 'home-feed' feature (a display of a continuous stream of updates, posts, and content), where users would not principally interact, but observe each other – and by observing, desire and thus imitate one another. As discussed by Thiel in a 2008 interview, this 'good mimesis' feed option was essential to avoid 'rivalry' (a central Girardian term, especially 'mimetic rivalry' that devolved into spiralling harms and scapegoating) among users. This is one of the major driving forces behind Facebook's (and similar platforms') channels of interaction, one that has since found countless replications that not only imitate the formula (mimesis again) but also expose and increase its potential.

## Individuals and the 'everything'

Who are these users whom we are supposed to be inspired by, according to Thiel, while we practice 'good mimesis' (as opposed to the bad mimesis that he claims may 'blow us all up by this next century'[4])? On the one hand, it seems evident that they are the VIPs users may now interact with daily. On the other hand, lie the common people, who fall into two centrally dubious categories: both 'real' and 'friends'. Let us look more closely at the matter.

Sherry Turkle, among others, has discussed the controversy of using a single profile as self-presentation, not only for your acquaintances but also for all those other users that you call 'friends' (2011). Facebook's concept of 'friend' has already in a sense created a sort of neologism that allows users to view and interact with all of their personal and public information (Vaidhyanathan, 2018): the circle closes, everyone becomes a VIP or a fan, and everyone may imitate one another. As such, an online world is created where everybody is a friend and by this definition, no one (Hari, 2023); it is merely a system of information exchange and news that is not limited to social life but also expands to one's personal, political, philosophical, religious, and/or sexual orientation. The more real the user is, the more they are 'true', and the better that they are represented and may be represented. The concept of using a single profile to represent all of these aspects of our identity is, I believe, very important to be understood and, mostly, forewarned – a point also raised recently by internet critic/enthusiast Marie Le Conte (2022). By being one individual (both everyone and no one), the user is constantly subject to observation and valuation by a non-quantifiable set of users. Subjugation as such becomes even more controversial and problematic: the single profile fulfils the purpose of Deleuze's notion of the 'dividual' data-doubles (Haggerty and Ericson, 2000). In this scenario, the 'individual' is no longer separable from its digital entity, consequently developing into an even more simplistic reality: a single, fully measurable cell of data.

Combining the essence of the individual's likes, tastes, feelings, relations, ideas, thoughts, purchases, styles, and emotions into a single tool is not simply a data gold mine (Zuboff, 2019) but a central social engineering and control achievement.

From an engineering perspective, Zuckerberg has proven very successful in timely purchases of the most influential social media platforms that combine private messaging (WhatsApp) and image trends (Instagram). Alongside his investments in smart glasses technology and crypto payments, it is evident that the entrepreneur had a direct interest in owning and managing the largest possible data exchange of users across most platforms, forming a specific 'closed' ecology where users interact under a single gatekeeping enterprise allegedly breaching Antitrust laws (BBC News, 2025).

This is also apparently the ambition of investor Elon Musk, who by purchasing the social media platform Twitter for $44 billion in 2022 (Conger and Hirsch, 2022) attempted the realization of his 'everything app' ambition. The renamed X.com has been, according to *PC Mag*, an 'obsession' (Humphries, 2017) for the entrepreneur since his PayPal days (Novak, 2017), a platform that aspires to turn into a 'super app'. Rather than developing it from scratch, Musk must have believed the data available on the platform was worth that expense. In any case, X's ambition is no longer Twitter's initial purpose of a quick and immediate public forum, but a Western version of multi-faceted platforms long used in Asian countries, such as WeChat or Grab social credit models (Browne et al, 2022).

WeChat indeed represents the potential for social control among platforms, something that was not fully available in the Western world to date, at least not officially or voluntarily (Chan, 2016). Back in 2022, on the *All-In Experience* podcast, Musk said that the US needed a super app: 'It's either convert Twitter to that or start something new. It does need to happen somehow' (2022). 'If you're in China, you kind of live on WeChat', Musk continued. 'It does everything. It's sort of like Twitter plus PayPal plus a whole bunch of things all rolled into one, with a great interface. It's really an excellent app, and we don't have anything like that outside of China.'

But what exactly is WeChat, and should Musk's comments be considered a threat? Released in 2011 as Weixin (微信) – meaning 'micro letter' – WeChat, as it is known in English, is part of Tencent Holdings, one of China's largest internet conglomerates. For a decade now, it has been China's most popular mobile app.

WeChat represents the quintessential social media tool, encompassing everyday social interactions and enabling strict state control over content and interactions. This dual role is crucial both from a surveillance perspective and for social control in China. Smart devices in China have become the central tools of citizenship, restructuring economic activity and social interactions to benefit the companies that own them (Hjorth et al, 2020).

Furthermore, WeChat stands out for its institutionalization beyond a simple platform, allowing users to engage in the digital economy and follow institutionalized media and centrally managed groups (Plantin and de Seta, 2019). It has been subject to extensive Western academic and journalistic scrutiny, particularly regarding its networked authoritarianism (MacKinnon, 2011). The social credit system, a digital surveillance mechanism to reward good behaviour and punish bad conduct, has been a focal point of this scrutiny (Liang, 2020). Kai Strittmatter has perhaps most emphatically criticized it, referring to it as the 'Little Red App', akin to an upgraded version of the Little Red Book (Strittmatter, 2020).

The intricacies of the social credit system are beyond the scope of this book, as its practices, regardless of its current efficacy in China, may seem culturally intolerable in the Global North, at least for now. It is, however, a fine-tuned case study that contrasts the excitement regarding the most-boasted about involvement of social media in aiding, if not provoking, the Arab Spring of 2010 and connecting activists worldwide. Moreover, it is worth noting that platforms like WeChat and Weibo excel in designing web-based products that effectively operate within the constraints of the 'Great Firewall of China'.

According to Strittmatter (2020), before Xi Jinping's rise to power, the internet in China was seen as a pressure cooker that would eventually explode if tightened too much. Xi Jinping offered a new reading on the potential of growing such a tool, long seen merely as a Western menace. Rather than suppressing and limiting its use, the internet was fully embraced by the party as its great 'harmonizing' quest. With the centralization of communication tools such as Weibo and WeChat, the party managed to allow for individual expression, while controlling and suppressing that very expression with remarkable efficiency. As with Mao's 'Thousand Flowers Blooming', the Onlife approach to the web allowed censorship and surveillance of the most minute details. With the implementation under Xi Jinping's regime of the 'Great Firewall scheme' (Wang, 2020), 'anyone who spread a *rumour* that was shared more than 500 times or received more than 5,000 clicks would risk up to three years in prison, given the apparent seriousness of the actions in *upset[tting] the social order*' (Strittmatter, 2020: 72) This is especially interesting considering that the objective of the 'censorship' was not to limit access to the web, but quite the contrary: the desire was one of propaganda, where a single narrative is repeated and endorsed or 'harmonized' through billions of different yet uniform voices. It is fundamentally the governmental channel to 'gauge the mood of the nation' (Strittmatter, 2020: 72). Such an approach was not only effective in blocking and imprisoning, without warning, popular individuals with millions of followers, but also in monitoring via social media bots and actual web-police the content of the web.

These Orwellian techniques were used to suppress the memory and remembrances of instances of political agitation, such as the 1989 uprising (Lim, 2014), or to block and filter messages, such as during the Hong Kong Umbrella Revolution of 2014 (Wong and Zheng, 2024), as also characterized by the new AI DeepSeek platform. But the information itself has become a central tool to monitor general discourse and build up the dossiers that secret police can access and monitor. This was evident with the so-called 'Penguin Patrol' and its 50-cent troll army (Guest, 2022), which in exchange for a small wage (that is, 50 cents per comment) would flood the web with comments and images to divert attention from political themes, while also reporting agitators and dissidents (Huang, 2018).

Furthermore, it seems that with the COVID-19 pandemic, WeChat saw an upsurge in the Onlife biopolitics of experimental social control techniques. Like the contact tracing technologies used by Western countries, China integrated a 'Health Code' system that applied to the WeChat accounts of users.

The Health Code system was implemented in over 300 cities in China to assign users a colour code, which determined their access to various activities and places. It covered at least 900 million users (Liang, 2020). Showing one's health code and scanning venue QR (quick response) codes became prerequisites for all public places, including public transport and shops (Yu, 2022). The colour coding system classified individuals into one of three coloured QR codes: green (low risk, unrestricted movement), yellow (medium risk, 7-day self-isolation), and red (high risk, mandatory 14-day quarantine) (Yu, 2022).

To create colour-coded identifiers, the Health Code system utilized three categories of data. First, individuals were required to input personal information such as their name, national identification number, and physical health conditions (for example, fever, fatigue, dry cough). Second, spatial-temporal data obtained from applications like Alipay and WeChat were utilized, including geolocation information from GPS and network providers to ascertain if a person had been in any high-risk infection areas. The duration of time spent in these risky locations was also taken into account. Last but not least, the Health Code system analysed user connections and online transactions to determine their potential exposure to carriers of COVID-19.

Such a system was an advance on the ongoing digital surveillance system that WeChat allowed for – known in the West as exemplary of the 'surveillance state' and digital dystopia (Strittmatter, 2020) – to rate and rank individuals and gamify obedience by rewarding people of good character and behaviour and punishing those seen to exhibit bad behaviour and characteristics.

While the social credit system has perhaps generated more moral panic in the West, without being uniformly and systematically implemented in all Chinese regions, the COVID-19 crisis made its application more precise and effective. The problems of this system appear in anecdotes across the web, with a particularly explanatory event described by Dr Haqing Yu (2022). According to Yu's account, in August 2021, a post titled 'The Journey of Yellow Code and Green Code' surfaced on WeChat. It described how, during a flight from Xining to Lhasa, the plane was redirected to Chengdu due to severe weather conditions. Passengers expressed concern, as Chengdu was designated as a COVID red zone, potentially affecting their health status codes and access to Tibet. The captain proposed a solution: if passengers refrained from using their phones in Chengdu, their health codes would remain unchanged. Following a brief delay, the plane resumed its flight to Lhasa. Upon arrival, passengers activated their phones with their status remaining green, enabling their entry into Tibet (Yu, 2022). The Onlife paradox is self-evident, with the passengers, whatever their health conditions, bio-monitored because of their whereabouts, regardless of the vacuum presented by the aeroplane.

This is extraordinary if we consider Strittmatter's (2020) warning that China could offer an example for the world to follow. Indeed, the global appeal of surveillance and control via WeChat is further evident in the other elements mentioned, including its geopolitical control over residents located abroad during the COVID-19 pandemic.

There are many examples of these circumstance in Antonella Ceccagno and Mette Thunø's insightful ethnography of Chinese residents in Italy during the pandemic (2022). In this context, WeChat has proven to be vital in distributing centralized information on behalf of the party but also in setting up mandatory surveillance groups during the pandemic, with the purpose of remotely monitoring citizens abroad. Such aspects, conceived of as 'diaspora surveillance', allowed for the structural geopolitical management, control, and mobilization of an otherwise historically disembedded community (Ceccagno, 2015).

In Italy, which is among the epicentres of the Chinese community outside of mainland China, WeChat offered an alternative news source to the Italian media and enhanced systematic digital monitoring practices that peaked with episodes of vigilantism (Negro and Hu, 2022), a practice that has infamous precedents in the Chinese community (Ong, 2012; Huang, 2021).

The Onlife, therefore, becomes an ever-growing powerful global tool to systematically apply the means of control within a hyperconnected structure that truly renders communication trivial, immediate, and effective, but so is its potential for oppression, which may clearly tackle protesters, silence dissidence, and disperse crowds. But its scope, and problematics, are evolving further.

## Meta and beta

As mentioned in this chapter, the global structure of social media operates in a multilayer dimension, one that fundamentally touches upon all of the mediated senses. With its 'Move fast and break things' motto (Taplin, 2017), Zuckerberg did not simply reinterpret the Schumpeterian axiom of 'creative destruction' made of endless innovation (Klein, 2008), but revised the entire concept of socializing. It comes as no surprise then that in the aftermath of the company's moment in the spotlight during the Cambridge Analytica scandal, with its data leaks, and even the need to apologize to parents in early 2024 at a senate hearing (CBS News, 2024). Ever since, Zuckerberg attempted to envision a new social media world, a so-called *metaverse*, but this also came to represent a similar pattern of problematics that perhaps allies with his controversial admiration of Emperor Augustus (Vervaet, 2019) and the plain 'emperor-style' rebranding of his public image (Montgomery, 2024).

As such, along with the digitalization of photography as a central driving force of the lucky bet made by 'The Facebook', and the timely investments of both controversial renegade Sean Parker and ambiguous philanthropist Peter Thiel, the metaverse appears as another multisensorial level of experience for the digitality of harms.

This new envisioning of the company is, in the words of Zuckerberg himself, the result of 'lockdown boredom', which led him to envision the need to go beyond the limitations of computer-based interactions (Metz and Thorbecke, 2022). Of course, this debate has long been proposed by

Silicon Valley gurus such as Jaron Lanier, who to date is not only claiming credit for the development of VR technology but is apparently 'fighting' to keep it from turning (fully) from a dream state utopia into a nightmarish reality (Lanier, 2018).

It is somewhat ironic that the 1992 novel that allegedly coined the neologism 'metaverse', *Snow Crash* by Neal Stephenson, described the future (and our present) as a messy fixture of 'social inequities, sexism, racism, gated communities, surveillance, hypercapitalism, febrile megacorporations, and corrupt policing' (Bell, 2022).

Zuckerberg's metaverse not only seems to fulfil the prophecy of a highly polarized dystopia but also underscores the significant challenge of policing the rampant anarchy that leads to continuous abusive behaviour. This issue mirrors the problems seen in online gaming and general cybercrime. However, the so-called Web 3.0 hyperconnected potential proposed by the meta environment is crucial. It is important to note that Meta is not merely a gaming environment: it represents a conceptual advancement for a social extension. This advancement has already transformed social interactions and now aims to redefine the social norms established since the advent of the internet's Web 2.0 phase.

With the metaverse, Zuckerberg opened the social sphere to a visual, auditory, and sensorial experience, which he deemed: 'the next evolution in social connection and the successor to the mobile internet' (Ginsburg, 2022). What is central to this development, other than say, videogaming, is the real-life interaction with individuals in their Onlife existence. Users are not simply role-playing, but they are getting on with work duties, influencing, promoting, and generally living within a meta (beyond) interaction, just as *Second Life* attempted decades before (Boellstorff, 2008). It is thus, basically, a 3D version of Facebook – but it is also potentially a 3D version of what is wrong with Facebook. The matter is almost self-evident: just as *Snow Crash* is set in a world ravaged by economic crises, Zuckerberg's metaverse was conceived during a period of social crisis brought about by COVID-19 isolation and general social distancing. It was designed as a tool to address the crisis, specifically the challenges of everyday in-person interactions for both work and leisure. The so-called face-to-face exchange is becoming obsolete with the technological advances of Web 3.0.

Innumerable articles have immediately raised awareness of what is wrong, and what may get worse, with the metaverse, highlighting its addicting, immersive, and 'inevitable' potential. According to print media, being sexually harassed, assaulted, and actually raped on the metaverse became a 'thing', even at the very beginning, as reported by *The New York Times*,[5] *Vogue*,[6] *PC Mag*,[7] and *The Guardian*,[8] among others.

Of course, one must be progressive in thinking of the future: books, pens, Moleskine notebooks, dictionaries, keys, cash, and so on, have all been taken-for-granted objects up the 2010s and are now one by one turning into practical, electrified Onlife equivalents. The same perhaps will happen to virtual coffee drinking with friends and concert going – as *Second Life* prophesied and made a ton of money out of at the time (Wagner, 2023), something Zuckerberg must surely be well aware of.

Yet, the *Second Life* example is significant: Facebook is no 'second life', but as I have discussed in this chapter, it is *a form* of life, if only another version of it. As such, it can be inferred as an Onlife development of it that is by no means escapism.

At the time of writing, it is still too early to say whether the metaverse and the like have turned into a total dimension to which, once immersed, there are few means of escape. However, returning to the Onlife conceptualization of the 'digital bleeding into the everyday', the new VR and XR (extended reality) technologies are progressively involving users in more mundane circumstances. Technologies tend to take over everyday spheres: this is particularly true within the Onlife. Mobile phones progressed into smartphones that allowed greater and greater means to film, control, observe, and check in on users, all aspects of which have been highlighted over the last decade by media scholars, from Siva Vaidhyanathan (2018) to Geert Lovink (2019). The means to communicate have not only changed, say from the use of 'smileys' to emojis and now avatars, but have also developed with greater interaction and immersions.

From a criminological perspective, significant changes in social communication and the environments shaped by advancing technologies raise several implications. New technologies introduce means that are not immediately understood, especially when used in public. An illustrative example is the 2016 incident where, according to Reuters, the careless use of Google Maps directed a travelling motorcyclist into a crime-ridden slum in Rio de Janeiro, resulting in a fatal shooting (Reuters, 2016).

Within augmented technologies, the initial uses of smart glasses in the early 2010s have created an uproar of irony and memes. The infamous Google Glasses, initially released in 2014, provoked so-called 'glassholes', a term loved by the magazine *Vice* (Franzen, 2015), which led to a beating in a pub that went viral, and even to the banning of the technology from other venues to prevent further similar incidents (Schuster, 2014). This is no place to go into detail on what exactly went wrong with the Google Glass experiment: one can only propose that the social acceptance of filming strangers and 'zoning out' in public has changed exponentially, especially since COVID-19. What is certain is that ten years later, the technology and potential social acceptance of these types of products have come a long way. Investments, too, with both Western and major companies in the Global South, including Samsung, all being involved in developing and integrating 'face-computer' technology for the 'metaverse' by early 2025 (Hector, 2024).

In particular, '*Facebook/Meta* invested $10 billion dollars in 2022 alone into XR development, including AR [augmented reality] headset research and development; *Microsoft* received $22 billion USD from the US army for AR headsets, software and services in 2022; *Google/Alphabet* have made multiple billion-dollar AR acquisitions' (O'Hagan et al, 2024: 2), with Apple also entering the US market with its Vision Pro device in early 2024 (Nellis and Chmielewski, 2024).

Such augmented reality devices allow practical interaction with the Internet of Things (embedded sensors, software, and tech extracting data), but also imply a change in what everyday interactions will imply (Chung et al, 2023) and the social media conviviality beyond the screen.

In discussing the social implications of new VR devices integrated with the future of social media, O' Hagan et al (2024) have highlighted the potential impact of integrating augmented reality into our daily lives, including the societal challenges and risks associated with this shift in perception, such as the potential for abuse, manipulation, and information disorder that may arise from digitally enhanced experiences.

In particular, they highlight how the new augmented reality may not simply alter the fabric of perception, but render such alteration harmful in a variety of scenarios, as 'such devices will inevitably arrive at consumer friendly, socially acceptable form factors, designed to be comfortably worn and used all-day – what has varyingly been referred to as everyday, pervasive, ubiquitous augmented reality' (O'Hagan et al, 2024: 1). The means of 'penetration' appears to be a growing concern of the AR potential integration into devices, where users will find it very difficult (if not impossible) to opt out – a recurring point I associate with the Onlife.

But what are the potential harms involved in the use of these augmented headsets? Quite generally, their stated intention is to 'empower users, communities, business, governments and others to alter, augment, diminish or otherwise mediate our perception of people, places, objects, media and more' (O'Hagan et al, 2024: 1). But other than mediating our perceived experiences, their design is one of reshaping the fabric of interactions within anticipated dystopias – where everything may be doubted, anything shaped within the virtual space: be it a troll or a 'semi-sociological' discussion on mass hysteria where birds are really surveillance drones (McIndoe, 2023). While I will discuss in more detail the augmented dystopias of virtual 'unreality' in Chapter 7, the communal aspects are central to this chapter's argument. As a team of computer scientists at the University of Washington already noted by 2018, the use of AR technologies offers an uncharted, albeit cryptic, mode of interaction between users who 'share the same physical space and may interact with shared virtual content embedded in this space' (Lebeck et al, 2018: 392). As such, AR applications may display varying sharing functionalities, where certain virtual content is set to private while others are made public. The issue of privacy implications and data security breaches that can arise from using wearable AR devices in public settings is a frequent subject of study in the field of computer science. These devices may inadvertently expose individuals to risks such as revealing confidential virtual content without their knowledge or inadvertently sharing private information. Virtual mirrors and digital spotlights have nevertheless offered practical solutions long before the current technologies (Butz et al, 1998).

## 'There's a *Black Mirror* episode for that'

The uptick of confusion and negativity is a recurring element in the criminological exploration of the Onlife: the future of social media is no different. In this chapter, I have highlighted its most blatant problems and distressing occurrences, which constitute a systematic, ongoing endangerment of what it means to live a social life within a perpetually connected environment. In summary, the problems we are facing as global users include corporate cluelessness and the disregard of moral values mixed with tactical and even creeping social control manoeuvres, all appearing on the verge of expansion, just as the unstoppable 'liquid' condition of devices progresses within hybridized spaces.

AR devices, seamlessly integrating into everyday objects, are now blending in with regular glasses: the rapid advancement of sensors, cameras, and algorithms present significant opportunities and challenges for users interacting with their surroundings. This evolution risks widening the gap between those who can afford and utilize AR devices and those who cannot.

Popular Netflix's science fiction series *Black Mirror* did anticipate much of this in multiple episodes such as 'Arkangel' and 'Nosedive', and it is undeniable that with continuous improvements in these technologies, users may gain capabilities similar to the *Terminator* vision, enabling them to perceive and analyse human emotions and behaviours with unprecedented precision. If this proves true, a new power dynamic will inevitably arise where technologically equipped users hold a distinct advantage over others, deepening class exclusion (Melossi, 2003) and integrating within the 'crimmigration' context (Franko, 2020) and systematic surveillance systems (Bigo, 2006). Within mundane contexts, from job interviews to a date or a police investigation, an online integration of hyperconnected emotion sensors could analyse a simple smile, while algorithms could estimate someone's age based on visual cues – forming a new horizon of bio-sociality and criminality in controlling, influencing, and managing bodies.

5

# Cryptic Corporations of Harm

## Encrypted barriers

Control of information has become a central element of the everyday use of smart devices. Users consult devices accessible only through strictly individualized biometric features, such as face recognition and fingerprints, inserting keys and opening new screens that unfold our intimate space. They store an increasing amount of information at the tip of our fingers, which includes both vital and trivial matters, from work-related to anything intimate. The content of the device is personal, and the information is not simply private, but secret. By this means, secrecy has for evermore become a key dimension of modern life. It is a pervasive aspect of our technologies and is particularly embraced within smart features and devices (see Knight and Saxby, 2014; Knights and Morris, 2015) To hide is an action perpetually suggested to the user, and they need to constantly generate hidden content. But more than that, our text messages and chats appear to be 'secret', protected by encrypted technologies, yet such protection is flawed: we can easily screen-shot conversations and share them online – with serious criminological implications (Lavorgna et al, 2022). Such conditions are in no way marginal, nor marginated.

This chapter looks at technological innovation replicating elements of harm and criminality on a structural and corporal level – with direct effects on users, consumers, and producers. It offers an analysis of profit-based Big Tech misconduct, with particular emphasis on Amazon's web-based dynamics of control over consumers and staff; gig economy abuse (Uber and the like); technological planned obsolescence; and environmental harms and green criminology perspectives. Such perspectives focus particularly on the malpractices and criminogenic offences committed during the COVID-19 pandemic and beyond, the impressive increase in profits and also regulations, as well as instances of data colonialism, surveillance in the Global South, and algorithmic racism.

Acting cryptically, protecting device content with advanced biometric technology, storing secrets, and leaking them have become integral to Onlife interaction. Corporations operate similarly – they design products to present a facade of 'freeware', friendly interfaces, personalized vouchers, and flash discounts. These elements not only encourage loyalty and purchases but also enable a deeper understanding of consumers and direct access to their most personal data. This exploitative reality extends beyond Vance Packard's *The Hidden Persuaders* (1957). As I argue in this chapter, it represents a systematic biopolitical strategy of encryption and revelation. This approach appears to promote harm and crime in secret and perpetuate a 'disinformation society'. This new social reality promotes a 'free-for-all' mentality at the expense of everyone else, including the environment.

The smartphone stands as the epitome of tools facilitating the management of cryptic existences. Flat and lucid, the very design of the smartphone, the quintessential Onlife device, deceives attention – its coating almost deflects light (think of the anti-glare features). Its design is nonetheless appealing, especially that of more expensive models, though overall their structure is quite uniform across the different brands. The imagery of Kubrick's film *2001: A Space Odyssey* acknowledges such a scenario, with the 'supercomputer' antagonist HAL 9000 representing the quintessential silent observer, vigilant and latent in its functioning, yet never fully allowing the users to be at ease. Also, it is striking how the alien monolith resembles so precisely the smartphone, with its slim, dark, lucid surfaces. Smartphones appear quite evasive. While active, though with its screen off, it makes no sound and hardly emits lights (very few models any longer have an LED light to indicate notifications, though always-on screens are becoming more popular). Contrary to other computational devices such as personal computers and laptops, which, depending on the model, produce and emit overt noises, flashes, beeps, and whirring sounds, giving very clear and somewhat transparent evidence of their functioning, smartphones and tablets appear seemingly inactive, even though, covertly, they are perfectly responsive.

As such, the smartphone is marked by an opaqueness in its operations, employing a vague and even 'insidious' approach to searching and communication. This omnipresent device resides constantly in the user's pocket, seamlessly transitioning between a mobile connection and an offline 'aeroplane mode'. Even with the screen apparently 'off', a smart device could be recording, filming, or listening: providing not only essential services but also serving as a surveillance and monitoring tool. Within its confines lie our most sensitive and private information, offering a convenient window to express and share these details with anyone, at any time, and from anywhere, all at the touch of a fingertip (Serres, 2012). By having such a tool always at hand and accessing its features at any given time, we abide by a novel form of Goffmanian front and backstage alternation (1956) – heading back and forth between our intimate and public spaces. Anyone owning a smartphone, and thus more generally participating in the Onlife phenomena (which is seriously complex to evade; Szakolczai, 2023), partakes to a certain extent in the ecology of secrecy.

## The malicious normality of smart functionality

Interpersonal electronic surveillance and covert monitoring – such as unauthorized tracking of someone's online activities and communications through cyber-creeping or cyberstalking – along with other forms of cyber harassment, including threats, intimidation, and the non-consensual distribution of intimate or sexual images or videos (commonly known as revenge porn), are recurring issues that contribute to an increasingly prevalent and controversial reality. What is permitted, and to what we have 'given' permission, loses its grasp in virtual scenarios. So much takes place without us knowing, behind our backs (Pasquale, 2015; Forssell, 2016). Yet, it has a specific, enduring effect on us, both as children and adults (Shariff, 2014). A wide range of harmful and criminal scenarios unfolds in an immense variety of situations and areas such as technology, law, art, and finance. These issues primarily stem from social engineering tactics employed in electronic scams, fraud, and targeted data breaches. As engagement increases with technologies such as cryptocurrencies (digital or virtual currencies secured by cryptography, which makes them challenging to counterfeit and trace), deepfakes (AI-generated synthetic media that alter video or audio to superimpose one individual's likeness onto another person), and NFTs (non-fungible tokens, unique digital assets representing ownership of specific items such as art, music, or virtual real estate on a blockchain, typically Ethereum), the risk of blockchain-related scams is escalating. However, this chapter is particularly concerned with the interpersonal use and abuse of cyber-based systems. The elements of cyberstalking are significant: an 'invasive form of partner monitoring' (Marcum et al, 2017: 375) can take in apparently 'friendly' social environments, aided by social networking platforms that become in themselves social surveillance websites (Tokunaga, 2011). While no longer talking in 'real life', users remain virtually and formally 'friends' and are thus observed and controlled, oftentimes unknowingly. Secrecy again appears a central aspect of both harm and proliferation. Such episodes take place globally and in an all-aged (Hjorth et al, 2020) and pluri-gendered reality (Burke Winkelman et al, 2015), from university campuses (Marcum et al, 2017) as well as within the internal communications of co-workers in organizations (Lowry et al, 2016). It also replicates on a multiplatform level, with shifting rules and regimes across devices and various apps offering both instant messaging as well as picture sharing (Srinivasan and IlamParithi, 2018). The recurrence of stalking and bullying are particularly connected in this scenario. Such dynamics show evidence of 'more psychosocial and emotional damage than traditional offline physical bullying because of the increased volume, scale, scope, and number of witnesses' (Gillespie, 2006, cited in Lowry et al, 2016: 963).

Especially harmful and well-reported elements of this phenomenon include how personal information is made public and then endures as public property. This is already popular on platforms such as 4chan in the form of doxxing (Ball, 2023), along with real-life trolling and 'swatting' (making a hoax emergency call to law enforcement, often with the intent of provoking a heavily armed police response at an unsuspecting person's location). Doxxing is also particularly relevant as a means of committing gender-based violence (GBV) in cases such as revenge porn and sextortion (Henry et al, 2020b), which can be considered as a recurring and 'systemic violence' (Eikren and Ingram-Waters, 2016). Such elements of technology-facilitated sexual violence and harassment are not simply a feature of the 4chan channels – but reflect the de-facto intimacy that devices offer – high-definition filming and instant messaging combined with captivating and protective features – both at home and in the outside world (Dragiewicz et al, 2018; Woodlock et al, 2022). Such a scenario, fed both by angry ex-partners and hackers, replicates elements of harm within a virtually infinite scenario where images may be released, shared, and stored endlessly (Maalsen, 2024). This point, already raised by Ziccardi (2015), shows how there is no easy way out of any of these situations, and the difficulty is evident in considering legal responses to 'revenge porn' (Eikren and Ingram-Waters, 2016) or cyber gender harassment (Citron, 2009).

Of course, there are powerful arguments for the value and importance of this very secrecy. Angus Bancroft makes a very convincing argument in his book *The Darknet and Smarter Crime* (2020) on the significance of secrecy in everyday online interactions, in particular within crypto market exchanges, especially as a form of resistance and protection for 'total transparency' that instead is vouched by 'totalitarian countries' as a means to control (Bancroft, 2020) – a point further developed Ben Collier who, regarding the non-criminal (and prevalent) use of Tor technology, highlights its 'anonymity, decentralisation, openness, transparency, security, antihierarchy, freedom of speech, utopia, resisting censorship, and the classic hackery love and fear of computer technology' (Collier, 2024: 15). But as I will discuss here, the ambivalence of the Onlife agenda focuses on the cryptic modes in which users are insistently exploited, within various dimensions to which 'resistance' via secrecy offers very limited and highly contextualized aid.

## Overt and covert

Behind the scenes, social media platform Facebook has long preached an exciting 'breaking of boundaries'. Such audacity attracted the most innovative minds from competing companies, where they encountered significant red tape over new software development and implementation. One example was the recruitment of artificial intelligence (AI) technical engineer Joaquin Quiñonero Candela, who would leave Microsoft to introduce machine-learning models to Facebook in 2012 (Hao, 2021). His prime role was one of advancing the use of traditional algorithms that use hard-coded criteria set by engineers with machine-learning algorithms that undergo a training process using input data to identify correlations within it. As such, trained (learned) algorithms become capable of automating decisions based on learned information – be it individual choices as well as interests. Quiñonero and his team would become the 'right hand' of Zuckerberg due to their highly committed approach to maximizing user engagement to the extreme.

However, it soon became clear that the model was not simply improving the targeting of ads and connecting common interests, but directly favouring controversy, misinformation, and extremism (Lauer, 2021). In opposition to the highly glorified positive involvement of Facebook in the Arab Spring uprisings in Egypt and Tunisia in 2010 and the political unrest in Myanmar in 2018, its involvement proved quite different. As admitted in an official apology by Facebook's Newsroom at the end of 2018, the spread of false information and inflammatory language on social media led to an escalation in religious tensions and ultimately resulted in genocide against the Rohingya Muslim minority in Myanmar (Warofka, 2018). While the nature of toxic discourse and its effect in the Onlife is the focus of another chapter, it is central to note how the behind-the-scenes work of platforms such as Facebook may lead, in not even such a casual fashion, to concrete harmful actions and humanitarian crimes.

Manipulation is a keyword here, one that is correlated with the Cambridge Analytica scandals of the same year. As such, Facebook users have not only been a treasure trove for all sorts of personality profiling (Summers, 2018) (central to the capta-veillance problematics discussed in Chapter 2), but the information was resold back to them with the direct and concrete objective of altering public perception and targeting specific groups, emphasizing bias, feeding paranoia, and conspiracies.

Again, these are all connected themes that are not just limited to Facebook (and will be discussed further in Chapters 6 and 7). But Facebook, however, is important, as it is, and has long been, the most influential of those platforms working on the potential of the Onlife.

At the heart of this argument lies the significant role of developing such a platform into a mobile application, facilitating seamless integration with the everyday mobility enabled by smartphones. Even here, a notable anecdote proves the subjective influence Facebook had on its users' experiments (and being experimented on by these multi-corporations). Apple and Facebook had long quarrelled over the latter's integration into Apple's operating system. The dispute culminated in privacy issues being raised in 2019, although these only slightly affected users (Roose, 2019). The integration of the platforms would appear today almost a symbiosis (Haraway, 2016): without the iPhone, there would be no Facebook. But this perspective is not at all linear. Leaving aside the advocacy for privacy that Apple has boasted about since the Cambridge Analytica scandal, and closing a blind eye to what its Apple Intelligence system may entail or risk, Facebook proved its particular significance for Onlife users by actually proving that, effectively, without Facebook there would be no iPhone.

In the 2012 iOS 6 system upgrade, users were able to seamlessly connect their iPhones with various prominent social media platforms such as Facebook, Flickr, Twitter, and Vimeo directly through the phone settings. However, this feature was removed in the subsequent iOS 11 update, released five years later.

According to *Business Insider*, such an approach was apparent in part of the previous strategy to tackle Google, finding alliances with minor platforms in a phase of direct competition (Yarow, 2012). Albeit 'at war', these companies allied for specific 'phases' while upgrading different protocols, networks, and techno-systems that best suited their exploitative instincts: from data collection to forcing users to prefer specific services suggested by the hosting platform (be it Apple or Android, with little other competition). Users in all this had very little voice, while being evermore persuaded into accepting new upgrades, new devices, new deals, and so on.

## Adding addictions

While these dynamics are by no means a surprise, nor any longer a strictly 'covert' aspect of a platforms' design, it is surprising that they have not in any way lessened their popularity.

Rather, as noted by David Lauer, they are significant in the business model of Facebook (2021) and, as I argue, other similar companies. The perpetual 'hooking' aspect of today's Onlife devices finds a trace in a myriad of different dynamics of usage (Lauer, 2021). Such is the rhetoric used about most consumer items, as noted in the 1950s by the journalist Vance Packard (1957). But to persuade users to spend and to purchase is quite different. Consumers may be subjected to desiring, and lured into purchasing, a specific brand. With the implementation of the Internet of Things in modern devices, everything surrounding us requires perpetual attention, a constant inflow of data, and continuous upgrades. But today's objective is no longer solely one of having drivers buy a particular car. It is to have drivers drive as much as possible. Smartphones work just the same, where the purchase of a mobile device is merely a business card into the realm of desires and purchasing power that a user consents to, knowingly or unknowingly (Harcourt, 2017).

The concern with deep brain stimulation via smart devices was a significant trend in the news in the late 2010s. Smartphone addiction, digital detox, and dopamine craving become buzzwords highlighting the modalities in which devices are designed in such a way to constantly call for our attention, endlessly scrolling and craving for more information or signs of appreciation (Waters, 2021). The principal causes of such 'freneticism' or 'binging' in relation to our devices have long been identified (but by no means limited): the value of the 'like' sign, feeding the most hidden need for approval and gratification, the endless scrolling feature, compromising our attention spans, they are all connected to the much-denounced dopamine, 'a neurotransmitter that plays a crucial role in our brain's reward system' (Nasywa, 2023). This recalls Gibson's (2016 [1984]) *Neuromancer*'s character Case and the other 'cyberspace cowboys' of feeling insects-under-the-skin strung out once they unplug from the matrix, and, indeed, as Mark Fisher noted (2009: 25), 'Case's amphetamine habit is plainly the substitute for an addiction to a far more abstract speed'. The use of this neurotransmitter has been associated with the rewarding, bright, and encouraging messages of computer games, the design of Gmail (the 'scroll to update' feature), the welcoming colours of Facebook (blue that stimulates attention), and Kindle reader virtual reward prices (that induces ongoing engagement).

Such an argument has been significant and popular in depicting the functioning of social media in documentaries such as *The Social Dilemma* (Orlowski, 2020), which, among other things, repeats the recurring trope of the de-humanizing 'Skinner-Box experiment', also known as a 'lever box' operant conditioning chamber (Skinner, 1983), highlighting the loss of agency in modern devices. To this, even the requirement of charging and keeping a constant eye on the status of an unquantifiable number of batteries, be they for phones, AirPods, e-cigarettes, external batteries, tablets, toys, and the like, take over the mind of Onlife users: they are perpetually subject and subjectified in an operational system that replicates itself further in all sorts of operational updates, not to mention the endless notifications from social media to simple nudges that the apps and devices constantly deliver (Hari, 2023).

But beyond the moral panic of the corporation's unethical 'persuasiveness', we can trace direct uses within more criminologically precise appliances.

As mentioned in Chapter 1, the Onlife in many ways resembles a hyper-modern casino: it hooks users into a constant playing mode, full of potential and with falsely mitigated risks. A smart device, craving perpetual attention, becomes the ideal fulfiller of this attention to whoever is willing (conscious or not) to resign to it. As such, the users act as psychological addicts, and the producers of content as pushers. But when looking at the more mundane and concrete acts of gambling, the usage of apps on a mobile device is comparable to having a 'casino in one's pocket' (Whelan et al, 2021).

Eoin Whelan and colleagues (2021) acknowledged the impact of mobile technology on the gambling industry, highlighting the expanded accessibility and opportunities it provides for individuals to engage in gambling activities anytime and anywhere. The prevalence of mobile apps is believed to contribute to a more impulsive and habitual form of gambling behaviour. They note how:

> While immersed in a mobile game, users become distracted from other stressful aspects of their lives. Seeking the gratification of relaxation predicts engagement with mobile games. It is worth noting that adaptive relaxation must be distinguished from maladaptive forms of escapism (i.e., coping with adverse emotions, negative life events, or psychopathological symptoms). (Whelan et al, 2021: 3)

To the Onlife user, the pitch is a regular trope: entertainment and fulfilment at the same time, anytime, and constant. The user is alone in having to face the arrays of both motor and cognitive impulsivity (Chowdhury et al, 2017), a dilemma that goes back to the 'routine activity' of criminological theories over guardianship (Cohen and Felson, 1979). According to Leukfeldt and Yar's application of routine activity theories to cyberspace (2016), interpersonal crime involves criminogenic situations, motivated offenders, suitable targets, and the absence of capable guardians. Additionally, several researchers (Salter, 2016; Stratton et al, 2017) have highlighted the role of technological rationality (Marcuse, 2006) – how the design of technology influences user behaviour – in preventing harm associated with social media (Woodlock et al, 2022). As such, the devices themselves are designed to replicate harm and cast users as 'actants' in systematically deviant and harmful ways. In other words, the device offers no filter or protection against turning into an 'obsessively passionate mobile gamer' (Woodlock et al, 2022: 11), and rather may represent, in the analysis of Italian scholar Juan Carlos de Martin, an actual threat to democracy (De Martin 2023).

## Peaks of the cryptoworld

As further noted by Whelan and his colleagues (2021), the advertisements promoting mobile gambling apps often feature individuals engaging in gambling activities in social or familiar settings, like the family home or a bar. As using mobile devices in social circumstances is a socially accepted trend, there is no filter to what one can do with minimal discreetness.

Regardless of the endless list of neologisms surrounding problematic smartphone usage, as cleverly addressed in Tanya Goodin's 'manual'

(2021), with the tip of a finger the user is open to another series of legal and potentially harmful exercises (Hildebrandt, 2020). With very little guardianship filtering, everything can become an indiscreet action, albeit with a discreet potential (Yar, 2012). One can be deviant, but in secret; be in public, but behind a phone – again, anytime and anywhere.

As such, other non-related practices may fall into the addiction category. Micro investments and crypto trading, with their volatile and 24/7 nature, share similarities with speculative gambling (Johnson et al, 2023). With initial investments as low as two cents, users may engage in previously limited markets – an aspect that, curiously, is not simply promoted on specialized applications but insisted upon by otherwise 'semi-conventional', 'online-only' banks such as Revolut and Chase that were previously inaccessible to most. Such dynamics are even more problematic in the immediacy of loan applications within a fraud environment (Awaludin et al, 2023).

But, again, the hidden nature of the system of harm and, potentially, crime, is the central trope. Cryptocurrency is the champion tool for promoting the hidden ways in which money can benefit users (as opposed to the alleged 'transparency' of banks or government transactions and investments). Criminologically, while hailed by some as a revolutionary financial innovation, cryptocurrencies have also sparked addiction concerns, as well as disinformation, disinvestment, and, specifically, the financing of terrorism (Holt and Udroiu, 2022), especially within ambiguous fundraising campaigns (Reuters, 2023). As reported in *The Guardian* in 2021, in the context of El Salvador, where the government has embraced Bitcoin as legal tender, the emergence of what some term 'crypto paradise' underscores the complexities surrounding this digital currency (Youkee, 2021). Moreover, the criminological implications of cryptocurrency adoption raise questions about its potential misuse in illicit activities, from online speculation to money laundering and even 'cryptic' neo-colonialism schemes (Renteria, 2020; Dilanian et al, 2021). Specific geopolitical environments in the Global South, particularly in Central and South America, have aided the idealization of these forms of easy, rapid, and low-risk investments that, nevertheless, do involve a series of hidden harms for both the Global North and Global South. Project Prospera, situated on the island of Roatan in Honduras, is a prime example of a direct Silicon Valley investment interfering with the local polity to the extent that it is even separated from the rest of the country in which it exists (Browne et al, 2022). In El Salvador, such forms of corporate philanthropy were long present after 12 years of civil war (Sánchez, 2000), and have become even more blatant and aggressive with the elitist lens. The country's self-named 'world-coolest-dictator',[1] President Nayib Bukele, could alone act as a case study of the criminology of the Onlife, but let us limit ourselves to discussing the crypto harms involved in his political manoeuvres. Bukele, since he was first elected in 2019, has overtly tackled the internal affairs of gang wars and drug lords with surprising success (Freeman and Perelló, 2024), to the enthusiasm of many supporters. But on the cryptic side, the coaxing of crypto investors and the creation of a tax (and crime) free safe haven had an almost immediate impact on the population. Though boasting of a plan for a tax-free crypto mining hub called 'Bitcoin City' in the year after embracing Bitcoin, El Salvador faced bankruptcy in 2022 (Alvarenga, 2022). This was anticipated by the chaotic roll-out of norms and incentives that citizens and shops had to comply with to integrate with the crypto-paradise trope. At the forefront of this initiative was the implementation of the 'Chivo Wallet', the government's officially endorsed Bitcoin e-wallet, which was aptly named after a Salvadoran colloquial term for 'cool'. Additionally, Chivo automatic teller machines (ATMs) were introduced as part of this rollout. President Bukele had not only assured the public that Bitcoin would uplift El Salvador from financial challenges and lead the country towards a prosperous future akin to the Asian Tiger economies, but the government offered a promotional incentive of $30 to individuals who downloaded and registered with the app (in a country where a full-time minimum wage only amounts to approximately $300 per month). However, following its launch, the app faced numerous technical issues and became a target for fraudulent activities, resulting in nearly a thousand reported identity theft cases within the first three months (Rauda Zablah, 2022). When looking at the government's (and thus Bukele's) pockets, El Salvador had acquired 2,400 Bitcoin tokens at a cost of over $100 million by 2023. However, due to fluctuations in the market, the value of the government's Bitcoin holdings has decreased by 60 per cent. The issue of Bitcoin-backed bonds, aimed at preventing default by the country, has been postponed, possibly due to a lack of investor. Meanwhile, according to the International Monetary Fund (IMF), the national debt continues to grow (Alvarenga, 2022).

To complete the 'behind the scenes' mismanagement of a country's push toward an Onlife reality, we find the encircling influence of China. After the US investment and debt plunge, with one out of three El Salvadorians living in poverty, China's banks represent a novel alternative, offering by the end of 2022 to buy the country's $21bn in foreign debt. Two years later, the cost of the crypto gamble reached its conclusion, to the expense, with no irony nor novelty, of the environment, with the country opening again its mining facilities (Mackey, 2024). The gamble, however, seems only to have changed the currency: the hidden damage of Onlife investments is only at its embryonic stage, pushing further the propagandistic assurance of progress, loaded with promises of fast internet, fast money, robotics, and alleged top-quality services, in a country where running water alone is still something of a luxury.

## Dark box

If in 2011 the already mentioned Marc Andreessen claimed 'software was eating the world' (Andreesen, 2011), today's disk spaces are doing the same with their hidden values and hidden functioning. At the time of writing, my computer is asking me to update my software for vague 'bug fixes', eating several GB of space – eating up space that will slowly, and relentlessly, fill up and which, as a consequence, will increase the lag and obsolescence of the device, with limited possibility to 'revert' back to the previous operating system (OS) so as to free up space. In the same way, sinkholes fill up with e-waste, while mines empty – with corporations seeking precious materials for their micro-components further and further into space, potentially opening up the horizon for the mining of deep space sources (Knapp, 2023).

The opaqueness of functioning from a macro level in the geopolitical manoeuvres of 'widening countries' can be well replicated in the micro internal components and workings of Onlife tools and devices. Opposed to the easy-fix analogue build of early electronic tools, contemporary devices are harder and harder not only to repair but to open. From the 'diabolical' Apple-patented pentalobe screw, which made devices notoriously difficult to open and repair (Wiens, 2011), to single-melted components (Merchant, 2017), Onlife devices are increasingly engineered as singular, unalterable, and non-manipulable gadgets. This design trend offers little protection against built-in obsolescence, which ultimately limits their usability and functionality. Typical users are left with little choice but to accept the devices as they are, flaws and all, with no means to address or adapt their operation. As such, the burden of hidden e-waste looms greater and greater over the environment, a reality that is facing a lukewarm governmental response or specific regulation on the 'right to repair', at least in the EU (European Parliament, 2024), but looms in developing countries such as Thailand (Mangmeechai, 2022) or Taiwan (Tsai, 2020). The release of toxic substances in unrecycled waste is comparable with the colonial (Qiu, 2016; Couldry and Mejias, 2019), environmental abuses (Taffel, 2022) that the mining and sourcing of the specific devices' components require, such as the rare metallic ore coltan (Merchant, 2017). The sustainability of lithium and generally rechargeable batteries is a particularly concerning point. In a world that pushes towards the Internet of Everything, potentially requiring all sorts of everyday objects to be independently powered, the environmental cost of sustaining all these components is an open question to which scholars such has Mike Hynes have highlighted the social, environmental, and cultural paradox (2021). On the one side, the devices being smaller and smaller will require minimal energy – and apparently the automation aspect will compensate for the emissions, as the World Economy Forum suggested in 2018 (Arias et al, 2018). However, this is contrasted with the somewhat foreboding argument of how this very technology has reduced work opportunities (Rotman, 2013) and led to the gradual withdrawal of human agency (Carr, 2014). The large-scale impact continues replicating cryptic functioning elements, a hidden corporation of harm over which Onlife users have little control or understanding. As noted in Sy Taffel's (2022) eye-opening article, it is exactly the very small, highly technological, and successful devices such as the Apple AirPod that exemplify the problems: 'child labour, water shortages faced by indigenous communities as a result of corporate mining activities, communities being poisoned by electronic waste, and many of the worst impacts of longer-term issues surrounding climate change are not typically experienced by those who can afford luxury commodities such as AirPods' (Taffel, 2022: 434).

Not being able to easily open, interact, revert, and modify devices returns us to the much-mentioned subjectivization of the body that the Onlife entails, with a systematic difficulty in opening and engaging with the 'inside' of a smart (Onlife) device. Long gone is the flexibility of early mobile phones in which users could easily access sim card slots and manually remove them without the use of tools. While, of course, the modern e-sim offers allegedly even more flexibility to change operator, to freely open and access the internal workings of a phone may be a life or death feature for any individual trying to escape, or even protect, his or her identity in an authoritative state, or a crisis within a political adversary territory. This is not limited to shadowy Jason Bourne-style international spies or drug lords, but even to political activists, asylum seekers, and free thinkers of all sorts (Aas, 2006): from homophobia in Central Africa (Freude and Waites 2023) to human rights violations such as the repression of the Uyghur in China (United Nations, 2022).

Function-wise and only recently, some EU states have openly attacked the opaque dynamic pricing offered on the websites of companies such as Ryanair and Amazon, both of whom fundamentally base their business model online. For decades now, prices of flights and products have been determined online through complex algorithmic calculations (Salanti et al, 2012). Through the utilization of a dynamic pricing model, ancillary revenue strategies, yield management techniques, and competition monitoring, for example, airlines can make real-time price adjustments to enhance revenue generation and increase seat occupancy on their flights. Furthermore, in such an opaque system much discussion (and further subjectification) is given to the fear prices may vary and be customized for specific users based on factors such as cookies and spending habits (Shen, 2017).

This is by no means (yet) illegal, but given the aggressive resistance of Ryanair to the EU suggestion, in 2023, of capping a minimum cost per flight (to allow greater transparency and assurance to consumers), it is clear that Ryanair and other companies have a particular interest for their calculations to continue, and to do so in a questionable way (Amante and Weir, 2023). Users may not know if by checking that flight too often they may be potentially 'punished' for not purchasing 'impulsively', an aspect that, as mentioned earlier, is key to the constant interaction with smart devices.

Feeding impulsivity is indeed central also in the workings of Amazon. Its controversies, from worker rights to environmental disasters, are also enough to fill a book on harm alone. But as with Bukele in El Salvador, let us limit ourselves to a series of cryptic workings on behalf of Onlife users. The desire to take advantage of the user's need to 'immediately' spend goes back to the early internet days, when characters such as Jeff Bezos and Elon Musk already dominated the scene, that is, before social media giants such as Facebook.

Bezos and Musk share an interesting business endeavour: not simply to offer users what they want (or what they don't want) (Stone, 2014), not simply trusting the website and the money you send to them, but to make them purchase it with as little friction possible. This was Musk's recurring ambition in the development (before the success of PayPal) of the original wholly digital online bank X.com (1999), because, in his words, 'People are ready to use the Internet as their main financial repository' (Tolliver, 1999).

With the likes of near-field communication (NFC) technology that has enabled contactless payments, which render digital payments instantaneous and without the need of 'inserting cards' or entering pin codes, Amazon has been prompting users towards 'one-click-purchase' since 1997, a concept which has revolutionized e-commerce spending (Fallon-O'Leary, 2023). Users no longer need to insert a personal identification number (PIN) code or the complex string of numbers on their credit cards: all purchases can be confirmed instantly. This is an aspect that the company, at the time, claimed 'increases the security of the system since customers do not have to re-enter sensitive data and that it also reduces the number of steps that would normally be involved in completing a purchase' (Kirk, 2011).

We return to the theme with which we opened the chapter. Through immediate purchases, in which Onlife users lose the sense of the physical threshold of money and spending, addictions thrive, especially among the young (Nyrhinen et al, 2023). Online shopping can evolve from a convenient option to a problematic addiction, especially with the widespread use of smartphones. This lack of self-regulation can negatively impact personal finances and young adults' ability to manage money and avoid debt. According to Nyrhinen and colleagues (2023), the ability to regulate one's behaviour is not innate but influenced by external factors. At times of crisis, such as during the COVID-19 pandemic, the allure of online shopping and the desire to reward oneself (Harcourt, 2017) with purchases can become even stronger, as noted by Amazon itself (O'Neill, 2023). As such, this constant exposure to temptation makes it easy to accumulate debt and further exacerbate the addiction. The 'Everything Store', where anything can be bought, collides with the 'Everything App', where everything can be done – as long as you rely on them.

## Harm economy

It is interesting to note how such a mechanism affects both the environment and the working conditions of those behind Amazon and other e-commerce giants (who follow the Amazon model). Even simply viewing an item allegedly initiates a complex and highly coordinated stream of moving, shifting, delivering, up and down, not simply in a warehouse but across a global network of warehouses and fulfilment centres distributed across the globe (O'Neill, 2023).

Such an aspect is also interesting from a theft perspective, especially of small electrical items from warehouses. Most of us will remember how much plastic was used to package earphones, controllers, and even batteries displayed in tech stores. According to Amazon's statement, European customers have received plastic-free boxes from their distribution centres since 2023 (Amazon, 2023). Such a change is apparently 'revolutionary' from an environmental perspective – although it is difficult to precisely know how much packaging is used and thus discarded when shipping a pair of headphones from a factory in China to a Western warehouse, which requires more extensive packaging norms. It also sheds light on the new control systems that prevent such theft in a systematic way. As proven by the confidence of the current carton packages of most electronic goods, from cheap earphones to high-end phones, purchases in the Onlife are traceable from the producer to the buyer with the most methodical details, with very little 'dark' spots where packages may be opened and the goods stolen. Nothing in the Onlife is potentially left to chance.

And while Amazon's immense warehouses eat up city suburbs – it is the low-class communities (Waddell, 2021) who pay the price of endless expansion, as well as the soil of the earth itself, with less and less land to store rain water (Calma, 2022) – it does even less where it offers jobs (Kassem, 2024). Amazon's working conditions have a direct effect on its employees, with them experiencing 'overwork, extreme stress and anxiety, and health problems such as joint problems' (Cole, 2023a, 2023b). The workers are subject to a strictly panoptic flow of information regarding their performance (Kassem, 2024), and management shares details of their relative intensity of performance in comparison to their colleagues with an 'opaque system [that] renders discussions regarding working conditions and the firm's mistreatment of its workforce very difficult' (Cole, 2023a).

Again, this all comes down to the issue of performance charting. The feature is not limited to Amazon, and as noted in the work of digital geographers Mark Graham and Mark Dittus (2022), it is a recurring pattern in the platform or 'gig' economy that fundamentally characterizes the Onlife.

In the gig (or platform) economy, a form of labour that grants flexibility and non-commitment, multitasking, and globalization, the subtle power structure proves distinctly Foucauldian (Gould, 2024). Using applications and platform interactions, particularly evident among delivery riders, the worker is constantly under a watchful eye, aligning with the concept of self-management, as indicated by Beck's 'risk economy' (2000). This environment paves the way for a scenario of self-discipline, where managerialism becomes the central concept governing the individual's self-direction, control, and efficient resource allocation (De Stavola, 2020).

Rather than being (evidently) oppressive, Ferrer-Conill (2018) points out the playful aspects of the digital labour environment, particularly through feedback loops and loyalty incentives that render the burden a ludic activity, particularly in an Onlife environment (Just et al, 2023). This playfulness extends to an environment where work commitments are infantilized. It underscores how digital labour is promoted as both liberating and socially empowering, particularly when contrasted with the paternalistic approach of job centres, especially among migrant workers (Harbisch, 2023). Game and informality are entrenched into the very structure of the gig economy, with early advertisements by Deliveroo, for example, emphasizing fitness incentives and framing work as a self-improving challenge facilitated by user-friendly platform designs and motivational communication such as emails, advertisements, and slogans (Stavola, 2020).

But 'coercion and control through algorithmic governance' (Turnbull, 2022: 283) is also systemic within services such as Uber, where the stalking by drivers, algorithmic bias, and transphobic violence are further exacerbated by a lack of transparency and minimal response (Turnbull, 2022).

## Crypto-data-mining

But what are the boundaries of the collection of everything, and how deep can this go? With the outbreak of the COVID-19 pandemic, we have seen the potential of contract-tracing applications in triangulating health status with personal movement, promoted by the introduction of social tracking devices and 'digital public health technologies' (Gasser et al, 2020). With contact-tracing apps and the so-called 'green pass' vaccine status, which were utilized by many affluent societies, the actual concept led to debates about privacy and concerns about the entire 'data' gathering system of corporations and state agencies (Floridi and Sotgiu, 2021). Though never mandatory (at least in Europe), these apps have been promoted as a necessary moral obligation for 'everyone with a cell phone' (Talesnik, 2021). Regarding contact tracing apps, the implication is that the more citizens comply with them, the better such tools function. Yet, following initial 'crash' incidents (underlining that more downloads meant a better service was not the case), these apps became central elements for the control and monitoring of the virus and its 'carriers' (Gasser et al, 2020).

## Subjectifying – 'enshittifying'

Considering the issue further within the broader understanding of the Onlife, such a dynamic of subjectivation and control takes place even in a broader field. Already in 2013, Radiohead frontman Tom Yorke (making an evident reference to Jaron Lanier's 2010 influential *You Are Not a Gadget*) noted the exploitative modes in which platforms such as Spotify act as 'gatekeepers' of musicians' income in unprecedented ways (Renshaw, 2013). Opaqueness and crypticism become again the central focus here, as the actual income generated is by no means transparent. Various sources claim different numbers, ranging from $0.03 to $0.05 per play (Jacob, 2021). But it is not the precise number that counts (considering the total income from all the various streaming services). Rather, what is interesting is that Spotify streaming has proven to be a reasonable solution to preventing the systematic illegal piracy and copyright infringements that the music industry has been subject to since the birth of Napster in 1999. Illegal downloading proved one of the most ethically challenging and controversial 'harms' of the music and general entertainment industry since the late 1990s. In strict 'cyber-crime' terms, users could easily harm the industry by simply clicking on specific file-sharing websites and torrent servers and downloading albums and films in a relatively unsanctioned manner, 'arguing for the users' right to copy and spread digitalized culture' (Wikhamn and Knights, 2016: 43).

However, as noted by a series of musicians (Rigotti, 2024), the paid-streaming services only fully support big names, while making it harder than ever for 'niche groups' to finance themselves. This has become even more blatant with the January 2024 Spotify announcement that it will no longer offer royalties to artists with less than 1,000 listeners over the previous 12 months.[2]

As such, through the monopoly of Spotify, which since 2008 has positioned itself as a music provider, 'in contrast to "piracy" alternatives' (Wikhamn and Knights, 2016: 44), musicians of the Onlife are covertly obliged to constantly update their discography and provide new content. They become subject to a system of control over their finances, and, ideally, in the words of Lanier (Naughton, 2013), of their everyday creativity.

Some internet critics have insisted on denouncing the so-called general 'enshittification' of the internet (and indeed Onlife experience): a systematic 'worsening' of platforms and services caused by constant updates, with less and less imaginary and more and more glitches (Doctorow, 2023).

Commenting in *The New York Times*, Julia Angwin (2024) noted that, because of the so-called 'enshittification' of Google Maps possessing an un-evolving monopoly over navigation systems, a father was led across a broken bridge in 2022 and drowned. It has been reported that the family have denounced Google and plan to sue for negligence (Gross, 2023).

Indeed, the focus of this chapter has been to highlight the various dynamics in which corporations, institutions, and governments take advantage of the hyperconnected blurry lines of the Onlife, promoting the dynamics of biopolitical power in opaque and hidden ways – with often unexpected and yet problematic consequences. Many of the crimes and harms involved are subtle, and not even directly quantifiable as such (or, ideally, they would be made illegal). Instead, they take place in the 'background', not even systematically, or simply incidentally – yet, taken as a whole, they represent the various criminal and zemiological actions that take place in the Onlife. As I have argued, the system of subjectification within the Onlife appears to be one that is taking it all: users are subject to capta, involved in cryptocurrency schemes, led to polarizing debates, involved in a data-for-all dynamics, drawn into a consuming maelstrom within environmentally and work-wise questionable systems, while the rhetoric is one of a 'rising tide lifting all boats'. The reality, however, is quite different.

As such, I would suggest as an example the 'not being afraid of making money' mantra of the 'cryptobros', who barely understand the blockchain dynamics of their technology but blindly follow the tax credits assurance of welcoming hosts or even collectively invest millions in exciting art projects with no notion of copyright laws.[3] Another is when blindness again comes to the vantage of the producers of devices. Firstly, we come across the direct ally of the e-waste: planned obsolescence. Secondly, the creeping subjectification of users from creativity to a mere workforce.

As I discuss in the next chapter, all of these are drawn into a maelstrom of problematic content and even greater mental, physical, and social harm.

# 6

# Toxic Onlife Infowarfare

## Sourcing e-reality

Any information found online comes with a level of doubt regarding its credibility. The internet is not only bloated with fake news, but the actual information found is often contradictory and, as mentioned in the previous chapter, capable of firing up endless debates. Depending on the source consulted, things can be good and bad at the same time, criminal and lawful, deviant and/or normal. For example, as noted on the academic blog *The Conversation*, individuals of various age groups worldwide appear to have been engaging in an obscure practice shared online known as 'jelqing', which involves violently rubbing their genitals to increase penis size (Taylor, 2024a). This technique has gained popularity through online sources, although it is not widely recognized by medical professionals due to the potential long-term harm and concrete danger of erectile dysfunction. Despite this, information regarding this practice can be found on numerous medical websites, including the popular (yet reasonably contentious) *Healthline* (Jewell, 2023).

The Onlife not only highlights the subtle influence of everyday toxic narratives – shaping choices and perceptions of symbols – but also exposes the dangerous misuse of otherwise harmless tools that reinforce these radicalizing narratives (Valentini et al, 2020). Once again, rather than the device in one's hand replicating knowledge, it only increases misunderstanding and a gives a false interpretation of things.

Similarly, while working on this chapter, I happened to be shopping in a major Italian supermarket and was approached by an elderly lady who could not read the symbols on the back of a bag of coffee. Close to my ear, the lady claimed that 'no matter my beliefs', I should be wary of the 'handshaking symbol' on the back of products. I was quite surprised by this, as I assumed she meant the 'eco-solidarity' certificate. When asked for clarification, she claimed that she had read in 'some group' that that sign meant – again, 'no matter my beliefs' – that 'they' had inserted the 'vaccine' inside it. I was far too deep into writing this book not to correlate the matter to COVID-19, and this claim intrigued me. However, to my surprise, she further claimed she had been very cautious about symbols and ingredients for the last few years since using the 'carrot app', which I later associated with the popular French-designed Yuka app, which specialized in offering in-depth information on commercial products to consumers. Now, some of this may very well be what Dave Beer refers to as the *Quirks of Digital Culture* (2019b), where 'On the surface it is often the case that the features of our digital culture don't seem to represent much beyond a fleeting moment, a surface effect, some brief flickering event or an attention-grabbing bit of gossip' (Beer, 2019b: 6).

Indeed, much of this and other web searches, however easily accessible the source, prove inconsistent and incoherent. The concept of 'detox' is another notorious one that particularly grabs the narrative of so-called 'life-coaches', advocating a healthy lifestyle and significant in many 'conspiritual discourses' (Barros and Sandlin, 2024). 'Detox' is used for all sorts of beauty, wellbeing, and relaxation purposes, but remains ambiguous. There is no clear scientific value to anything that 'detoxes' the body (and mind) – other than mere marketing. Toxins and detoxifications, however, are terms that stick, and significant branding has been created around their solution and cure. If anything, the argument is itself intoxicating, and ambiguous, as is the entire Onlife scenario.

Nevertheless, such a bombardment of information provides the grounds for what is known as 'evidence maximalism', a term coined by scholar Mike Caufield, noting how everything online turns into evidence to support a specific theory – making it harder to share a reality – whatever that reality is (Warzel, 2024b).

This resembles the problems around flat earth theorists who claim there is currently no specific proof that the earth is not flat (Burnett, 2016). Such a fringe argument is more complex than it would initially seem, especially since any argument around and against the theory itself makes use of scientific sources that are mediated, forged, and re-interpreted (Wolchover, 2011). In other words, they replicate the same instances of suspicion and misunderstanding that lie beneath all conspiracy theories or sectarian religious beliefs, where the truth is ingeniously hidden from us.

But the significance of flat earth theorists to this book lies in the fact that by navigating the web, any theory and idea may be debunked as well as supported: this is the power of the internet, and it has a growing effect on the Onlife. Not only may it develop, but it may also latently grow out of the virtual sphere and affect the everyday lives of individuals in damaging and harmful ways.

Such a discussion intersects with some of the arguments around the actual nature of flat earth theories. According to some, very few advocates of the 'theory' actually believe that the earth is flat; it is simply a form of trolling, as apparently many 'Redditors' confirm.[1] For others, it is a statement on the power of disinformation, just as 'Pastafarians' (for the most part), with their worship of the Flying Spaghetti Monster, seek to provoke religious bigotry, as discussed in *The Conversation* by Tony Meacham (2019), or birds are promoted as fake secret agents of the CIA (McIndoe, 2023). The internet does not help clarify such issues. It exacerbates and polarizes the conversation further within cheery and wishful thinking dynamics. Searching for information about flat earth theorists assists the production of clicks, stories, and moral panicking on human fallibility and gullibility. If anything, it justifies the need for further control over online traffic and content.

The internet as we know it is, at its core, concerned with collective contribution and shared content. This is the fundamental power force behind world-changing websites such as Wikipedia, where content is created based on collective knowledge or crowd wisdom (Surowiecki, 2004). However misleading in the specific, the general sense of these platforms is that human knowledge (and now artificial intelligence (AI)) will improve the overall quality of information shared, like a large group of people taking educated guesses on a specific topic. The 'average' result is the basis of Wikipedia's and other 'informative' platforms' knowledge. This is the core argument of Jaron Lanier's criticism of what he called the 'Digital Maoism' (2006) tendency of web collectivism. Information becomes overinflated and inexact, but it also becomes harder and harder to rectify, change, and contribute to in a manner that resembles the 'real world'.

This issue is also at the heart of the 'mind bleeding into the world' argument of David Chalmers (2017), where the mixing of the natural, the physical, and the artificial, both by the mind and by the world, becomes our future. AI augments the mind, virtual reality augments the world, and the two of them engage in some sort of interaction (Chalmers, 2022). The Onlife, with its blurring of instances, becomes a particularly fertile ground for conspiracy narrative and action. The blurring aspect of conspiracy is evidenced by the development of 'conspiritualism' ideology, implying the merge of conspiracy within Western esoteric beliefs (Asprem and Dyrendal, 2015). There, the objective is one of 'harmonizing' rather than 'harming'. However, with the outbreak of the pandemic, the discourse around body-spirituality, connected to medical hesitancy and the like (Parmigiani, 2021), and general 'deep-state' paranoia, developed new, problematic aspects that are fundamentally influencing the Onlife.

As such, the question of criminality – or better yet, the internet as a conduit for crime – becomes a key aspect of such an argument, whereby 'cybercrime in social science fiction as dramatic, futuristic and potentially dystopic proscribes public expectations of cybercrime as above the capabilities of normal folk, as sensational, disempowering victims and being beyond the scope of state protection (e.g. policing)' (Wall, 2008: 868). As David Wall points out, the sensationalism of media content 'blur[s] predictions about "what could happen" with "what is actually happening"' (Wall, 2008: 868).

As one might expect, this discussion has become increasingly complex. Lanier's (2006) concept of 'Digital Maoism', when specifically applied to David Wall's analysis of cybercriminality, refers to an era when the average user could be a misleading, confusing, influencing human being. Today, however, with the rise of computer-generated content and automated bots, this issue has taken on even more serious dimensions.

What arises from all this, and more will now be discussed, is that the credibility of online content has never been more ambiguous (and yet credible!) than it is today, and the conspiratorial nature of what goes on online has had a significant effect on the everyday life of individuals around the world.

## Another epistemological problem

A good definition of conspiracy theories is: 'paranoid psychological tendencies with the belief in particular stories of secret nefarious social networks' (Morelock and Narita, 2022: 1010), which describes in a somewhat more scholarly manner the (I would claim still historically accurate) stereotype, highlighted by historian and conspiracy expert Peter Knight, of 'an obsessive, petty-minded right-wing paranoid nut, a proponent of extremist politics with a dangerous tendency to single out the usual suspects as scapegoats' (2000: 3)

While there is an ongoing debate around the distinction between 'theories' and 'fantasies' (Wu Ming 1, 2021), taken generally, conspiracy discourse, characterized by the belief in hidden plots, can foster a sense of heightened suspicion, causing individuals to question not only narratives presented by politicians and the media but also the very nature of trust. Such is Adam Curtis's analysis for his documentary *Can't Get You Out of My Head* (Curtis, 2021), where he claims conspiracy theories offer more captivating and realistic alternatives to those presented by political and media sources. This reality raises questions about whether people are drawn to them for entertainment purposes and how these dynamics influence public perceptions of reality: they are, in other words, the modern equivalent of science fiction narratives, from such theories as Martian canals to the Yeti. What on the one side is a trope, an urban myth and perhaps even an obsession for some, turns into a systematic belief promoted online and engaged with offline within a toxic discourse. The question of 'who' exactly is involved in these conspiracies and 'who' believes them is a larger issue that we will not be able to cover in this book. However, it is important to recognize that the controversy surrounding freedom of speech makes this situation even more complicated.

The right to express any belief, even if it is unfounded, can clash with ethical concerns about potential harm. When examining the psychological aspects, it is important to distinguish between personal delusions and collective panic, which add subtle nuances to the understanding of conspiracies. The term 'conspiracy fantasy' implies that these narratives incorporate imaginative elements, while the introduction of dystopian elements portrays them as a type of speculative science fiction. The tension between perceiving everything as interconnected and dismissing events as orchestrated 'false flags' reflects a deeper divide within conspiracy narratives. Furthermore, the interplay of trolling and hoaxes within these theories introduces layers of complexity, blurring the boundaries between genuine beliefs and intentional misinformation, forcing individuals to decipher motivations and comprehend the impact on both personal convictions and societal dynamics. In particular, Caulfield and Wineburg (2023) note the pattern of:

- Connecting dots that are not there.
- Believing that big things are evidence of a form of big thinking, such as the flawed rhetoric #diedsuddenly (a hashtag often used to spread misinformation about COVID-19 vaccines killing otherwise healthy individuals) discussed in Caulfield's blog[2] or the alt-right trope 'go woke go broke' (where ideological marketing stances damage the company's finances) – that is, pigeonholing narratives that fit a broader political point.
- Thinking that on closer inspection all evidence against one thing is actually evidence of the very thing they believe.

Such patterns do quite systematically describe the awe and thus delusion around specific fantasies that, nevertheless, have a direct effect on the Onlife of individuals.

For instance, the recent theory claiming that the singer Taylor Swift was part of a government 'psychological operation' (psyop) to influence the 2024 Super Bowl[3] may have impacted how some people discussed the event. Particularly challenging is the sociological study behind the 'incel' (involuntary celibates) communities, and their rhetoric arguing that the denial of sex constitutes a 'reverse rape', and that such offences are as harmful as real rapes (Hoffman et al, 2020: 573).

Accordingly, the pressures of everyday life leak into online life and back again, travelling through socio-economic dimensions. The hybridizing of different theories in online spaces can shift from far-right to more moderate left-wing ideas within memes and through tropes like the 'transinvestigation'. This refers to a mix of 'trans' and 'investigation', where individuals become fixated on uncovering the supposed 'hidden' gender identities of celebrities and politicians (Lenton, 2024). These shifts include instances like the 'fanspiracy' (fan-driven conspiracy) surrounding Taylor Swift, where some far-right groups have labelled her an 'Aryan Princess' with a supposed secret/Nazi agenda. They base this claim on her perceived 'pale' appearance mixed with a 'godesslike' aura. Also significant are allegations based on media photographs that her social circles and partners are all systematically White, framing her as a crypto-fascist at heart (Sunderland, 2016). On the other hand, more liberal groups promote the 'Gaylor Swift' theory, speculating about her sexuality and suggesting she hides her attraction to women (Ferrigine and Saha, 2023). Some of these conspiracies are easy to neutralize: the 2024 Super Bowl conspiracy involving Taylor Swift only needed a specific date for its supposed realization to be quickly debunked on national television and fade away (at least from the mainstream click-bait and subsequent conspiratorial 'moral panic'). Other events, such as the whereabouts of the Princess of Wales, Kate Middleton, in online forums in early 2024, required a public confessional video to make the mainstream media feel bad – and ignite further online conspiracy debates on the falsity, manipulation, and false flag of the information released.

But the radicalization of these tropes and toxic discourse does not take place simply behind a computer screen, as 'every once in a while, as the Islamic State and incels have both displayed to devastating effect, somebody breaks away from these virtual domains to commit real-world violence' (Hoffman et al, 2020: 575). Secondly, like jihadists, 'violent incels have developed a culture of martyrdom, in which past murderers are venerated as heroes to admiring future generations' (Hoffman et al, 2020: 575). This admiration plays a crucial role in the idealization of the 'supreme gentlemen' and similar themes associated with incel Elliot Rodger's mass killings in 2014, as well as other figures within far-right online communities (Dignam and Rohlinger, 2019). These men, who view themselves as attractive or deserving, express anger over their inability to attract partners, which they contrast with what they believe is their otherwise appealing personality or appearance. These groups tend to place blame not on themselves but on what they see as an over-idealization of feminist values, which they perceive as contributing to their difficulties (Ging, 2019).

## Digital-storm-'gate' is gathering (over and over again)

As mentioned earlier, the problematics of the internet within the Onlife is the possibility to source, hopefully without reasonable doubt, the content and factuality of what we view, read, and click. This is a systematic problem that adds to the series of factual misgivings that the Onlife response leads to and the actors who promote, distribute, and construct content. At the time of writing this in 2024, conspiracy theories are increasing both on- and offline regarding the assassination attempt on former president Donald Trump, building upon the 'perfect storm' of the 'supersonic'[4] spread of rumours and inflated claims by public figures who should know better, including Elon Musk.[5] Confirming the previously mentioned axioms mentioned by Caufield anyone can search through more and more videos showing a prism of angles of the same event, with Reddit posts showing graphical replicas of the shooting location, the direction of the bullet, the 3D movement of the head moments before the bullet's impact. This political confusion is not novel, neither in the UK (Berger, 1995) nor, say, in the Nixon era. The impact of Onlife's novelty was significantly influenced by similar circumstances during the 2016 US election, involving many of the same actors (Aikin, 2019; Dignam and Rohlinger, 2019; Finlayson, 2021). Furthermore, the ambiguity and influence of President Donald Trump have been even more significant to the criminology of the Onlife, especially at its peak of toxic discourse during the COVID-19 pandemic. This influence remains significant for two reasons: first, it highlights the powerful role that online data and available information (of any nature) can play in shaping public opinion and behaviour (Geoghegan, 2022). Second, it underscores the rise of conspiracy narratives among the American public, exemplified by the spread of QAnon and 'plandemic' theories during this period of 'epistemic crisis' (Morelock and Narita, 2022).

Regarding the first aspect, with the Cambridge Analytica scandal, defined by some journalists as 'Facebook-gate' (Ziccardi, 2019: 111), it became worldwide knowledge that a private enterprise, with UK headquarters, could have an influence and impact on US political campaigns. Though Italian scholar Giovanni Ziccardi (2019) emphasizes that involvement in the actual election was very much alleged, what became evident after the 'data breach' scandal was the rapid and unpredictable distribution of user data to third parties. This included the analysis and creation of psychographic segmentations based on this data that would allow for predictions on user interests and tendencies. What these scandals allowed the public to understand was that all the likes and preferences submitted to such sites, which are designed to expose your secret preferences, are content incentivized within the platform with the aim of micro-targeting users and inducing a 'permanent persuasion' (Ziccardi, 2019: 120). International involvement in the 2016 US election had also become central, with troll-farming accusations from the media levelled at the Kremlin.

Such problematized relations between information, users, and votes were exacerbated by episodes of sheer incompetence – an argument articulated with masterful precision by the Italian writer Wu Ming 1 (a pseudonym; lit 'anonymous') in his book, *Q for Qonspiracy* (2021). The incompetence was evidenced by the leaking of 20,000 emails from US presidential candidate Hillary Clinton's private account in 2016 when her server was hacked in a targeted attack known as a spear phishing hack after she had, according to the BBC, 'broken government rules by exclusively operating a private server from her upstate New York home while secretary of state' (BBC News, 2016). The seriousness of the affair, which ended up being shared on Wikileaks, had significant (and in many ways surreal) criminological effects on the Onlife. Indeed, Clinton's emails did not have a particular impact because of what they contained – which had been largely decrypted and interpreted as mostly harmless exchanges – but what they 'appeared' to contain. The internet, that 'hungry gullible beast', as pointed out by Lanier (2010), reinterpreted those trivial messages as secret codes, filled with ambiguous meanings.

## Rabbit in the basement

The timeline of the events is significant to see how the spiral of conspiracy and confusion may, and has, blurred on- and offline. After the 2016 leak of Hillary Clinton's emails, a video known as 'Frazzled.rip' began to circulate online, featuring a deepfake (or better, a cheapfake) video of a supposed satanic ritual involving Clinton, her top aide Huma Abedin, and other members of the Democratic Party (Ball, 2023). This video connected the leaked emails to a narrative surrounding the harvesting of 'mole children' across the US, to extract adrenochrome from their blood to attain eternal youth. The height of the controversy focused on the family-friendly Comet Ping Pong restaurant in Washington, DC, which became the centre of false allegations claiming that children were being tortured in its (non-existent) basement. Does it matter that most of the content surrounding this video is (seriously) poorly edited and that most web searches (hilariously) lead to 'Rickrolling', tricking users into clicking and viewing the iconic Rick Astley hit song 'Never Gonna Give You Up,' which has become a recurring meme and a staple of the internet's (but especially 4chan's) ever-changing pop culture? It does, as it leads to the concreteness (albeit delusional) of otherwise alt-right tropes that were already infesting the web (Hawley, 2017; Massanari, 2017; Mihailidis and Viotty, 2017; Salter, 2018; Dignam and Rohlinger, 2019; Phelan, 2019; Drolet and Williams, 2020). However trolled, joked, and mocked, the conspiracy seems to constantly arise – with more and more perverted nuances (Ball, 2023). Indeed, according to Clinton's leaked emails, campaign coordinator John Podesta had engaged in a conversation with the restaurant's owner, James Alefantis, regarding a fundraising dinner scheduled to take place at the restaurant. Fantasizing about the 'bigger picture' of the leak, Wu Ming 1 (2021) notes that the initials 'cheese pizza' coincided with 'child pornography'. Consequently, 4chan community members, and later even Reddit forums, propagated by known full-time provocateurs such as Alex Jones, Mike Cernovich, and Jack Posobiec, also began to fabricate a secret language in which terms like 'dough' were equated with 'child', 'cheese' represented 'girl', and 'sauce' referred to 'orgy', among other interpretations (Wu Ming 1, 2021: 15).[6]

Such a milieu of confusion formed by systematic psychological manipulation (gaslighting) of information went beyond simple trolling and meme-generation. The massive and systematic targeting of Democratic Party candidates was part of an obvious alt-right-led political campaign in support of Donald Trump (Nagle, 2017). Trump's persona resonates with the ultimate potential and influence of the Onlife recall of untruth.[7] However, it is important to underline at this point that Trump is by no means the first to use such political manoeuvres. Among many others, Silvio Berlusconi has been referred to as someone who created the 'post-modern world where it doesn't matter what actually happened, but what people think happened' (Stille 2006: 20). I will discuss more of this in Chapter 7, 'Harms Against Reality'.

What is central to the Trumpian age is how it is not simply the media working as a political instrument to shape the world (Innis, 1951), but how individuals also digitally shape it to fit that very instrument and use it as a tool (and a weapon). To weaponize the tool of media is a central trope, one that has been picked upon by various media scholars (Nagle, 2017; Singer and Brooking, 2018), highlighting how 'individual actors, motivated purely by economic incentives, can, in an uncoordinated way, complement and extend the operational information of one set of actors to or against another' (Silverman, 2019: 385) and even invest in systematic, creeping radicalizations within targeted YouTube videos, podcasts (Klein, 2023), and other apparently harmless content (Perlroth, 2021).

As argued in Adam Curtis's (2021) documentary (and as such to be interpreted with a pinch of salt), with reality and fiction amalgamating, online fantasies found the ideal ground to leak into the real world: a quasi-infinite batch of men and women who could be seemingly made to believe anything, especially if it touched on some of our most basic instincts and sensibilities. We may note criminologically that the power of online conspiracies (and also more genuine campaigns) lies not only in their distribution but also in the frustration that inaction can lead to. This is where the already unhealthy practice of compulsive and endless scrolling online of modern anxieties finds a direct breach from the virtual to the material world. In the delusional mindset that fills the toxic narrative, if the conspiracy surrounding 'mole' children from which Democrats suck the life-force is true, and all these children have disappeared across the US, and if all these sick paedophiles are doing what they are doing, how is it possible that nobody is doing anything about it? Is such silence the hidden proof that indeed the Deep State of evil rulers is so influential, powerful, and real? Is it perhaps the very evidence that humans are selfish and doomed?

Indeed, the Comet Ping Pong restaurant owner and his employees received a long list of death threats, hate comments, and defamatory reviews as a consequence of the rumour. However, it appears that addressing the issue solely through online means was not enough. The perceived reality of the 'mole children' threat prompted 28-year-old Edgar Maddison Welch, a father of two, to arm himself and drive 600 miles to storm Comet Ping Pong. While driving, he filmed a video for his daughters claiming he could not let them: 'grow up in a world that's so corrupt by evil, without at least standing up for you and for other children just like you' (Miller, 2022). Maddison Welch stormed the restaurant, menacing its diners and heading for its basement, seeking to recover the alleged children (Ball, 2023). He thus unequivocally transformed a cryptic online fantasy into a real-life threat for unbeknownst diners. The storm of disinformation was at full potential, and that storm would soon gather all the various conspiracies into the prophecy of QAnon.

## Sparks of delusion

If we look ahead from the 2017 Pizzagate affair to the year 2020, at the peak of lockdown manoeuvres to tackle the COVID-19 pandemic, we can see the emergence of the most challenging period of the internet. Sophisticated deepfakes, bots, echo chambers, and algorithms putting national security at risk became not simply problematic, but everyday (Ball, 2023).

QAnon capitalized on the confusion of the 2016 US presidential election and consolidated it into a specific and very clear conspiracy against the established order, with an increasingly precise agenda and targets. Using alt-right digital propaganda and controversial, often violent rallies, which made use of ubiquitous media reporting (Sweeny, 2018), it even found itself a righteous leader in President Donald Trump (Ball, 2023). Trump undoubtedly derived advantages from the vagueness inherent in the current digital era. For instance, there was a well-known incident on 8 October 2017 when he seemed to provoke reporters with a remark alluding to the 'calm before the storm', while posing for a group photograph during a dinner honouring military personnel. He then dismissed reporters afterwards without providing any clarification (Baker, 2017).

Whatever the intentions of President Trump, his phrase 'calm before the storm' was soon picked up and mentioned in the 4chan thread 'Pol' (for politics). This is the same thread where the first post signed by a user named 'Q Clearance Patriot' appeared in October 2017, prophesizing the incumbent extradition of Hillary Clinton (Wu Ming 1, 2021).

The new contributor, soon known simply as Q, came to develop and embrace the various 'drops' of cinematic references, alt-right memes, and other incoherent information appearing across the web, promoting a systematic rewiring of fears on the current state of affairs. Very generally, the Q conspiracy and its anonymous contributors (known as QAnon) filled the gap of misinformation they deemed to be the objective of mainstream media (using the concept of the so-called 'red pill', in reference to the movie *Matrix*). It was not QAnon that was confusing and dispersive, they argued; it was the elite and the cabal that controls everything (Morelock and Narita, 2021).

The prevalent sentiment of 'something must be done' is evident in various Onlife incidents across the US, such as the 15 June 2018 Hoover Dam incident – where a man in an armored truck blocked traffic demanding the release of an alleged incriminating government report on Hillary Clinton, before being arrested with weapons in his vehicle (Ball, 2023), and the Gambino family shooting in 2019 – where a reputed boss believed to be part of the 'deep state' was thus shot and killed outside his home in Staten Island, New York (Southall, 2019). But it would be a mistake to assume that these phenomena are simply a US affair. For example, the QAnon and general conspiratory sentiments were further exemplified by the 15 March 2019 killing of 51 worshippers in two mosques in Christchurch, New Zealand (BBC News, 2019). The incident was live-streamed on social media, with QAnon conspiracists labelling it a 'false flag', adding to the many acts seemingly driven by the perception that decisive actions to challenge the Deep State are imperative.

Thus, the rise of COVID-19 in 2020 and its subsequent necessity for state-imposed restrictions further exacerbated the 'doomscrolling' narrative of a 'plandemic', which conspiracists thought implied further domination and covert abuse of children and the general population (Morelock and Narita, 2022). Even more significantly, the very narratives of these theories mix with colonial problematics and white-supremacist rhetoric, such as the ongoing alarmism of the 'Great Replacement' theory. In the Onlife's mixing of these tendencies, fascism even blends with ecology (Klein, 2023), and violent outbreaks occur along with gun violence and live-streamed crises, such as the 14 May 2022 shootings in Buffalo, New York – where ten people were killed and three others injured in a racially motivated attack (Kriner et al, 2022).

At this stage it is evident that what happens online is much greater than the simple trolling efforts of the flat earth theorists and their conspiracies. Instead, the narrative appears in the minds as well as the bodies of users: not only can they vote and change the course of an election, but they can also bear weapons and gather together. At this stage of the QAnon and other Deep State conspiracies, the complexity becomes baffling as the connections made cover historical events, various religions and cultures, state agencies, and even cinematic and science fiction references from across the globe.[8]

## Blame it on the messenger?

So far, I have highlighted the controversial means that politicians adopt to promote and maintain a toxic and harmful discourse in the Onlife scenario. I have mentioned the 'calm before the storm' example as it is central to the development of the proliferation of the 'Q drops' concerning the Deep State agenda (and perhaps vice versa). Another Onlife example is Trump's notorious 'covfefe' incident of 2017,[9] where an evident typo on his (or his team's) behalf was not acknowledged, nor immediately edited or removed, instead becoming an inside joke about some secret coding (Abadi, 2017). Other countless examples can be used, but they all return to the same point: mediated production of confusion is both absurd and productive, aided and promoted by spin doctors who navigate the digital fabric to alienate and promote polarization both on- and offline via various media.[10]

But from a criminological perspective, one also needs to consider who the real perpetrators are of this digital confusion that resonates in the Onlife. Edgar Maddison Welch, who 'stormed' Comet Ping Pong with barely any previous criminal record (Wu Ming 1, 2021), has since died in January 2025 (France 24, 2025), shot dead in his hometown by the police. Nevertheless, he had been, in his own words, 'addicted' to the internet, derailed by the sowing of the seeds of digital confusion. It was no surprise that he himself had also tragically turned into an alleged 'crisis actor' (Ball, 2023), perpetrating a 'false flag' that replicated even more cognitive dissonance, in the most classical sense of the term (Festinger et al, 1956).

Other individuals have less of a clear conscience. In particular, and as already mentioned, Alex Jones, founder of the website Infowars, highlights the current polarization of information found online. Since its beginnings in 1998, the website has demonstrated two central trends which influence the Onlife: one is the main income of the site, selling 'pseudo-scientific' solutions, including COVID-19 vaccine alternatives (Breland, 2020), and the other is distributing alternative views of current events to common news outlets. Infowars became particularly popular after the 2012 Sandy Hook school shootings (Van Den Bulck and Hyzen, 2020), claiming that related news stories were 'false flags' (deceptive tactics to conceal a real purpose) and the parents of the victims 'crisis actors' (individuals hired to play specific roles in emergency response). In line with the conspiracy trend, it argued that the tragedies were 'fake', staged events by the authorities designed to shape public opinion and impose restrictions on civilians' use of firearms (Wu Ming 1, 2021).

It was left to users to confront the mind-boggling possibility of these 'conspiracy theories' with 'hard facts'. In a surreal twist, on top of their grief, Sandy Hook victims' parents were bullied online (cyberbullied) and even visited at home (doxxed), after being accused of staging the events by so-called 'truthers' who claimed their children 'never existed' (Ball, 2023). The harm and damage from this targeting still lingers on years later. As one parent acknowledged, the confrontations continued to take place both on- and offline, meaning they could not simply move on or let go (del Valle, 2022). This resonates with the Pizzagate aftermath for Alefantis's Comet Ping Pong restaurant, where, even in 2021, protesters would still regularly meet, menacing the proprietor, his employees, and customers (Miller, 2021).

While Alex Jones, among the prime distributors of such misleading content (rebranded 'hate content'), has faced innumerable complaints and legal action against him (Hyzen and Van Den Bulck, 2021), the mass of highly misleading (yet profitable) content continues to spread across all sorts of legitimate social media platforms. Initially, bans and censorship appeared to be a (albeit very late) solution. The first to act was Apple Music on 5 August 2018, banning podcasts related to Infowars; this was followed in a couple of hours by all the major social media corporations (Hern, 2018a). This solution, known as 'de-platforming', was echoed by Twitter in early September 2018, making it evident how the whole thing was a delicate matter (Wu Ming 1, 2021). At this time, 'Jones and his message attracted 2 million weekly listeners to his syndicated and streamed radio show and up to 1.3 billion views to his YouTube channels, while Infowars.com had 20 million monthly visits – 80% from the US' (Val del Buck and Hyzen, 2020: 43). While at the time of writing it is still debated whether the system of de-platforming actually works (Klinenberg, 2024), it is evident how much profit this content gave to the platforms that hosted such presenters (as noted in Chapter 4). On the other hand, Alex Jones's justification was one of promoting 'free speech' to the extreme. Thus limiting the propagating of disinformation, whatever its nature, is evidence that some sort of state-sponsored censorship was taking place, that the internet was controlled, and that most internet content was manipulated and not trustworthy (Hyzen and Van Den Buck, 2021).

In light of this feeble rhetoric (let us call it a 'sophism'), it is somewhat self-evident how easily the COVID-19 pandemic theories (aka 'plandemic'), including the its connection to 5G network technology, and QAnon correlations, mixed with climate change deniers, conspirituals, and so on, has further propagated the theories of false deaths, false flags, and another staging of events, as featured with even more vigour on Infowars, Steve Bannon's War Room and other websites, shows, podcasts, and live-streams (Klein, 2023). After all, well attuned to the promise of endless content that the internet promotes, one of the recurring tropes of Q's 'drops' was the sentence 'Enjoy the show', a show that beyond the screen and inside everyday tragedies 'keeps going on', and more than that, 'nothing can stop what's coming', another recurring trope of QAnon supporters (Ball, 2023).

It is hard not to wonder, as Naomi Klein has done in the book *Doppelganger* (2023), and with the re-election of Donald Trump, that with the Alex

Jones case, Steve Bannon's show, and Naomi Wolf's growing popularity, what can be done about this form of discontent and hate content, which seems to only infuriate and spread further frustration and anger? To date, solutions to the problem of hate discourse online have followed two basic directions: banning online content and pursuing legal action against the producers of said content. However, the drawbacks of this approach are akin to putting a lid on top of a boiling pan hoping the content will just cool off – and Trump's astonishing November 2024 electoral win has proven so.

## Stalking (in) the 'dark forest'

There is a striking quote from the hardcore science fiction novel *Roadside Picnic* (1972) by the Strugatsky brothers: 'You can imagine anything at all. And real life is never what you imagine.' The novel and Tarkovsky's film *Stalker* (1979), which was inspired by it, share the ambiguous description of a mysterious 'Zone' that is isolated by the military and is accessed occasionally by clandestine 'stalkers'. The area is extremely dangerous and is so for the most unforeseeable and mysterious reasons – however, access to the Zone is highly desired, as it is believed that some of its areas may grant wishes. The truth around this is hard to grasp, and while some stalkers have lost their lives in the most bizarre ways, others have gained incredible wealth – especially by selling in a clandestine market the oddly energized objects found in the Zone. Some of them are antigravitations, others release some sort of dark matter. What are they and where do they come from? No one knows, but some have opined they are nothing but the waste of some 'visitor' who may have passed suddenly through Earth, had a picnic there, and left forever.

I have discussed the randomized and paranoid discourses built online around QAnon escalating into every day, creating Onlife crimes and harms. Such a complex condition is evident in Naomi Klein's highly autobiographical book *Doppelganger* (2023), where she describes her frustrating attempt to protect her person, image, and memory from being merged, confused, gaslighted, and vacuumed into that of conspiracy writer and advocate Naomi Wolf.

There is no easy way of stopping this form of content other than systematically de-platforming the main actors involved and preventing their profiting from such content. However, a systematic study of the recurring patterns would, I suggest, help to prevent the rise of conspiracy theories inflated with the concepts of distrust in authority and general scientific knowledge, and prevent further radicalization into 'extreme' mentalities. 'Q drops' act as the metaphorical mysterious waste of *Roadside Picnic*, charged with unclear energy and promoted in a black market of fantasies and conspiracies. Such dynamics become evident with the spread of a counter-QAnon culture, known within conservative circles as BlueAnon (Lorenz,

2024), indicating the subverted left-wing conspirator thinking around Trump's murder attempt on 13 July 2024 – further replicating the means to contradict and interpret what goes on- and offline.

The cultural criminological perspective on discontent is central to how the Onlife problematizes and ultimately 'neutralizes' its occurrence. Notably, the producers of information and those who believe it are clearly distinct groups of users. Who takes advantage of conspiracies, who distributes them, who laughs, who cries – these are all very broad dynamics that need to be addressed to truly connect discontent with the desire, irony, or vicariousness of producing harm in the Onlife.

Whether left or right, liberal or conservative, the dynamics remain the same. At its core, the argument touches on fundamental Enlightenment principles fostering the meaning of 'truth' (Grišinas, 2024), particularly Kantian ideas of rationality and critical thinking – concepts that are frequently undermined in toxic discourse (Morelock and Narita, 2022). Platform design and the assumption of digital literacy place the burden on users to 'know better', to read, stay informed, and constantly remain 'up to date', urging them to apply 'discretion' to the content they encounter while being 'overflooded with fake utterances, hallucinated by the AI, pictorial (mis) representations, and sheer volumes of extra-factual information that fill our newsfeeds everyday' (Grišinas, 2024: 16). As Plato pointed out long ago (and struggled with himself), reasoning with sophists – those who use clever but deceptive arguments – remains one of the most challenging intellectual tasks imaginable. Lovink writes (2022a) that the 'don't engage' technique would seem the most effective, but this 'hiding in the dark forest' approach – inspired by the Liu Cixin novel of the same name (2015 [2008])[11] – is no longer either acceptable or enough. In the novel, the concept of 'cosmic sociology' introduces a framework for understanding super-societies and the ways in which they can protect themselves from other, potentially hostile civilizations. This perspective prompts a re-evaluation of our current online environment, as we can no longer consider ourselves safe from various forms of harmful exposure. Indeed, the conspiracy building around celebrity figures such as Taylor Swift or Kate Middleton would confirm this: silence only exacerbates further the 'click-bait', endless content consumer culture we are living in. Silence for any Onlife user becomes potentially even controversial, especially when choosing not to engage in political discourse, which, from vaccinations to social identity movements and major conflicts around the world, has become so vivid. Furthermore, in current circumstances, the Onlife has evident repercussions on the everyday lives of users, ones that, as I will discuss in the next chapter, systematically puts questions of reality and comprehension of surroundings in jeopardy. But, as I suggested in Chapter 4, this should not come as a surprise, especially in a world that is so polarized, not simply from a political perspective, but also from a social one.

As mentioned earlier, though QAnon highlights the peak of this phenomena, it would be wrong to assume this level of toxic discourse was limited to the US political spectrum. COVID-19 conspiracy theories are again fundamental in engendering power structure insecurities and social control theories. Italy, for example, where I happened to spend most of my lockdown days, suffered a high level of casualties yet proved to have impressive levels of 'resilience' during the first months of the pandemic. This was particularly true until lockdown was substituted with other forms of more subtle restrictions (including curfews) and political endorsement of the vaccine campaign. At this stage, the discontent towards the measures and the politicians behind them began to coalesce into a toxic debate that tore apart institutions, workplaces, families, and friendships. As mentioned by the Italian author Wu Ming 1, the Italian authority's use of media and TV channels led to confusion, incoherence, and pure malevolence (2021). It is notable, however, that the rhetoric of the virus spreading silently across homes, infecting communities, and jeopardizing lifestyles, parallels how conspiracy theories, toxic online discourse, and their effects on everyday life made unknown citizens receptive hosts. As mentioned in many blogs and online forums, anyone could become infected. In this rhetoric, the virus and the conspiracies aligned, with few guidelines to truly 'protect' individuals' mental health and social welfare.

Just as the forbidden 'Zone' only creates further fascination and new 'stalkers', it would seem we can do little to limit the emergence of QAnon-like fantasies. But perhaps something can be done concerning more politically led delusions. Indeed, there is a lengthy list of ambiguous policies which have ignited debate and controversies and leaked back and forth in the Onlife dimension. Across Europe, there has been since 2020 heated discussion over the concept of '15-minute cities' and related protests involving 'low emissions zones' as well as general discontent over licence plate recognition cameras and the like (Partington, 2023).

The concept relates to a somewhat classical notion of how a city would function with the ideal social capital of having all necessities within a 15-minute walk from one's home (one could simply read page 138 of Jane Jacobs's *The Death and Life of Great American Cities* (1961) to agree and move on with the whole matter). Indeed, the '15-minute city' was deemed as an interesting utopia that came out of the pandemic years where traffic was diminished. It became evident, taking Paris as a case study, that one could cross most cities with a bus and a bike in more or less 15 minutes while taking the car would actually take longer (O'Sullivan and Bliss, 2020). So the car, historically the object of consumer freedom, became rather a subversion of that – something authors such as Ivan Illich had long noted in his ode to cycling (1974). It is no conspiracy, and perhaps not even too much of an opinion, to say that by driving you are not free; you are stuck in traffic most of your life. However, when one mixes these notions with the 'far right' intolerance of the 'lefty' green-washing agenda and connects the limitation to movement enforced during the pandemic, the correlation might heighten an already heated 'climate change deniers' debate (de Nadal, 2024). Rather, to insist on a climate-pledge agenda involving phrases such as 'machine-with-tree substitution' in Paris (Poon, 2024) – and have media and politicians use the same terms of 'replacement' and 'substitution' as the conspiracy theorists who claim that an 'ethnic cleansing' agenda is replacing 'white-with-non-white' populations – is an odd rhetorical choice. To overlap this 'replacement' discourse, particularly in the context of rapid and controversial changes to our social and economic environments, serves as yet another means to indoctrinate or inadvertently lend credibility to harmful ideologies, blurring the distinction between legitimate environmental actions and dangerous conspiracy theories. Nevertheless, political ambiguity, provocative statements, and basic human anxieties have led to most of the commotion, leaking from online forums to heated rallies against further impositions on citizens' freedom: a fundamental warning is one of not mixing conspiracy talk with fundamental public dissent, which only hegemonizes expressions, opinions, and dialogue.

As with many of the aspects of this book, an undertone of this chapter has been that the internet has generated great confusion in people's lives, with shades of it being an epistemic crisis (Morelock and Narita, 2022). The so-called world wide web offers, on the one hand, a huge collection of information – which could ideally be an excellent thing – but that information can also be highly manipulative and open to misinterpretation. As I have discussed in previous chapters, this is especially caused by the very nature of the distribution of information. Free speech, as claimed by most conspirators, is accepted as the necessary direction for all civilized societies, however, the scope and width of its grasp are beyond anything ever imaginable and within such a limited timeframe. As Umberto Eco (2015) noted shortly before his death, and amidst considerable controversy, platforms like Twitter have facilitated indeed a remarkable exchange of information. This exchange could have, for instance, heightened awareness of the horrors of concentration camps during the Second World War. However, it has also provided a platform for the 'trivial conversations of imbeciles after two glasses of wine' on a wide range of topics, occurring on a global scale.[12]

An effort for greater communication would be welcome in an environment where, on the contrary, the more contemporary sentiment is one of 'people read crazy stuff online' and use their devices erroneously, and therefore 'should not be trusted'. Of course, such argumentation can be even more problematic and spark even more controversial sentiments. This could possibly lead, as suggested by academics such as Frank Furedi (2020), to an 'elite' taking democracy away from people because the very people can't be trusted anymore – which is the same argument of many of the protestors and conspiracy theorists around the 'red-pill' hidden truth regarding 15-minute cities, ultra low emission zones (ULEZs), and the like. Q-affiliated militants claim that they are fighting for the greater good: they represent democracy and the protection of it. What can be done in this toxic Onlife dichotomy, which only seems to be heading towards more polarization, misinformation, and violence? Further suggestions are offered in critiques of the internet by Geert Lovink (2022b) and the work of the Institute of Network Cultures, which is aimed at encouraging political debate and human involvement, not 'clownesque' provocation and systematic scapegoating, but one of 'disrupting the disrupters' and the platforms where they interact (Lovink, 2022a). I will return to this topic in the final chapter, but first, let me offer some further considerations on the systematic assault on reality that the Onlife entails.

# 7

# Harms Against Reality

This chapter discusses the elements of a web-induced digital world where the boundaries between what is concrete and relatable are in perpetual jeopardy, with a constant threat to the distinction between what is real and what is 'fake'. The advent of deepfake software, which can easily alter faces and manipulate screen interactions, and the implementation of the dark web have given rise to new criminological and zemiological realities. From astroturfing (a deceptive tactic in which organizations or individuals fabricate grassroots support for a cause, product, or idea) and sock-puppets (artificial online identities created by an individual or organization to manipulate discussions, promote products, or influence opinions without disclosing the true source) to catfishing (the act of creating a fake online persona, typically on social media or dating platforms, to deceive another individual), these virtual phenomena gain increasing importance as misinformation proliferates rapidly across the internet. This chapter examines the increasing hijacking of reality, the hyperreal elements within artificial intelligence's (AI's) potential, and the responsibility of indefinitely altering the 'Onlife' dimension.

## Creeping abnormalities

Most of this book has been authored by AI. Well, no, it has not. But as a reader, you would not necessarily know that – at least not yet, or in this edition. My 'name' is on the cover, and you might assume I conducted most of the work and research. However, that's not necessarily the case. While Leonardo da Vinci's original handwritten notes of his various Codex are accessible, contestable, and comparable, the digital authorship of the very words you are reading – printed, shared, and digitized – is about as anonymous as it gets. We place our trust in the name on the cover, just as we do with webpage content, statements from leading politicians on social media, or videos depicting conflicts in the Middle East. Yet, this trust is based on scant evidence – a presumption that diminishes with every passing moment, every update, every page refresh. Distrust for reality is creeping into our everyday life engagements.

In the previous chapter, I discussed the evolvement and menace of 'conspiracy theories' that transpired online with significant effects on the everyday lives of individuals, leading to episodes of crime, harm, and victimhood. Virtuality allows a much more potent credibility of ideological convictions and medialized sensationalism.

In Chapter 5, I pointed out that the Onlife is not only open for all sorts of function creeps, but its very devices are subject to various latent functioning designs, hidden patterns, and silent processes. Devices practice capta in stealth mode, enabled by visibility- and signature-reduction features. They are covert and latent tools that allow an entire array of functionalities without users being fully aware of when and why. Latency is another fundamental aspect highlighted throughout the book, describing the nature and functioning of Onlife technologies – the retroactive, concealed, and idle performance of capta systems collecting data and monitoring features that users are not fully aware of, nor particularly concerned about, until it is too late, such as with cases of blackmail, sextortion, and ransomware.

Here, I discuss aspects of these virtual dimensions and how they become even more significant with their engagement to the false information being bombarded at the web, especially in light of the potential new technologies on the horizons (AI and virtual reality (VR) among many) (Milivojevic, 2021). They influence perpetually and permanently the Onlife dimension that in itself is integral to our everyday sense of reality. This chapter problematizes the ease with which not only users and actors can alter the sense of reality, but also how, with the immediacy and spread of Onlife tools, governments and state agencies can change the law, impose restrictions, and modify policies and previous tolerances. As such, the Onlife today becomes a structure that enables the ever-increasing hijacking of reality, that is, both of normative axioms and social interactions.

The deceptive conditions of rapidly evolving media have long proven their influence. Before 'deepfakes' – highly credible digital modifications of videos, including the features, voices, and sounds of politicians and oligarchs – were indeed possible, with an evident caveat of limitations and much moral panic, as noted by scholars Simon and colleagues (2023).

Since 2023, as we emerged from the geopolitical and sanitary instability that COVID-19 caused, we thus rapidly shifted into another ongoing crisis of social, political, and economic crisis with AI, Deep Learning and Computer-Generated Content. On top of that, we have dived deeper into the Onlife, which has presented us with even more challenges and, to date, few apparent solutions to a more confusing than ever condition.

And this confusion, when massively and systematically (ab)used, is the focus of this chapter.

## Brave new neuro-1984

George Orwell's' *1984* is today an almost over-cited phantom of our times. As I am writing, an idle camera lens integrated into my laptop is pointing directly at me. The same happens when I raise my phone and tablet. Big Brother watches and cares for us with every googling, image, and social media update. With the integration of AI into smart devices, phones not only hold all our information but will judge, consider, evaluate, and edit my very perception, my very mood, and notify me; perhaps soon, via AI, our brainwaves might become fully transparent and spied upon by our employers in our own office – a dystopic possibility discussed at Davos in 2023, as reported in *The Guardian* by Hamilton Nolan (2023). Some of this is science fiction, some an inversion of the notorious 1984 Ridley Scott-directed advert for Apple which claimed: 'You'll see why 1984 won't be like *1984*'. As such, in this chapter, I concentrate on another aspect of the dystopic novel. The protagonist's Winston Smith's responsibility in his work was one of systematically and effectively fabricating reality. Or better, tune reality to current standards and government needs. Winston takes care when skimming incoherent (read controversial) content from current news reports, to render the current state of affairs always precise and consistent. Yet, in a sudden realization, Winston notices it is a lie. His government is waging war against a country that not long before they were at peace with. Winston cannot remember, nor anyone else (or at least they will not admit to), the real dynamics of what happened, why or when: nor can he be certain of how the events developed, their progress, and their result.

His condition, and the general milieu of Orwell's 'IngSoc' is one of a quasi-dream state, where nothing is fully palpable, and where any condition or interaction may rapidly, suddenly, shift into some sort of menace or antagonism. A certainty is there, to suddenly disappear in a mist, with the mind struggling to admit if it ever existed at all, as if it all was a gaslighting brain fog.

In Kazuo Ishiguro's novel *The Buried Giant* (2015), we share a similar sense of constant change mixed with the feeling that something that has been lost is physically depicted in a memory fog that surrounds the characters, who live incessant days, each one the same, all missing something: no long-term memory is available, everyone looks ahead. But ahead, there is nothing. Yoko Ogawa (2020) was directly inspired by the same idea, bringing a further cryptic tale of a contemporary island where *The Memory Police* unexpectedly raid people's houses to remove suddenly 'banned' objects.

There are two significant aspects of this complex argument. One is the technological detrimental effect on human cognition, one that Nicholas Carr described notoriously as the 'shallow' state that the internet produces on the mind and memory (2014). The ever-changing nature of its information flow, the permanent upgrading, updating, refreshing, reloading, scrolling, and looping of its features and elements represent, all in all, the loss of sense and control over what can be framed, sensed, remembered, acknowledged – to the extreme of feeling, as suggested by Tanya Goodin, of having 'too many tabs open in one's brain' (Goodin, 2021). This is particularly problematic when it targets and affects children, causing anxiety, stress, and feelings of inadequacy – as well as affecting sleep patterns (Teachout, 2024). In many ways, it confuses what we may sense as real. And while, systematically, the ambiguity may be criminally tackled, unreality itself becomes a means of promoting confusion, distrust, and self-doubt.

Another central theme is profoundly analysed in Naomi Klein's (2023) book *Doppleganger*, which highlights the unsettling Onlife blend of confusion and misinformation. This merging of online and real-life events fuels conspiracy thinking and, especially, wishful thinking. The result is a confusing mix of identities, events, terms, and concepts that resembles a quasi-senile condition.

As discussed in Chapter 4, the influential aspect of what constitutes Onlife today, and its potential impact on everyday life, further shapes the much-discussed mindset of the general public with inherent biases (Innis, 1951). This argument parallels the moral crusades against cable TV and media in general, highlighting particular criminological interests such as Gerbner's 'cultivation theory' and his idea of a 'mean world syndrome'. His theories posit that excessive exposure to mediated violence fosters an inflated belief that the world is more violent and brutal than it actually is (Gerbner and Gross, 1976), contributing to moral panic over video games and similar media. Such are the warnings of Huxley's *Brave New World* (1932), whereas we are potentially creating a system where, rather than a rigidly enforced dystopia, reality is repressed through endless entertainment, drug-induced tranquility, and an almost hallucinatory sense of progress – one that propels humanity toward an illusion of positive evolution (Postman, 2017).

Indeed, William Gibson's premonitions of a 'mass consensual hallucination' (Gibson, 2016 [1984]: 6) become central when trying to define and understand the new individual – not simply as a passive observer of the consumable media, but as a persuasive, cyberactive, cyberpunk, and cyber-potential-criminal (Wall, 2008). Information is the currency of Gibson's novels. And indeed it is the 'spice' of the intercalating information flow energy that constitutes the World Wide Web. The producers of the content, the information flow, are no longer citizens, but users who interact and interchange with this flow of 'energy', or information, contributing to the cyber verse, the info-sphere, the new frontier of being together and exchanging. We have already mentioned the geopolitical potential for the content generated to be ultimately fake, corrupted, toxic, and nonsense (Singer and Brooking, 2018). What if it is also computer-generated?

Such a reality was already highlighted in 2017, when journalist Adrianne La France, writing for *The Atlantic* (2017), suggested that most of the content on the web is generated by bots, with reports of 'bad bots' cyber attacking users with increasing precision.

As mentioned in Chapter 4, the seriousness and consequence of such conditions have brought forward dystopian visions of what the internet is and what it can turn into. Particularly significant was the discussion on what was known as 'the dead internet theory', popularized in early 2021 by an anonymous user named 'Illuminati Pirate' on the Agora Road online forum.

The supposed theory is as simple as it is captivating: 'Most of the internet is fake'. It proposes that most web content, the 'likes' attached to it, the pictures, and reviews, are created by deep learning, and computer-generated technologies that diminish the means of interaction and creativity, and moderate content, re-proposing the same boring and manipulated content. Such theorizing is only more credible with every new advancement of AI, but it also creates an even greater ambiguity concerning the agenda behind the content it was created for and with. Is Illuminati Pirate itself a bot, and has the conspiracy theory itself been planted to create further confusion among online users?

As I will argue here, much of the rhetoric of this misinformation and confusion has been repeatedly focused on the users themselves, on their lack of judgement, with an overall reference to ineffective education, poor parenting, and general 'poverty' – both economic and moral. Instead, this chapter wishes to analyse the dynamics of a virtual ecology that deliberately misleads its users, polarizes views, and confuses audiences, with serious and harmful implications that need to be addressed for what they are: harms against reality.

## 'Dreamstate'

I mentioned the film *Stalker* (Tarkovsky, 1979) and the book that inspired it, where fiction and 'reality' systematically blur, as a metaphor for our hyperconnected age and the enduring effect it is having on the everyday lives of individuals, from those who seek answers online ('The Zone') to the very confusing meaning they receive from the media. 'This Man' is a sociological prank created by Andrea Natella, who promoted an online campaign in 2006 claiming people worldwide were dreaming of a mysterious, somewhat upsetting, individual. He even launched a website (thisman.org) where thousands of individuals effectively claimed to have been visited in dreams by the fictional figure, underlining, among other things, the suggestive and influential power of online myths and legends (a theme that is well connected to the conspiracies outlined in Chapter 5). Natella's provocative project, still alive today and actively inspiring films and games – with a particular enthusiasm for its merchandise in South Korea – even managed to fool *Vice* magazine into running a piece on it in 2015 (Butler, 2015), suggesting the porous 'dream state' condition of today's fictionality: not only had users across the world equally shared the prank (or were inspired by it), but they even self-influenced each other in, effectively, dreaming about this very creature of fiction.

Emerging at a similar time, another criminological parallel may be drawn, especially when dreams turn into nightmares. The so-called pop-culture icon 'Slenderman', a monstrous creature, emerged from the 'Creepypasta' forum-based horror-themed website, building upon its fan base and even becoming a recurring trope via films, graphic novels, and other conventional and unconventional media. Slenderman hit the news and reached a moral panic status in 2014 when two Wisconsin 12-year-olds attempted, according to internet folklore, to 'evoke' and please the creature by luring a fellow schoolmate into the woods and stabbing her repeatedly (Hale, 2022).

Of course, vampires and lycanthropy have long been part of folklore around the world, and one cannot blame pop culture because of some fanatics breaking into cemeteries and stabbing corpses. However, more and more commentators are blaming the web, or at least the porous structure of the internet, which is seen as problematic in the way in which it is ever harder to distinguish fabricated content from the truth, fiction from science fact (Klein, 2023; Warzel, 2024a). In the 'Infocalypse' argumentation by political commentator Nina Schick (2020), the future of the internet is systematically one where the hyperinformation flow, as forewarned by Virilio (1998), will not simply be overwhelming, not only toxic, but influential without users even realizing. The dream state takes hold, with its effects 'sleepwalking' out of the screen and into our lives and shaping our memories (Alegre, 2024), particularly with the advent of AI photography, where images and individuals may be shaped and modified at will, or even inserted into the background (Warzel, 2023). In the somewhat provocatively titled book *This Is How They Tell Me the World Ends*, journalist Nicole Perlroth (2021) highlights how cyberweapon threats are intrinsically designed, and insignificantly applied, within the everyday appliances that we engage with. Again, the sleepwalking metaphor applies, bombarded by the mediatic confusion of what is represented and what may be interpreted – with apparent cyberattacks and globalized threats constantly in the background of our existences. One of these is characterized by the Russo-Ukrainian War, and the crimes it involves, showing again the rapidity of virtual dreams turning into physical nightmares.

## Creeping 'shards' of mediated war

The conflict in Ukraine escalated in 2022, when the world was still recovering from the COVID-19 pandemic. News outlets, en masse, suddenly revealed the menacing line of Russian tanks on the Ukrainian border. For William Merrin and Andrew Hoskins, this would begin the first of many 'mediatic wars' turning into 'sharded' realities (Merrin and Hoskins, 2024). In contrast to previously photographed and videoed conflicts ranging from Vietnam to Iraq, the battlefield is now systematically represented and recorded, often live, on social media channels – both on Western and Southern platforms. The potential for altering facts, or promoting propaganda on the motivation and justification for the war, led to notoriously controversial actions, as with the ban on European servers accessing the pro-Putin international outlet Russia Today (RT), a website that shared a powerful and successful business model. Indeed, *RT News* gained considerable traction among European readers by featuring a range of 'respectable' contributors, including prominent figures such as celebrity commentator Slavoj Žižek (2022) and sociologist Frank Furedi. However, it interwove this content with fake news and subtle pro-Putin propaganda, effectively disseminating it to unsuspecting audiences (Hsu and Myers, 2024).

This technique of gradual fact-alteration is not new. It has been apparently a key strategy in the pro-Putin 'spin doctor' playbook, including playing a significant role in shaping public perception during critical events such as the Brexit referendum and Donald Trump's 2015 presidential campaign (Geoghegan, 2022). As such, content is subtly produced to alter and influence a specific set of voters, supporters, or even simple incidental viewers. Again, this is a long-debated sociological and media studies theme, focusing particularly on echo-chambered and targeted content (Pariser, 2011), especially in light of the Cambridge Analytica revelations (Ziccardi, 2019). In Ziccardi's words, the means of dissipating information becomes a 'technology of power' that may alter and shift perceptions and influence opinions, forming de facto the ideal manufacturer of public consent in Chomskyian terms (Woolley, 2023). 'Fake news' becomes a systematic apparatus of which politicians, both in the Global North and West, have swiftly taken advantage, pushing the boundaries to a 'post-truth' environment.

Combining reality with truth is problematic and complex. Nevertheless, it is evident that what we are witnessing online, and with its demeaning effects Onlife, is a technique designed to alter, confuse, and scramble our concrete understanding of the world. This process is difficult to pinpoint and even harder to limit, but it has a significant impact on the everyday lives of individuals, especially when the technique of fabricating and reporting content becomes a para-military tactic to send a message: and falsity is the medium of that message.

## Criminogenic reality

The concept of 'harms against reality' might sound anachronistic – after all, as mentioned earlier, we are used to living in a post-truth, virtual state where reality itself almost sounds cacophonic. However, it also serves as a warning.

In 2012, crime theorist Eric Wilson described the para-criminal yet systematic attempts of the late Silvio Berlusconi to create a dreamlike political scenario. This blurred the lines between the illusory and the delusional (2012: 303), allowing Berlusconi to manipulate Italian political public debate and secure judicial and parliamentary immunity for decades. Since Trump's presidential elections, such dynamics have become almost trivial. However, the speed at which they have become trivial is part of the same haunting warning bell.

Wilson connects this rapidity to Paul Virilio's concept of the 'dromosphere' (1998), where the boundaries between the 'real', 'visual', and the 'virtual' progressively blur. While this idea isn't new (Virilio originally wrote about it in 1991), Wilson's notion of 'crimes against reality' highlights how criminogenic phenomena represent the optical negativity of telematic illusions. Here, the 'deep' state forms a metaphorical composition of space, crime, and light (deep = dark = crime), facilitating a parapolitical war made of images and sounds that decompose our modes of perception (2012: 311).

Earlier in the book, I discussed the 'dream-state' condition that weakens our understanding of everyday life, marked by ever-changing, inexplicable moments of joy (the release of a new iPhone model!) amidst constant, gruelling images of global tragedies.

As noted by Wilson (2012), the German word for 'dream' is '*Traum*', which sounds similar to 'trauma'. The term 'trauma' comes from the Greek word for 'wound', indicating a forceful rupture associated with conflict and violence. If the essence of neurosis is conflict, then every act of repression is a self-inflicted wound. Consequently, every dream that symbolically reveals the presence of repressed material signifies trauma.

The twist I want to explore is how systematic tools, like fake news, create criminogenic effects across various fields, from politics to the economy. These tools, coupled with AI, enhance the credibility of manipulated perceptions, deepening the illusion. This complex blend of misinformation and technology undermines public discourse and erodes the foundations of reality itself, making the boundary between truth and falsehood increasingly indistinct. The rapid trivialization of these dynamics underscores the urgency of addressing this pervasive manipulation before it further deteriorates our collective grasp on reality.

## Malinformation

Returning to the nature of the European and Middle Eastern conflicts characterizing the first half of the 2020s, the Onlife condition of the hyperconnected world has rendered the possibility of creating not only immediate, live recounts of what was going on, but a specific misinformation of what parties, corporations, governments make us want to believe.

The weaponization of such information is nothing new and, as I have mentioned in Chapter 6, the infamous role of spin doctors has been central to geopolitical manoeuvring and the alteration of reality. Documentaries, such as Adam Curtis's analysis (2016) of the recently passed away Gleb Pavlovsky, who worked intensively to shape the image of Vladimir Putin (Seddon, 2023), as well as films, from *Power* (Lumet, 1986) to *Wag the Dog* (Levinson, 1997), just to mention a few, all offer semi-satirical, semi-dramatical takes on the power of manipulation of the masses via intensive media use, one that goes beyond simple 'misinforming'.

This is the argument of Iranian-Canadian journalist and activist Hossein Derakhshan, who with Claire Wardle produced a report (2017) for the Council of Europe pointing out that the current state of affairs is not simply subject to misinformation (false information shared without harmful intent) and disinformation (deliberately false information designed to mislead, harm, or manipulate), but is significantly characterized by what they coin as 'malinformation', a lexical blend of mis-/dis-information and malware/malicious software (Mir, 2023), whereby true information is distributed but in a misleading context (Wardle and Derakhshan, 2017). An example is editing a video of a public official to remove its crucial context, thus making their statement appear extreme and damaging their reputation (Wardle, 2019).

Such argumentation is similar to the 'cheap-fake' problematic, involving the use of badly edited or produced deep-fake technology (Paris and Donovan, 2019), however, given the political intentions to create confusion over a certain event, the investment in the type of 'malinformation' may be very 'deep'. Personal commitment to 'wanting' to believe has been evidenced in the spread of online scams via psychologically damaging 'catfishing' scams (Lauder and March, 2023), where the means to manipulate develop 'an online relationship with someone who turns out to be completely different from the identity that they had portrayed' (Lauckner et al, 2019: 290). As with the previously named 'sock-puppets' (Caled and Silva, 2022), catfishing has proved extremely lucrative within the Onlife in forging identities to prey upon users via various means of scams, identity theft, and other forms of deception within the already mentioned 'Dark Tetrad' (Craker and March, 2016).

While each of these tactics serves to destabilize and confuse, making it difficult for individuals to discern truth from falsehood, with 'malformation' the direct attack on the 'reality' of specific events becomes harder to pinpoint, especially when the extent of information is so vast, and 'posters' so intense.

## Astroposting

The hyperpower of posting is central to another evident concern of the internet and significantly harmful to the understanding of the Onlife, that is, the concept of virtual 'astroturfing'. The concept of astroturfing is not new: developed in opposition to grassroots campaigns or sentiment, astroturfing is 'when an entity artificially creates an impression that there is widespread sentiment in favour of or against a product, policy, or concept, when in actuality no such sentiment exists, at least not to the extent imputed' (Schill, 2014, cited in Chan, 2022: 508). Trivial examples are when toothpaste companies advertise the need for white teeth with the support of dentists, or, quite plainly, promoting artificial grass over genuine grass during a major sports event. Jovy Chan claims astroturfing today goes beyond simple social media false marketing towards fake 'facts', but the menace in falsifying actual support and general credibility, 'especially when pluralistic ignorance is at play' (Chan, 2022: 528) is a concept that is as significant as ever in the Onlife.

As such, other than directly trying to manipulate the content that individuals read and thereby shape their opinions (for example, through catfishing and sock-puppetting), agencies, corporations, and governments themselves may target content and weaponize physical 'astroposters', referring to the troll farm style of 'frontline staff carrying out the instructions and actually creating content on the internet, be it manually, or via sock puppets or bots' (Chan, 2022: 509), to suggest general consent over a specific theme, with both financial or simply destabilizing purposes (Woolley, 2023).

During times of crisis, such as the dissent against lockdown measures during COVID-19, opinions can shift significantly (Schill, 2014). In the political arena, the perceived threat of astroposting – defined as 'pumping up the credibility of certain beliefs or opinions' (Chan, 2022: 524) – was particularly evident in Italy during a brief period when I was there. A group known as the 'mattoncini' (little bricks) emerged, consisting of 'COVID deniers' who collectively posted dissent against anti-COVID-19 measures across all major social media platforms, often identifying themselves with a 'brick' emoji alongside their content.

Although the group was allegedly focused on trolling other users, their use of hashtags like #nonrespiro ('I can't breathe') – a phrase also associated with the tragic last words of police 'chokehold' victim Eric Garner and a powerful slogan of the Black Lives Matter movement (Klein, 2023) – took on a darker tone when repurposed to oppose the mandate of face masks for trivial reasons. On a broader scale, such incessant and repeated messaging on a large-scale on the then Twitter and Telegram channels can create the illusion of widespread agreement, falsely portraying a non-existent majority consensus. The 'mattoncini' (who would later target the health minister, rallying against the so-called 'sanitary dictatorship', and thus hoping to destabilize the government) were apparently only a handful of posters (Globalist.it, 2021), tweeting intensively from the same account, much like the previously mentioned '50 cent army' in China.

As noted by Chan (2022), beyond simply 'trolling', astroposting may have serious repercussions (and practical advantages) politically also within authoritarian countries, especially with the purpose of 'sow[ing] distrust and instigate[ing] arguments ... creating uncertainty, and disrupting genuine conversations' (2022: 521). This technique is particularly successful in suppressing civil movements, 'especially at its early stage where the direction is unclear' (2022: 521): examples of this can be seen in the previously mentioned state-backed operations against protesters in Hong Kong as well as in Middle Eastern and African countries.

## Astrobots?

Luciano Floridi's (2024) contribution to the AI debate is very clear in claiming that it is not, by any means, a neutral tool, and must be addressed as something directly influencing the Onlife. Specifically, Floridi envisions how 'AI can and will be used, ever more commonly and successfully, to manipulate people's views, preferences, choices, inclinations, likes and dislikes, hopes, and fears' (2024: 64). For Floridi, the central menace posed by AI is its persuasive means, something he centrally connects to the Onlife, forming a *hypersuation* scenario by means of the 'intensive and transformative power of AI to influence beliefs and behaviours through personalised, data-driven strategies' and thus forming an 'automate[d] production of high-quality content in ways that are increasingly accurate, rapid, affordable, flexible, indistinguishable from human-generated alternatives, and tailored as required' (Floridi, 2024: 64; see also Huang and Wang, 2023).

Some of these actions may be purely random in their appeal, in other words, politicians and other ideologists may take advantage and either push or taint specific trends. This mass shift of 'astrobotted' opinions – computer-generated rather than just 'astroposted' – demonstrates how troll farms, hacker communities, and state-led operations can weaponize social sentiments. Systematicity in the process was revealed in 2023 by the 'cryptic' (see Chapter 5) manoeuvres of shadowy agencies such as the Israeli 'Team Jorge' (*The Guardian*, 2023; Leloup and Reynaud, 2023), by intertwining troll armies, cyber espionage, and a mass of influencers. As analysed in an independent investigation by the international network of journalists called Forbidden Stories, Team Jorge members allegedly work as disinformation mercenaries, assisted by bots and computer-generated content that also work well within the Onlife, utilizing such techniques as delivering via false accounts sex toys to a political candidate as to stir up a personal scandal or remotely forging fake results for COVID-19 tests to entail mandatory isolation (Andrzejewski, 2023)

The automation of delivering and distributing harmful, misleading, fake, and malicious content exacerbates the issue, further subjecting users to these virtual schemes. Two sides of the problem are unveiled. Firstly, the systematic and automated power to distribute, click, produce, and share such content onwards via bots, algorithmic devices, and other means. We return to 'the dead internet theory', where, seemingly, the internet is made entirely (or predominantly) by bots that systematically forge computer-generated reviews, content, opinions, and articles with the unprecedented and uncontrollable ubiquitousness of distribution, rapidity, and effectiveness. Secondly, via deep-fake technological means, the forged is not only hard to distinguish from genuine content but may alternate original material, either slightly manipulate it with credible features, or with increasing precision, create new, falsified, and mimicked content altogether.

A well-described example is highlighted by neurophilosopher and author Erik Hoel (2024), who captured this unsettling reality in an essay titled 'Here lies the internet, murdered by generative AI'. Hoel argues convincingly that not only is all online content now potentially tainted and fundamentally corrupted, but it may also corrupt itself in a recursive cycle – stealing ideas and recycling themes in a typo-filled, self-plagiarized, degraded exchange of books, songs, art, and other creations, resulting in a copy of a copy of a copy.

This perspective is further illustrated by the online collective Clusterduck, which created a practical example through an episodic documentary inspired by Adam Curtis's style, titled *The Future Ahead Will Be Weird AF* (Dal Dosso, 2023). The narration, generated by AI to mimic the distinctive cadence of the renowned British director, accompanies a script written by Silvia Dal Dosso. The short documentary explores the rapid evolution of AI, characterized by chaotic and cacophonic experiments, ultimately leaving us with little choice but to sit back and enjoy the ride. Long and quickly gone are the days in which a Photoshop digital modification could be easily spotted by odd lighting paradoxes or AI monstrosities revealed by small, imprecise details: the new integrations of AI technology and the constant intake of human-generated content, however potentially limited, constantly jeopardize and alter the understanding of reality even more so. Everything is evolving at an astonishing pace, including our ability to grasp the processes behind the abuse and misuse of AI technology, which are perfected by the time they reach the public. Examples range from AI-generated photoshoots depicting Syrian/Palestinian/Sudanese children (depending on the captions) surviving bombings to the widely circulated image of the late Pope Francis in a flamboyant puffer coat. But more than being simply weird, hard to comprehend, read, and interpret, AI is proving more and more efficient in altering and replicating reality in ways that are harder to distinguish and limit, forging memories and the interpretation of what is and what was (Hoskins, 2024).

## (Cheap) fake 'I'

In early 2025, the Italian Prime Minister's voice was replicated via AI requesting money transfer to pay a diplomatic ransom (Le Monde, 2025). Many of these crimes were already possible in pre-COVID-19 times – when perhaps the technology was not as perfected, and the associated risks were likely underestimated, leading the menace of 'deepfake' technology to more serious levels (Schick, 2020).

The problematics of deepfake technologies have been enlisted within a series of more or less criminal and harmful Onlife environments (Paris and Donovan, 2019; Alegre, 2024). Many of the situations characterized as dangerous, particularly by the news media, have been rather amateurish – and have become known as 'cheapfakes'. Fake videos of world leaders have been apparently been attempted on many occasions (BBC News, 2022), with limited success in being convincing to the global audience (at least, as far as I know). Rather, a more practical and potentially lucrative application, according to Alex Hern (2018b), is the face-swapping technology used in pornography, claiming pop-culture icons such as Emma Watson, Daisy Ridley, and Scarlett Johansson, who by 2018 had become victims of such abuse. But by the same year, deepfake porn had also become used as a political weapon, as with the public shaming of Indian activist Rana Ayyub, with the targeted aim to 'undermine her credibility and silence her' (Alegre, 2024: 55).

While the sharing of deepfake pornography is, by 2024, a practice universally banned on all major 'clear-net' platforms (as opposed to the so-called 'dark net'), it is, however, somewhat ironic that the creators of the most notorious AI computer-generated platform, ChatGPT, flawlessly worked on and almost released a new model with a synthetic voice feature that allegedly, but quite convincingly, imitates the voice of Scarlett Johansson. The actress, as previously noted a recurring victim and popular target of deepfake pornography, with the literally unstoppable copy-pasting her of image (Harwell, 2018), impersonated a 'futuristic' AI assistant in the movie *Her* (2013), which, it seems, was the inspiration and justification for using it in the chatbot. The excuse for doing this, however, in contrast to its use in pornography, was that it was not plagiarizing a human being/voice; it was a pop-cultural tribute to an iconic film![1]

Indeed, Scarlet Johannsson's legal action in 2024 over the ChatGPT-4 system (which was quickly rectified by the AI engineers), concerning the very perception of what can be used and with what modifications, proves that there is a consistent and ongoing problem within the media industry that needs a systematic new approach. While it is possible nowadays to ask Chat-GPT to rewrite this content as romantic author Victor Hugo, the digital persona of media figures is rapidly shifting into a grey area of financial exploitation.[2] Aided evidently by the excessive availability of visual images, AI may be already superficially used to produce deepfake advertisements that include top-budget stars. But again, the problem, as with the voice in *Her*, goes back to Magritte's 'Ceci n'est pas une pipe' argument. What is being replicated is not Scarlet Johannsson, but an imitation of her. The same is happening with the growing list of exploited media figures – actors, comedians, and politicians – who are used, abused, and simulated to promote various commercials.

## Virtual tourists and beta terrorists

In Chapter 4, I discussed the meta experience of an augmented social media dimension, particularly focusing on the integration of headsets, which is becoming a natural part of the Onlife. For the late philosopher and scholar Roberto Calasso, writing in 2017, the experience created by VR headsets brings the otherwise ambiguous and 'embarrassed' notion of tourism to a new, awkward stage where one can be a tourist without even travelling, everything becomes navigable from one's couch (Calasso, 2017). The headset is the ultimate object of impermanence: just as tourists visit places knowing they will soon return home, VR explorers can remove their headsets at any time and return to their couches. In contrast, the augmented tendency is one of virtuality touring within users: we become the maps on which information navigates – while the user navigates the outside world.

AR devices allow users to overlay their view of the real world with superimposed informational text or imagery. AR will likely become integrated with powerful AI assistants capable of identifying and remembering real-world objects and scenarios. Additionally, we may well envision that other tools will facilitate persistent shared online digital overlays or 'metaverses', with content generated by a wide range of stakeholders.

O'Hagan et al (2024) highlight the effect on social interactions, for example, by 'allowing people to selectively convey information about themselves to others and adapt their appearance to the context, breaking down interpersonal barriers' (2024: 2) These include situations such as uninvolved bystanders inadvertently becoming participants in other users' AR experiences, similar to video gaming (shootings), or encountering unsolicited or inappropriate AR content, particularly of a sexually explicit nature. Users may change their appearance and the appearance of others, using controversial 'blackface' filters (a form of digital makeup employed by non-Black performers to caricaturize individuals of Black descent), sexualizing or 'otherwise appropriat[ing] the identity of others for socially unacceptable and abusive reasons' (2024: 3). With the Pandora's Box of digitalization potentially opened, a user's vision may also be altered to fit specific corporate or governmental agendas or experience censorship, both consensually and non-consensually. Frowns may be turned into smiles, frictions 'harmonized', and social unease such as homelessness, rubbish, and graffiti 'digitally washed away' (Eghtebas et al, 2023).

Such spaces – already integrated by local communities, advertisers, and governments – can, to use Calasso's analogy (2017), become open environments where the system's design also allows entry to criminal subcultures, organized crime, and extremist groups. Tourists may turn metaphorically into (meta)terrorists, or terrorists insinuated within the touring of everyday life 'sacrificing' – in the name of a 'belief' – the understanding of reality: manipulating the experience, tackling the ideas, and corrupting the understanding of what is, or what we may *believe*. Reality is another of a long list of victims.

## Conclusion: Mass hierarchies

As discussed by Aldous Huxley in *Brave New World Revisted* (1958), C.W. Mills's warning over the 'power elite' controlling all sorts of information becomes a means for a 'Permanent crisis [that] justifies permanent control of everybody and everything by the agencies of the central government. And permanent crisis is what we have to expect in a world in which over-population is producing a state of things, in which', in his haunting words, 'dictatorship … becomes almost inevitable' (1958: 14).

If the online fabrication of Taylor Swift's racial identity, sexual orientation, and political views as a way to 'fill the void' left by her perceived absence from the hyper-public sphere of the digital age (a phenomenon not limited to celebrities, as Josh Harris suggested decades ago), then the apparent 'disappearance' of Kate Middleton from public life in early 2024 provides a striking, AI-driven example of this trend. Online communities, using AI-generated false imagery and fuelled by a constant media maelstrom, caused the Princess of Wales to struggle, amidst other health matters, proving her 'state of being' beyond doubt. As reported in the UK edition of *Vogue*, this situation forced her to contend with the effects of digital manipulation and ongoing conspiracy theories, effectively becoming a victim of blackmail to prove her existence beyond the digital realm (Taylor, 2024b).

Instead, we seem to be returning to writer William Faulkner's 1955 (2003) consideration of the breach of 'privacy' because of media. In his essay entitled 'On Privacy', he discusses the loss of the American 'noble' principles of individual liberty and indeed the freedom of the press. Faulkner wrote the essay after being repeatedly asked to participate in an article concerning his life as an 'author', while, instead, his stance towards the editors was as simple as it was firm: a writer's visibility and indeed 'publicity' is compressed and contained in the 'work' that he delivers to the editor, which thus becomes 'open' to confrontation, study, praise, or criticism. But the author must be left alone. His editors were unconvinced: they claimed that the public wanted to know about his private life, and the less he was willing to give them, the more they would pay to have it. Whether he wanted it or not, someone would write the article sooner or later: the more he resisted, the more this someone would insist.

For Faulkner, such 'mass hierarchy' is the machine of public appetite and the commercialization of the private: there must exist a form of 'good taste' to be practised in respect of every individual, a good taste that nonetheless already in the 1950s sounded dramatically anachronistic. This is, as he writes, 'terrorizing (not scandalous: we cannot be scandalized as we have watched it grow [the loss of privacy], endorsed it and even used individually, when necessary, for our private gain)' (Faulkner, 2003: 25).

Just like a private acre, which you can define, fence, and limit, the private life becomes an object of possession – and with the mass media potential of fake content, it becomes rapidly a means of 'obsession' – to which there is little or no means of protection. As such, Floridi's argument to resist hypermutation via privacy may be somewhat unattainable.

As noted in his revised version, Huxley claims that 'There are many roads to *Brave New World*; but perhaps the straightest and the broadest of them is the road we are travelling today, the road that leads through gigantic numbers and accelerating increases' (1958) – and indeed, the very acceleration of convulsionary states becomes in itself a means of oppressive, of demagogic power. Interestingly, for the moment, not even the algorithms themselves manage to offer some sort of protection from this malaise that may constantly dispose of the Onlife.

Discussing regulation, the whack-a-mole condition of trying to catch up with the latest AI model update, and its subsequent greater potential, has opened an interesting and quite fresh debate among academics, Nobel prize winners, journalists, politicians, and corporations. Overall, the objective is one of trying to watermark the computer-generated content (Veltman, 2023), be it a voice simulation, a book reproduction sold online, or a tweet for that matter (Kapoor and Narayanan, 2023).

In reality, actual 'rational' human beings may be capable of doing the job better. For example, in April 2024, Elon Musk's AI content moderator for 'X', a chatbot named Grok, gathered enough false data to assume that Iran has struck 'Tel Aviv with heavy missiles' and informed the social media users of this (Thomas, 2024). Huxley's original parody of Churchill's famous quote, 'Never in the history of mankind has so much been owed by so many to so few', is 'Never have so many been manipulated by so few'. To further emphasize the dystopian control, we could extend the quote to 'Never have so many manipulated those already manipulated so much by so few'.

Apart from the highly censured use of deepfake pornography, it is perhaps safe to say that the real dangers of AI misuse come not from the grassroots level but from those in positions of power – repurposing the 'knowledge monopolies' highlighted by Harold Innis (1951) and so significant in the conspirator discourse. Some things never seem to change. Nevertheless, new developments in AI technology can be used paracriminally, with the systematic misuse and improper application of these tools – as with Team Jorge and who knows how many more shadowy disinformation mercenaries. But 'tracing' is another term for capturing, and the dynamics of capta make the Onlife even more susceptible, with increasingly precise methods to ascertain exactly who created specific content, as well as when and where it was created.

Once digital alteration tools are released into the market and integrated into our hyperconnected Onlife, they present a problematic approach to software. This software not only infiltrates the world but cannibalizes it, with users often unaware and unable to systematically resist both grassroots and VR-led, meta-terroristic astroturfed abuse.

8

# Obscuring Ignorance: A Hard Reset of Limitless Boundaries

## Closing the (first) circle

In Aleksandr Solzhenitsyn's novel *In the First Circle* published in 1968 (Solzhenitsyn, 2009), the 1970 winner of the Nobel Prize in Literature explores the lives of prisoners in a Soviet labour camp during the Stalinist era. Rather than dwelling on the stark horrors of the Siberian nightmare, as Arthur Koestler does in the chilling 1940 novel *Midnight at Noon*, Solzhenitsyn offers a more nuanced perspective focusing on a softer, quasi-gentle reality, depicted over the course of three days within the 'sharashka' section of the Gulag. The 'sharashka' is a low-guarded area reserved for scientists and intellectuals who benefit from better conditions than those in the hard-labour camps in exchange for working on experimental and ethically dubious scientific and technical projects for the state.

In contrast to their fellow prisoners in the deadly labour camps, Solzhenitsyn utilizes the metaphor of scientists living in a 'limbo' state – like the pagan thinkers in Dante's Inferno. They are decently fed, kept warm, and even allowed an element of romance with their guards. However, the subtle burden of living in an 'ivory tower' weighs heavily on the main characters, leading them to question their morality and their sense of freedom, which has been reduced to mere survival within the confines of state-approved silence.

Among the research conducted by the secluded scientists, emphasis is given in the novel to the 'study' of the human voice and how an agent may precisely identify and correlate an individual to a specific phone call without reasonable doubt.

For Solzhenitsyn, the human voice represents a significant analogy for a unique and personal attribute that can be manipulated and used as a tool of control and repression. By precisely recognizing the voice, a diplomatic whistle-blower may be revealed to the secret police. Two key characters of the novel, both scientists working on the project, wonder what other technologies may also be used and abused by their oppressive government and how far the morality of scientific curiosity and ethical principles may go.

The study of the human voice is quite fitting to the closing considerations of the previous chapter. Indeed, the synthesis of the human voice is among the ultimate achievements of AI technology – one that is being increasingly implemented within media and potential criminal activity. I would like to emphasize the analogy, illustrating how the study of its simulation directly impacts our understanding of the Onlife, alongside the associated criminal and harmful implications. A voice is not merely a portrait, offering a fleeting glimpse through time and space; rather, it serves as a far more enduring biopolitical instrument. The metrics of the voice, once synthetically appropriated, may appear more complex as a technology, but once achieved, are ever easier to replicate, reproduce, and distribute. The voice loses the meaning not simply of reality, but of the person, who no longer owns it. A face caught on camera is the reflection of biological features, skin, and muscles; a fingertip is solely an identifiable fragment of a body – a voice, however, is the reflection of the will, be it screaming, be it singing.

Another 'circle' themed book, Dave Egger's *The Circle* (2013), offers a corporate retake on the Big Brother political satire and interestingly infernal condition. Mae, the protagonist, is hired by an otherwise paradisiac (semi)fictional social media company that slowly englobes her into a hyperconnected, all-demanding work environment – where all the entertainment and amenities are provided for – to the point that the young protagonist gives up leaving the campus, meeting outside friends, and even visiting her parents. Slowly, the 'circle' fully encloses Mae, in a manner reminiscent of the 'sharashka', with the subtle use of total surveillance, enhanced by the launch of minuscule webcams hidden across the globe, envisioned by an enthusiastic corporate agenda that endorses transparency and endless entertainment with the sophistic 'chanting': 'Secrets Are Lies, Sharing Is Caring, Privacy Is Theft' (Eggers, 2013: 305). What is truly chilling is the novel's subsequent unfolding of the worldwide users' enthusiasm for such a social network experience – to endlessly watch and endlessly be entertained by others' lives (with obvious tragic consequences).

In such a scenario, the individual becomes not only pure 'data', but a constantly subjected one – a theme that Eggers will pick up in the sequel *The Every* (Eggers, 2021), adding the criticism aimed at Facebook to, evidently, that aimed at Amazon. Either way, technology allows the entire system to become subject to the surveillance rhetoric and metrics-driven technology. To think differently, as hinted at in both novels, becomes a problematic stance.

The oppressiveness of a furtively closing circle that subtly controls our existence is indeed a common trope in conspiracy thinking, especially within the rhetoric of the 'boiling frog' – where a frog will comfortably linger in a pot of water over a flame until it is too late for it to realize that something is wrong. But I would suggest that the indications of there being something wrong with the Onlife are self-evident, without this or many other previous books needing to overstate (or jinx) this. Rather, as I mentioned in the introduction when discussing the film *Molly's Game* (Sorkin, 2017), the Onlife criminological and harmful elements can easily find an analogy in an entertainment-led, drug-filled, alcohol-driven environment: users know they are drawn into something that may very well cause them harms, debt, or a sense of guilt. Molly's job, however, even if you get burned, is to make you stay in the game regardless. This is how the internet's data-craving, click-baiting reality endures, and how the Onlife is becoming an accelerating nosedive into a virtual reality (VR) connected and artificial intelligence (AI) driven scenario.

But what are the means to envision something else, another solution to our current state? I have mentioned Geert Lovink, who, along with Donatella Della Ratta, Tiziana Terranova, Franco Berardi and many others in their highly stimulating circle, has attempted to envision a relationship with technology that may 'liberate itself from capture' of the 'online [read Onlife] trap' (2022b: 26). To this, a great deal of countertendency has been proposed by Foucaultian biopolitics scholars such as Giorgio Agamben on his blog 'Una Voce'. There, Agamben envisioned, and promoted, a 'community within the society' – and thus a systematic and targeted withdrawal from the malaise of the modern era.[1]

Again, this is nothing new: perhaps yet another utopistic variation of the *Walden 2* experiment proposed by B.F. Skinner in 1948, made of a selected and yet isolated community that can thrive secluded from the 'corruption' of modern society. Using the already mentioned 'dark forest' analogy by Lovink (2022a), this all leads to a means of selected isolation, hoping for the best, expecting the worse – be it global technological breakdown, as in the plot of Rumaan Alam's novel *Leave The World Behind* (2020), or truly a 'Brave New 1984' where we all become digitally induced, AI monitored, and hyperproductive users. This is far from Gramsci's stoicism that is instead promoted by Floridi (2024), admitting the need for some pessimism of the intellect but fostering optimism of the will: I agree 'we must be optimistic' (Floridi, 2024: 63). Indeed, optimism is also the approach of Mbembe's life-work, where he diverts from the colonial analogy of 'darkness/evil', to evoke instead the idea of a 'long night', from which we need to envision the means to 'emerge' (2021).

I thus close this book by discussing what may be the urge to control, understand, reflect, and consider the appropriation of our persona in the Onlife. If Floridi, in the first pages of the *Onlife Manifesto*, noted how the Onlife's 'abundance of information may also result in cognitive overload, distraction, and amnesia (the forgetful present)' (2015: 18), I add to that discussion the need to control and forget 'data' as a means for a 'right to be ignored', that is, a means to envision a 'clearer' online experience where users are less subjected and influenced, and rather more in control.

## 'Itchy finger trigger warnings'

We, as users, currently need a means of fully securing our digital existence and limiting its leaks, propagations, distribution, and manipulation. The notions of privacy that have acted as a silver bullet to back up all progress, promising no effect on the user/consumer, have long proven inefficient, ignored, and anachronistic. Yes, cherry-picked news reports of Apple Inc's protection of its users' data during FBI criminal investigations (Selyukh and Domonoske, 2016), and the like, may give some confidence that, of course, not everything is strictly fatalistically vulnerable, as proven by the 2025 request of the UK government to pull out of encryption for new Apple costumers (Kleinman, 2025). Still, as discussed with my 'capta' argument, data is most certainly taken – within a specific layer of anonymization and a degree of scrambling. We may still today 'obfuscate' content, attempt means of resistance, install the Tor browser (accessing the so-called deep web), navigate via a virtual private network (VPN) (creating full anonymity of communication), and renounce smart devices. Still, it is uncertain how far into the future we will be legally bound to give up 'all that' and instead fully embrace the biopolitical scenario that Agamben foresees as the 'bare life' (2004).

Particularly problematic is the need for a proper awareness of what the Onlife entails and the criminological implications it may lead towards. In her discussion on the *Onlife Manifesto* (2015), Nicole Dewandre (2015) mentioned Mary Midgley's (Floridi, 2015) analogy of the 'bad smell philosophy' – things that may go wrong suddenly, dramatically, while being taken for granted in everyday life. One could not say that the Onlife, and the internet in general, have not been filled with warnings. Quite the opposite, scaremongering about the risks of dark-web purchases, the ease of digital drugs, the downloading of 3D-printed firearms, the menace of binaural beats (with virtual sounds producing psychoactive effect) (Barrat et al, 2022), the trivial online ordering of high-resemblance 'spoof-masks', custom-made balaclavas, and the like are nothing but drops in the ocean of systematic, rhizomatic criminal markets, deviant behaviours, and potential harms that take place regularly, incidentally, and constantly. The 'drop' is indeed a good analogy for this liquid state of constant, endless evolution of digital dynamics: a single drop that, in the long term, may shape, influence, and infiltrate the everyday lives of individuals, even in otherwise apparently 'free', liberal, democratic societies. Generative AI, as discussed in the previous chapter, has been a quintessential proof of this: ironically, but perhaps not coincidentally, the warnings have come from the main investors and developers of these computer-generated models, Elon Musk and Sam Altman, among them (Floridi, 2024). But one may wonder if the hype was not in itself another astroposting phenomenon to raise awareness, create content, share content, process data, and continue the vicious cycle of reinventing the wheel while flying on a jumbo jet. We have little means to prevent such a structure, especially because of how powerful the information flow has become today, how systematic the plutocratic forces have become, and how feeble our understandings of the systems we trivially use within the Onlife are.

To close the previously mentioned 'circle' I offer some final notes on attempting an 'offlife' or 'post-life' subcultural existence, even if only partially. This idea, facilitated, for example, by not being necessarily restricted to smartphone usage, allows the user not to produce incessant content and capta food. A rather drastic example might be to use a simple/basic phone (though it is uncertain for how long these will be compatible with the network) which, for the time being, is a device that still possesses some communication qualities but which acts as a deterrent to 'capturing' data. Anyone finding the phone and picking it up may read its text messages. Does this make it less of a protecting/protected machine? After all, anybody finding your notebook, with scribbled thoughts and ideas, has a similar 'insight' into your life. Yet they are only fragments: and this is the central difference between smartphone and GSM (Global System for Mobile Communication) technologies. The smartphone embraces all aspects of our lives, the GSM only offers partial 'windows' – text messaging, some pictures, and phone numbers (with often contact names). The design of its features renders them cheap 'informationally': they own very little of us. They can only vaguely be used against us – compared to the harms and fears of losing one's smartphone.

Of course, the question of whether to abandon technology altogether or to engage with it while advocating for change is a complex one. Suggesting that avoiding smartphones is the solution could be likened to victim-blaming, where individuals are held responsible for their own exploitation due to their circumstances (Hari, 2023). Instead of focusing solely on individual choices, addressing the systemic issues contributing to technological harm is crucial. So, we should strive for a more equitable and beneficial technological landscape by remaining actively involved in the digital world while working towards positive transformation.

## Surveillance and its resistance

As I have discussed in Chapter 2, the taking and keeping of data appears to have become a central element of internet navigation: data are taken and kept from users – analysed and monitored, on a regular and spiralling basis.

This is nothing new – and it is beginning to become a recognizable trend. Nonetheless, the wording is important, because it gives a different light on what takes place, how and why. The word 'data' is indeed perhaps too kind, if not simply misleading. What rather takes place – what is involved – is not a giving of our information, but a taking. In this perspective, the datum (given) must be redressed as capta – something taken. It is nonetheless a somewhat anachronistic reckoning that today needs to be directly considered. Capta, arguably, are the currency, and justification for the abusive power of the systems that are built around us.

The exploitative dynamics in which information extraction (capta) takes place on a normative basis during internet navigation or smartphone use in general are characterized by an alternation from voluntary public exposure (on social media and networks) to some form of 'background' recollection. The implication is that the secretive behaviour emerging from such an Onlife ecology is a response to overexposure. However, 'hiding' behind a passcode, fingerprint identification, face-recognition technology, and privacy policies only increases and amplifies the role of secrecy in our everyday lives, enhancing its meaning and function.

The privacy terms and conditions, updated incessantly, effectively become the first paradigm of any new device or technological improvement: the issue and an explanation of the privacy measures taken are always outlined, and the phrase 'we respect your privacy' is a dogma when considering any 'web-based' technology. But such measures can also be witnessed in the forms to be filled in and signed: these are only 'formalities' and are often unread, not for lack of interest, but for hyper-abundance of it. Along with these are the perpetual suggestions that we should control our data, especially with passwords and pins. Today's technology allows citizens to control and personalize their information, and to control, with basic technical knowledge, the information of others. Perhaps unsurprisingly, Netflix's docudrama *The Social Dilemma* (Orlowski, 2020), discussing these very issues, was one of the most viewed documentaries on the platform.[2] Social media is central to this idea: its pretence of being an agent of transparency is turned on its head, it becoming a promoter of masked lives instead: the information flows among secret peers, is controlled and analysed by secret algorithms, is sold to unknown third parties and is thus further analysed and processed and then resold. We may presume most users by now know instinctively that some of this goes on – nonetheless, who the specific actors are, what they know and do, is a mystery. What is public is a shade of reality; what goes on behind the curtains is secret and hidden – a point that is rendered even more clear with Dave Beer's[3] consideration of algorithms as the villains and heroes of our times. What we store on our devices, what we see online, what we write digitally, and film via smartphones is constantly at stake (Ziccardi, 2015); whatever is stored online can be perpetually leaked. Users are allowed to see everything online, and consequently become guardians of the Foucauldian-inspired panoptic gaze; however, the 'all-seeing place' becomes an actual 'space' where everything is watched, judged, contained, and controlled. As an update to Foucault's and Bentham's ideas, the contemporary 'eye' is not only electronic (Lyon, 1994), even 'artificially intelligent', but also remote, never forgetting, invisible, and ever-growing (Mayer-Schönberger, 2009), and it is owned and controlled covertly by corporations as well as governments (Pasquale, 2015). With the online and offline consumption of surveillance, the use of satellites, drones, but also marketing algorithms, GPS tracking, and consumer triangulation, the effects of a liquid state of permanent data-grabbing become evident: a specific system where the more visibility is achieved, the more secrecy is required.

Opposed to this attitude (which, one must admit, is quite marginal yet substantial on behalf of anyone who actually takes 'care' about surveillance) stands a total dedication and trust towards such services and devices: implied in many ways by the European 2024 Data Act (European Commission, 2024) and by the Privacy Sandbox initiative that will potentially provide advertisement without using third-party cookies (Wong, 2024), both of which propose to give more agency to users – but one may wonder if they will give more users to the agencies.

Here we confirm the long-debated concerns regarding the ineradicable nature of the data: the truly worrying factor of such change is the 'agency' of our data in operating systems, the pictures, files, apps, and programs that define us, follow us, both online, offline, on software and hardware, so that it becomes harder and harder to control it, not to mention get rid of it. Unfortunately, contemporary systems are only concerned with the first option because of its economic value. The memory of our data becomes the 'trap' into which users have fallen, which must be constantly protected, monitored, secured, and surveilled.

Facebook, again, is the evident proof of the inability to totally control our data just by using the privacy settings: indeed, the platform is itself holder of some of the most effective surveillance licences, such as for an algorithm that recognize dust patterns on a user's phone camera, in order to associate users in the pictures and create connections (Hill and Mattu, 2018).

By 2025, concerns about the nature of 'leaking' are not only negligible, but are also obscuring the true nature of a far more complex issue, akin to a double-edged sword. In contrast to Barlow's (1996) utopian vision of internet freedom, of a limitless and uncontrolled space of interaction, the future ahead is one where Internet of Things integration becomes an endless feeding of data that feeds endless automated, cannibalistic software. We believe we are in control of our data but, rather, we are controlled by the sense of control (Agamben, 2009; Klein, 2023). Users become the ultimate consumers – consumed and consuming.

## Forgetting as freedom?

We have mentioned on many occasions the importance not of recollection, but we also need to sensitize the idea of forgetting. In Nietzsche's last works especially we see a great indulgence in the importance of the individual to forget. It is an activity that allows the human to overcome their weaknesses, and indeed the key to managing the phantom of resentment. It is 'an active and in the strictest sense positive faculty of repression' (Nietzsche, 2007: 1). Such 'active forgetfulness' becomes a central element to understanding our necessity to tackle the instances of secretive counter-conduct. It is, arguably, a specific art of forgetting.

Such a view is found throughout history. Rodotà, in particular, notes the practice of declaring 'damnatio memoriae' ('damning the memory to oblivion') in imperial Rome (Rodotà, 2014). In cases of serious imperial offences, all traces of the names of those involved or found guilty would be destroyed and removed, leaving no trace – a theme that is echoed even in the rationale behind the so-called 'cancel culture' (Wrethed, 2022). But more than that, as has been proved by the vast number of records collected by the Soviet secret police (Verdery, 2014) – a malevolent 'planting' of false evidence, of data being used against us (Kapaló, 2020), as a means of 'malinformation'.

## Surveillance without control?

A police officer once shared with me a humorous yet revealing anecdote. Some remote homes had repeatedly been broken into by what seemed to be the same individual – a dealer. Despite having a known warehouse nearby and being arrested multiple times, the dealer often avoided any serious charges. What was the nature of his trick? During the break-ins, the dealer videoed himself using his personal smartphone inside the houses. If later caught and prosecuted, the offender would present this footage as proof of being merely a thief, not a dealer. Theft, being a minor offence, often garners some victim sympathy, while dealing is a far more serious crime. This is another clear case of sousveillance, as noted in Chapter 3, where the thief used video evidence of his crime to create an alibi, rendering surveillance cameras ineffective as deterrents or sources of incriminating evidence.

Indeed, as we have seen, many of the themes in this book revolve around the idea of surveillance, the desire to see what surrounds us, and the suspicion that something is going on while we are not aware of it; yet, at the same time, we want to have control over it. The results of such a condition are easily recognizable with the current 'army' of security systems, both in homes and in workplaces, in retail shops and on public transportation, extending to leisure and even education. Any space requires an object that knows what is going on and who is present, even with some assurance concerning their direction or motivations. Surveillance becomes thus a condition, as we have seen (Lyon and Bauman, 2013), of constant monitoring, controlling, and preventing, with the potentially surreal and limitless installation of tools. We could, nonetheless, play with the idea of what might be an alternative technology, as a kind of *forma mentis* or 'way of thinking' that may somewhat 'release the pressure' of this overarching 'Onlife' trap or cage. Regarding technology, an evident problem lies in the object and use of lens/camera. It allows the view of a determinate space, with ideally a viewer (or the threat of one) that monitors remotely whoever enters the space or behaves suspiciously. This technology is being evermore integrated with microphones, motion sensors, alarms, face recognition technology, and night vision. Lenses have become a fundamental feature of social interaction, a tool which we seemingly cannot do without – and indeed we cannot buy devices without them. Also, we have seen how some of these technologies, cheaply available on most e-commerce sites, promote hidden cameras that are invisible to strangers or anyone being filmed. The conditions of such tools are odd for a number of reasons, for, as we have seen, there is the problem of privacy, of 'misinterpreting' information, of social sorting, especially when they are used to prevent crime.

The perspective of home security could be intrinsically reconsidered, preferring eyes in the home that indeed exert some sort of control over the situation and 'visually guard' property, relying on some sort of 'sensory'-veillance. Smart sensors would aid us in surrounding spaces, doors, and walls, only activated in close proximity or actual contact cases. There would be no need to 'record' and 'hold' audio/visual data, the product of further capta. Instead, by 'passively' having sensors on alert, rather than actually observing, such a system could become, ideally, a return to the notion of watchdogs: they do not know who or what exactly they are seeing; they know if it is right or not.

Transporting the issue into the Onlife, the idea of a protected environment falls into the idea of a 'gentrified' one, where the unregulated digital world would be neatly, monetarily, and obediently channelled. As discussed in Lingel's (2019) gentrified internet analogy, Facebook serves as a prime example – offering ideally a clean, safe, and censored environment where users are subtly discouraged from discussing certain topics or posting specific content. Moderators and fellow users 'gently' encourage proper behaviour, aligning with Trottier's theories on social media as surveillance (Trottier, 2015). However, as we have seen, this is far from universally true. Instead, it increasingly applies to more exclusive scenarios, with the rise of paywalls, paid content, and heightened privacy and security measures.

With COVID-19, we saw the means to trace the whereabouts and control the movements of users implemented, sometimes willingly and at times mandatorily. Is this a new frontier of social sorting, as already suggested by David Lyon in the late 1990s, and now as relevant as ever (Lyon, 2022)? If in the pre-pandemic era data analysis, social sorting, and bio-security were tackled and debated on a daily basis, today they appear to be a necessary norm – or at least a necessary evil (Williams and Dienes, 2021).

Wrapping up, I have tried to make sense of the overarching scenario of what controlling devices are capable of, how they are used, and what they may corrupt into. Another necessary question is, what can be done about it? Is there something in the design of the products that must change? Is it a question of 'digital airbags', mentioned by Pagallo (2015) when referring to the dangers of the online scenario? Certainly, a system that would prevent harm in a non-coercive manner that is ideally non-paternalistic nor necessarily authoritative would be ideal (Pagallo, 2015). Also problematic is limiting freedom of speech online on a corporate basis while insisting on the civility of discussion within the Onlife. Geert Lovink has been looking at these aspects for a long time and, for him, solutions are fundamentally within an 'un-learning machines' process, 'enstupiditing' devices to limit their multitasking opportunities and generally attempting to constitute new communities that do not turn inwardly but invest 'outwardly' toward integration, communication, and comprehension in a proactive stance (2022)

Finally, another utopian and yet simple solution is to embrace transparency in the Foucauldian understanding of an 'aleathurgy', or 'speaking truth', as discussed at the College De France in 1981 (Foucault, 2014), one that could well shape the ideal dynamics of trust among peers, that is, to monitor, if necessary, but via a shared perspective; not only to see but to show that one sees. In other words, reduce the system's opacity into an interactive scenario that clearly, and directly, blatantly reveals the involvement and abuse of what is seen and what is controlled.

## The fogginess of digital war

Drowsed by the notion of empowerment and informed decisions, users themselves risk becoming 'zero-day' entities: vulnerable pieces of information subject to the very information that shapes and guides their thoughts, choices, and ideas – but most of these are channelled, sponsored, and promoted too – at times with hidden modes and ambiguous persuasions and systematic virtual astroturfing – central tools in suppressing protests, shifting political trends, and crushing dissents via 'harmonizing techniques', notable in the party rhetoric in the Peoples Republic of China.

The saying 'don't put too many eggs into one basket' appears prophetic: by connecting all out existence into a device (something envisioned by Bill Gates in 1995 with his Wallet PC) – and thus becoming fully part of the Onlife – human agency becomes systematically politicized and blurs indefinitely everyday online crimes and harms with everyday intricacies.

Returning to the pressing issue of the zero-day threat in our time, it is worth noting that despite the numerous warning signs and our growing acceptance of vulnerabilities in everyday systems, this scenario does not yet resemble a 'Chekhov's gun' argument – inevitably destined to go off by the third act. Much like nuclear weapons, which loomed ominously over the world during the Cold War period but did not lead to humanity's annihilation, the digital menace (including the advancements of AI (Milmo, 2024)) is undoubtedly threatening but has not, and may never, bring mankind to its ultimate end. While I have in Chapter 7 discussed the 'sleepwalking' state of our current Onlife experience and the AI-driven menace where all information is untrustworthy, we to date have not yet broken down into a *Terminator*-style 'Infocalypse' that takes over humanity (Schick, 2020).

Is it too early to say? Perhaps. Or maybe Yuval Harari was right in *Homo Deus* (2015) to argue that current human ambitions, unlike those of the previous century (and history in general), are now focused on more noble pursuits, moving beyond the obvious 'bad business' of causing apocalyptic cyber-attacks and similar threats. Besides, any serious cyber-attack from a relatively minor government to a G7 super force would likely escalate a series of concrete armed responses that would hardly justify the effort, however trivial. While this is a possibility, the likelihood is minimal – as *The New York Times* author Lazaro Gamio suggests (2024), we need to worry instead about new and more significant outages caused by human errors, rather than human malevolence.

## Rhizomatic crime prevention

The implications of the Onlife, with its harms and wrongdoings, appear, as I have been discussing, to be shifting towards a condition of systematic control, channelling lives, monitoring occurrences, preventing wrongdoings, and influencing choices. With the rapid, consistent, and overarching financed implementation of smart city integration, digital citizenship, and the appropriation of hyperconnectivity, VR, and AR, this is very likely what the future holds. The biopower structure forewarned by Agamben (2004) becomes more evident every day, although the road to get there fully is still long and winding. Just as social media did with the 'online' twenty years ago, AI technology has acted as a breakthrough in changing the game of the 'Onlife', both socially and criminologically. While it is still, at the time of writing, a confused, glitched, patched, faulty, bug-driven enterprise and tool, its potential is becoming daily not only clearer but integral in the everyday lives of individuals. With the new machine learning operating systems integrated into phones and computers, to be Onlife will soon be *OnAI*. Subjectification through and by technology may seem natural, making the object of power more precise yet subtly obscured, and shaping the everyday habits and behaviours of individuals in more directed and influential ways.

The most trivial criminological objective of this is, of course, crime prevention and general pre-crime calculus concerning who, when, and why someone may commit a crime, with its ongoing bias (Sankin et al, 2021) and systematic episodes of discrimination. This condition is already used in various jurisdictions, with a notorious example in Amsterdam since 2016 where the use of complex algorithmic calculus and policing puts 'hot-spot' minors under surveillance using the ProKid + algorithm (Van Brakel and Govaerts, 2024). To this, we may only envision further dystopias involving automated indexing of features and normo-profiling, diving into a new horizon of 'aggregated algorithmic image of normalcy',[4] and other means of systematic discrimination.

As mentioned by Hayward and Mass (2020) and Floridi himself (2024), the criminological implications of such a pre-crime system may very well soon include AI. Perhaps we even need to consider the pre-crime potential of AI right now – one of advancing the rhizomatic means of doing harm, causing mistakes, subjectifying but also discriminating, marginalizing, segregating, and undermining users, citizens, minorities, and activists across the world, with more precision but perhaps less and less humanity, tolerance, understanding, and justice – a new positivist thinking that may have the least durable answers.

## Better and worse

The 'enshittification' of everything, as mentioned in Chapter 4, is a central worry for users of the Onlife in general – and one again needs to be careful of the idea of the 'good old days' when things used to work, people were not wasting their life on social media, playgrounds were full of educated children, and so on. As Serres noted in his last works (2018), it is indeed very much a limited ideology, especially one inflated by far-right romanticism. In opposition to the process of infinite scrolling that is nothing other than a variation of the endless zapping of television channels, or the mob-mentality of burning down self-driving cars (Pearson, 2024), it is important to hold ground in what is, in existentialist terms, a right to say no to the systematic wrongdoings within systems and platforms that replicate power and harm structures.

Let us approach the matter once more with Harari's stoicism from *Homo Deus* (2015). Unless for some reason the servers are truly jeopardized or there is an unexpected (but not too unlikely!) solar flare that kills our connection indefinitely or a significant outage turns us back to practising cave art (less likely), the Onlife is here to stay. More than that, the Onlife has changed the world, and in many undeniable aspects for the better. We have more of everything, but more than that, we have a better understanding of many things, better access, and more awareness. As I have mentioned, a central warning of this book is how easily this very access may be denied, and the Onlife has redefined the 'terms of exclusion' citizens may or may not be subject to, remotely, precisely, and immediately. Today, users may lift their phones and, with the sole limitation of their right state of mind, learn about almost anything, or at least shape their minds about it. We may set coordinates on GPS and reach a destination with all possible means of transport. Freedom has never felt so immediate and fresh, particularly in light of Arendt's concept of 'natality' (1958), which refers to the capacity for 'beginning' – especially the constant ability to start anew. The Onlife existence, as noted by Hildebrand, is exactly this (2015: 86).

But this possibility may be just as easily revoked. Imagine the shock if the smartphone you (heftily) paid for, use regularly, store your most private information on, and access your finances through suddenly decided, because of an institutionalized action, to no longer recognize your face, fingerprint, or password. Biometric keys as such would turn into biometric locks. But such limitations may become more nuanced. The freedom of such services could become just as easily spaces of denial, states of exclusion. And this is not simply a monitory exclusion of having to 'pay' for them, but a biopolitical means to control and exclude. For example, GPS may be used, but perhaps only within a limited, targeted space. Social media is easily accessed, but perhaps only to view, never to comment or share. Google is available but only reveals a limited set of targeted results (work, shopping, home). Much of this is truly the rhetoric of the conspiracy fears around COVID-19 vaccine passports or the fear that the West may turn into a super-communist state, as controversial commentors such as Naomi Wolf claim (Klein, 2023). But beyond such dream-world paranoia, it is undeniable that, in the hands of corporate colossuses, virtual space (one that is becoming with the current VR technology increasingly 'haptic' – a buzz word for sensorial – experience) could become significantly tailored to a single user: no longer the democratized space of interaction that is practically identical, except for content, to all users – but one where access is limited to an elite. Again, the smartphone (and soon VR headsets?) acting as gatekeepers would be not simply the currency of the exclusion state, but, as mentioned in Chapter 4, the engine to further promote the virtual simulation and its effects in the hyperconnected Onlife scenario.

The problematics of the Onlife, as I have hopefully made clear, are in many ways based in often insignificant processes. These are themselves mixed within cryptic dynamics, hidden manoeuvres, and subtle, recurring methods. As I have discussed while highlighting the surveillance element that increasingly nuances our everyday existence, the means to forget may not be sufficient. In fact, we might be fundamentally deceived into permitting endless data collection, only to later find that, if ever needed, the ability to retrieve this information becomes less probable due to advancements in quantum mechanics and memory capacity. Rather than simply being affected, as in the concept of 'sharashka', we find ourselves in a peculiar limbo where the Onlife appears to be a permanent fixture, yet we have limited control over the type of Onlife we desire. Of course, there are a series of policies, protocols, and acts that are set up, discussed, envisioned, applied and debated – the Data Act across the EU is one among many – and the 'right to be forgotten' is the starting point of many privacy directives. But as I said, forgetting might not be enough. Perhaps haunted by the IBM computing abuse and the Fujitsu Post Office scandal in Britain,[5] I prefer not to be evaluated solely based on the metrics that reflect the future within the context of the hyperconnected reality known as the Onlife. To this dimension, given the long enlistment of problematics around the creeping elements of hyperconnection and online and offline blurring, I envision a 'right to be ignored', which I propose in three axioms. First, the means to be ignored in a strict Faulkner sense (see Chapter 4), regarding being free of being monitored, collected, updated, digitally uploaded, and constantly subjectified. While it can be argued that all technology is progressing towards the 'quantification of everything', this tendency does not necessarily reflect the fundamental principle of nature: it serves as a counterbalance to humanity and the technology that has been developed to support it. This is particularly important with respect to the isolation of individuals – do they wish to live 'off the grid', as Philip Egre allegedly has been doing since 2009 (Albergotti, 2021) – or effectively within an 'offlife' condition, a topic I have discussed elsewhere (Szakolczai, 2023).

Second, an active 'right to ignore', that is, preserve the privilege not to submit to technological advancement in any form, be it digital, virtual, or, effectively, Onlife. But it is also meaningful for those who wish to remain 'ipotechnological' (low-tech) or, as Lovink puts it, engaged in degrowth, machine unlearning, artificial stupidity (2022b).

Finally, it is important to sustain within criminology and zemiology a means for the 'right to be ignorant': this is not simply the means to 'not being informed', and thus not be part of the hyperconnected age for whatever reason, but to be ignorant is also the means to be present, by not being immediately identified. To be ignorant of each other is the baseline of early internet discourse, where users would interact solely by usernames (Hayles, 2005).

## Right to be ignored

As such, what can be practically done, especially if we are to consider a 'right to be ignored'? As I said, my intention is not to draw some luddite criticism, but rather to highlight the dangers and misconceptions surrounding the concept of an 'Onlife ecology' and its potential to evolve into the worst 'totalitarian' scenario. In accordance with Stefana Broadbent and Claire Lobet-Maris (2015) writing for the *Onlife Manifesto*, 'Ecology is also a means of spreading forms of cultural vigilance which can be promoted in schools and the media'. The requirement and care in developing and seeking ' "clean technologies", that is, technologies which are sustainable in respect to our attention and our capacity of self-determination and accountability regarding the processes they perform to fabricate identities and differences' (Broadbent and Lobet-Maris, 2015: 112).

This involves addressing systematic issues that recur within this framework. Instead of perpetuating these problems, we should consider re-evaluating our approach and updating the norms that govern interactions online through small means of *moderation*, that in themselves could perhaps do without the need for *regulation*. This would require recognizing and addressing the following dynamics of data within the development of the Onlife until we have 'full' control over them:

- Cloud connectivity: because of its perpetual Onlife hyperconnection, the devices are always at hand and 'connected to the net'. Its invasive aspect, the possibility to be always online, updated, and synchronized is inevitable. Wi-Fi-based devices, such as computers and baseline tablets, offer limited functionality, and yet may continue to work while 'offline'. Perhaps they could even work without ever going online – and, as such, be integral media (to listen to music, watch films, read, and play games) without necessarily producing capta, and thus being part of the Onlife. That is, turn aeroplane mode on more often?
- Triangulation of biometrics: the satellite positioning system is integrated into most smart devices, including cars and computers which increasingly apply biometrics to unlock, recognize, and activate each other. Nonetheless, its features are strictly smart and most surely avoidable and unnecessary to the everyday commuter. Other than for navigation and identification purposes, their features are solely one of tracking – an object that is strictly in need of protection from most users, yet it is basically implemented and endorsed. Interesting in this context is the recent tracker devices (Airtag and so on) that allow GPS monitoring outside of the smartphone – rendering surveillance even more mundane. Instead, the hardware reintegration into the Onlife would appear more sustainable, practical, and beneficial to the autonomy of the self. That is, turn the GPS signal off?

- Camera integration: appears 'intrinsically' part of every mobile device, indeed lenses may represent the main and most popular feature of constant monitoring, with the risk of abuse. This is no place to question this 'plethora' of lenses, though one may doubt the actual need to record – whatever the quality – all of these instances. As understood through Vaidhyanathan's work (2018), never have we been surrounded by so many tools to film and record as today. In this reality, we are evermore 'under the eye' – perpetually under surveillance and 'blasé' about this very surveillance. By achieving an 'offlife' reality that is less implemented by cameras, we could possibly achieve an environment with less 'requirement' to report, record, and prove our whereabouts, our peers, and whoever we see. That is, cover your camera?
- Hyperconnection/immediacy: all internet-based communication conveys the immediacy of the messages being expressed and the thoughts behind them. While there should be by no means any limit to the free flow of thought, this does not necessarily need to transpire into any context. Basic 'netiquette' (etiquette of the net) may be associated with a limit on the temporary boundaries where users engage. As is already somewhat possible with the automated features of Android smartphones that adjust based on location, one may envision potential for filters to limit engagement when users are at home. When in the office, filters may temporarily pause 'outside' interaction – to then physically 'release them' once the location or time changes. This is also potentially important when acting upon toxic content, distributing it, and sharing its features. Surely, a piece of misinformation shared in a light-hearted manner at 2 a.m. during a hen party may today have a similar 'viral' effect as content authentically published by a journalist during regular office hours. However, the significant distinction between these two scenarios is often overlooked in the current landscape.[6] That is, set time/location limits on devices?
- Crypto features: as discussed in Chapter 5, the design of the Onlife is one of overall cryptic and opaque features, especially with the devices that we superficially engage with: the absence of LED indicators or audible signals clearly indicating recording or filming are inherent features of the smartphone. This ambivalence, and lack of clarity, which allows users to film and record, while giving barely any signal that they are doing so, is significant. The message, I argue, is one where transparency, clarity, and painlessness are not a common goal – but rather, it would seem, act as a disadvantage for the user. Such a condition is highly problematic and needs clarity that may, yet again, softly induce users to act within less 'elusive' boundaries. That is, reducing, if possible, the use of devices in public settings and encouraging users to minimize all forms of ambiguity regarding their activities, including what they are doing, reading, or watching.

- AI pretence: another advertisement, used to introduce Google's Gemini AI at the 2024 Olympics, shows how to write a computer-generated fan letter to an inspiring athlete. Unsurprisingly, I am not the only person to think this was a really badly conceived commercial (Nyce, 2024); but it confirms the need to insist upon the censure of fake content recreated by AI, especially because there is no *need* for AI to pretend it is an enthusiastic fan, and by doing so, it neutralizes the enthusiasm of being a fan who would write a letter, or be inspired, or whatever. The use of AI to 'pretend' is the first step to legitimize further the means of 'harms against reality': and as long as this is endorsed, this will only continue and worsen our means of interaction. That is, use it how it best works for you, but stop pretending AI is actually you.
- VR rationality: the reasoning behind this point is semi-ironical. Opposed to the Kantian logic of some rational understanding among users, a more general, de-colonized approach to our understanding of the surrounding environment is to be welcomed. A word, more difficult to pinpoint, would be 'sensitivity': to be sensible to the uses of these technologies and the effect they have and will have. For example, with VR and AR altering filming and analysing reality, rather than simply having some sort of 'green light' mounted on the lenses, as claimed in 2023 by Zuckerberg, a specific 'soft' notification across users in the likes of the contact tracing apps would be more reasonable, sensible, intuitive: the user would be notified of what sorts of augmented alteration is taking place around them, and have their visual either screened or banned from their view. That is, augmentation needs trigger warnings.

Of course, this is a criminological book and I have insisted on highly negative conditions requiring drastic solutions. The technological means of interconnection are by no means lacking powerful positivity: grassroots engagement, interconnected solidarity, knowledge, and interpersonal mobility in which Onlife devices are increasingly becoming central actors are flourishing. As a result, completely disconnecting and disengaging from the digital world is not necessarily the best solution, nor one I vouch for. Hyperconnectivity has proven as harmful as it is helpful, but it is effective in many ways, for example in assisted living devices and caregiving (Carnemolla, 2018). Although there is a tension between care, risk, and surveillance within the use of these devices (Reid, 2021) the benefits are evident (Maalsen, 2024).

The offlife 'paradoxical' reality that is being described would thus imply the use of the same tools, only coming to terms with the 'data' as given and not bending to the 'capta' dynamics. Use the tools but not give in to their most invasive features. Enjoy the peaks of virtualization and a smart environment, but with meaningful limitations and a mindful approach. By this, I have sought to find more meaningful and compatible ways to 'live' with our technologies, to improve them rather than turning away, so as not to become outlived by them.

## The art of the Onlife

In this book I have highlighted how the Onlife has and is progressively heading towards new horizons of criminological, criminogenic, harmful, and zemiological means. In the last chapter, I have suggested and considered some small, albeit significant, proactive and resilient means to improve the Onlife, ideally, potentially, not simply as a means of survival, but promoting it as an art.

As a self-evident caveat, 'to be ignored', the 'fear of missing out' (FOMO), and nomophobia (the 'fear of losing/forgetting one's device') (Goodin, 2021) are notoriously among the major phobias of a younger generation, with their Onlife existence so entrenched with social media, hyperconnectivity, immediacy of information, distribution, evaluation, means of confirmation, liking, sharing, following, and subscribing. Indeed, most of those born post-millennial have never experienced a time when computers were bulky and not very mobile, connected to the internet by a cable, leading families to the 'tragedy' of having to choose between receiving a phone call or checking Facebook. Arguably, hyperconnected generations do not know the alternative, and it is not being offered to them. Within the Onlife, they continue to walk under the gaze of more and more cameras, with increasing control over their content. Despite the idealism of 'free communication' and an infinite information space, there is no guarantee of what content will be banned tomorrow, or which country, state, or community will find itself isolated. We as users, parents, friends, academics, intellectuals, and policy makers, have a responsibility to propose, promote, and envision a cleaner environment where we are allowed to 'opt' out – even if this only to stand outside and see the big picture of what is surrounding us. We currently lack laws that mandate the use of smart devices, and perhaps we should advocate for the opposite: laws that protect the desire and means to be techno-minimalists. It is important to recognize that some individuals still adhere to this lifestyle, and social sciences should dedicate more attention to their experiences, as criticized almost two decades ago (Glotz et al, 2005). In this context, to counter the 'dark forest' analogy of hyperconnectivity and entropic risk, where escape and exposure are constantly at stake, I envision a brighter forest of mangroves. This is central when we consider that mangroves are not simply the hybrid vegetation capable of thriving both from salty and clear water – but are deemed as essential wildlife hotspots and a 'crucial buffer zone, preventing soil erosion, shielding communities from wave action and storms, and minimizing losses of life caused by extreme weather events',[7] as stated on one of the many organizations investing in the protection of coastlines via mangroves forests. A sustained mangrove society may entail a true symbiotic community where it can emerge from the digital midnight and its criminal universe and cosmic harmscapes. In the light of this hope and ambition, we collectively have a responsibility and a quest for improvement that may no longer be ignored.

# Notes

## Chapter 1

1 See https://www.etymonline.com/word/*krei-

## Chapter 2

1 See https://adnauseam.io

## Chapter 3

1 See https://www.apple.com/airtag
2 See https://computerhistory.org/profile/konrad-zuse
3 See https://hbr.org/2013/03/a-new-type-of-philanthropy-don
4 See https://en.wikipedia.org/wiki/Songdo
5 See https://bearresearch.org/#research
6 See https://sitn.hms.harvard.edu/flash/2020/racial-discrimination-in-face-recognition-technology
7 See https://www.bbc.com/news/uk-england-somerset-58959930
8 See https://www.nationalgeographic.com/magazine/article/using-facial-recognition-on-grizzlies-and-more-advances
9 See the highly informed website and association passamontagna.info that provides text and updates on the passes and activism in both French and Italian.
10 See http://elahi.wayne.edu/track

## Chapter 4

1 Pizzorno shows how the idea of identity, as understood by Mauss, came from the Etruscan word of persona, or personare ('to resound through') (Pizzorno, 2005: 9), which means 'mask'. This person, a mask, is an ever-changing entity that may promote himself differently in different situations. In an anthropological description of various uses and costumes, a recurring point in found in Pizzorno's article: masks are tools of power. They alter reality, offer special statuses empowering the living and also the dead, sending spirits away or attracting them, depending on the specific ritual.
2 This precise sequence of 'Opticons' is inspired by Ryan Casey's doctoral thesis (2021): 'Left to their own devices: a technosocial ethnography of penal electronic monitoring in Scotland'.
3 See https://www.youtube.com/watch?v=esk7W9Jowtc
4 See https://youtu.be/esk7W9Jowtc
5 See https://www.nytimes.com/2021/12/30/technology/metaverse-harassment-assaults.html
6 See https://www.vogue.co.uk/arts-and-lifestyle/article/sexual-assault-in-the-metaverse

7 See https://www.pcmag.com/news/metaverse-predictions-it-will-be-harmful-addictive-and-inevitable

8 See https://www.theguardian.com/commentisfree/2024/jan/05/metaverse-sexual-assault-vr-game-online-safety-meta?Metaver.se

## Chapter 5

1 See https://www.theguardian.com/world/2021/sep/26/naybib-bukele-el-salvador-president-coolest-dictator

2 See https://artists.spotify.com/en/blog/modernizing-our-royalty-system

3 See https://thenextweb.com/news/cryptobros-spend-millions-rare-jodorowsky-dune-book-copyright-analysis

## Chapter 6

1 'Most Flat-Earthers are just trolling, and the general public fell for it' (2020). Reddit. February 11. Available from: www.reddit.com/r/unpopularopinion/comments/f864ga/most_flatearthers_are_just_trolling_and_the_general [Accessed 6 December 2024].

2 See https://hapgood.us/2024/04/27/the-structure-of-a-diedsuddenly-argument

3 See https://knowyourmeme.com/editorials/guides/why-do-people-think-taylor-swift-is-a-psyop-a-growing-conservative-conspiracy-explained

4 See https://www.theatlantic.com/technology/archive/2024/07/trump-assassination-attempt-conspiracy-theories/679012

5 Musk claimed, soon after former president shooting in Pennsylvania, Secret Service incompetence was 'deliberate': see https://x.com/elonmusk/status/1812296672510111853

6 Various forums even assert that the restaurant's signage exhibited clear satanic symbolism, with four triangles encompassing a star and a crescent moon within the lettering.

7 Without getting into too many of the possible examples, one can simply remember the beginning of his mandate, when under pouring rain he claimed in front of national television (and the Onlife community worldwide) that the sun was shining for him. When later questioned on the matter (given that behind his broadcast footage you could even see Melania Trump next to him holding an umbrella) he declared: 'The truth is [that the rain] stopped immediately. It was amazing. And then it became really sunny. And then I walked off, and it poured right after I left. It poured.'

8 A striking visual representation of the narrative can be consulted via https://deepstatemappingproject.com

9 From Twitter (later removed): 'Despite the constant negative press covfefe'.

10 This theme is central in another of Adam Curtis's documentaries, *Hypernormalisation* (2016), which astonishingly anticipated most of Trump's political rule and success.

11 *The Dark Forest*, the second volume of the *Remembrance of Earth's Past* trilogy, poses the axiom that the universe is filled with intelligent beings that hide from each other as to avoid turning into reciprocal preys.

12 As argued during Eco's Laurea Honoris Causa in Comunicazione e Culture dei Media at the Università degli Studi di Torino in 2015: see https://www.youtube.com/watch?v=u10XGPuO3C4

## Chapter 7

1 Such tongue to cheek pop-culture references within tech-bros (especially within Elon Musk's grasp) is a recurring feature, at times even apotropaic, as using a 'Ripley' look-alike from the *Alien* movie franchise as a dummy for the SpaceX experiments (see https://futurism.com/spacex-dummy-ripley-demo-1-crew-dragon).

2 'In the ever-evolving theater of the modern age, where shadows and light dance upon the grand stage of technology, the digital personas of those we once revered as media figures are being inexorably drawn into a nebulous realm. This domain, neither fully dark nor entirely light, thrives on the burgeoning tendrils of financial exploitation. It is here, amidst the echoes of authenticity and the whispers of artifice, that the essence of these individuals is bartered and sold, their identities fragmented and reshaped in the relentless pursuit of profit. The boundaries, once clear and distinct, now blur into an indistinct twilight, where the very nature of fame and influence is commodified in the ceaseless marketplace of digital currency' (ChatGPT 4o Model) – gross!

## Chapter 8

1 This aspect has even picked up significant scholarly debate, with the controversial idea of forming new monastic retirement communities with (spiritually) like-minded people – see *The Benedict Option* (Dreher, 2017).

2 See https://www.independent.co.uk/arts-entertainment/films/features/social-dilemma-netflix-film-media-facebook-twitter-algorithm-addiction-conspiracy-b454736.html

3 See https://medium.com/the-graph/algorithms-as-the-villains-and-heroes-of-the-post-truth-era-1a6532baeacf

4 See https://mushon.com/tnm

5 Where technological malpractices have devasted the lives of otherwise unrelated individuals; see https://www.postofficehorizoninquiry.org.uk

6 It is almost (but not quite) needless to say that such ideas have many problems, especially when tackling the invaluable notion of free speech. However, society is, after all, built on values that need or do not need to be respected, but, in any case, dialogue and recognition is needed as part of its etiquette. Some topics are universally deemed 'not appropriate' for, say, a family dinner – and postponing discussion to a more suitable time is not necessarily an infringement of civil liberties: at least, to claim that does sound quite immature to me.

7 See https://mangroveactionproject.org/mangroves-matter

# References


Aas, K.F. (2006) '"The body does not lie": identity, risk and trust in technoculture', *Crime, Media Culture*, 2(2): 143–58.

Abadi, M. (2017) 'Trump and his White House have made some embarrassing spelling mistakes – here are the worst ones', *Business Insider*, [online] 3 April. Available from: https://www.businessinsider.com/trump-typos-spelling-tweets-unpresidented-2017-4?op=1&r=US&IR=T#covfefe-1 [Accessed 24 November 2024].

Adams, S., Purtova, N. and Leenes, R. (2017) *Under Observation: The Interplay between Health and Surveillance*. Cham: Springer International Publishing.

Agamben, G. (2004) 'Bodies without words: against the biopolitical tattoo', *German Law Journal*, 5(2): 168–9.

Agamben, G. (2009) *What Is an Apparatus?* Stanford: Stanford University Press.

Agre, P.E. (1994) 'Surveillance and capture: two models of privacy', *The Information Society*, 10: 101–27.

Aikin, S.F. (2019) 'Deep disagreement, the dark enlightenment, and the rhetoric of the red pill', *Journal of Applied Philosophy*, 36(3): 420–35.

Ajana, B. (2020) 'Border control/immigration', in L.A. Schintler and C.L. McNeely (eds) *Encyclopedia of Big Data*. Cham: Springer, pp 1–4.

Ajana, B. (2017) 'Digital health and the biopolitics of the Quantified Self', *Digital Health*, 3. Available from: https://doi.org/10.1177/2055207616689509/FORMAT/EPUB

Alam, R. (2020) *Leave the World Behind*. New York: Ecco.

Albergotti, R. (2021) 'He predicted the dark side of the Internet 30 years ago. Why did no one listen?' *Washington Post*, 12 August. Available from: https://www.washingtonpost.com/technology/2021/08/12/philip-agre-ai-disappeared/ [Accessed 30 July 2024].

Alegre, S. (2024) *Human Rights, Robot Wrongs: Being Human in the Age of AI*. London: Atlantic Books.

All-In Experience (2022) 'Elon Musk on Twitter's bot problem, SpaceX's grand plan, Tesla stories, Giga Texas & more', [podcast]. Available from: https://podcasts.apple.com/it/podcast/e69-elon-musk-on-twitters-bot-problem-spacexs-grand/id1502871393?i=1000561681595&l=en-GB [Accessed 24 November 2024].

Alvarenga, D. (2022) 'Will this be the first country bankrupted by crypto?' *Rolling Stone*, [online] 26 August. Available from: https://www.rollingstone.com/culture/culture-features/el-salvador-bitcoin-law-volcano-bonds-nayib-bukele-1388472/ [Accessed 29 November 2024].

Amante, A. and Weir, K. (2023) 'Ryanair fights off European squeeze on its ticket prices', Reuters, 19 October. Available from: https://www.reuters.com/world/europe/ryanair-fights-off-european-squeeze-its-ticket-prices-2023-10-19/ [Accessed 14 November 2024].

Amazon (2023) 'Amazon introduces 100% recyclable packaging for customer orders in the UK', *Amazon News*. Available from: https://www.aboutamazon.co.uk/news/sustainability/amazon-packaging-fully-recyclable [Accessed 9 December 2024].

Andreessen, M. (2011) 'Why software is eating the world'. Available from: https://a16z.com/why-software-is-eating-the-world/ [Accessed 29 November 2024].

Andreessen, M. (2023) 'The techno-optimist manifesto', Andreessen Horowitz (a16z). Available from: https://a16z.com/the-techno-optimist-manifesto/ [Accessed 14 November 2024].

Andrejevic, M. (2002) 'The work of watching one another: lateral surveillance, risk, and governance', *Surveillance & Society*, 2(4).

Andrzejewski, C. (2023) 'Team Jorge: disinformation', *Forbidden Stories*. Available from: https://forbiddenstories.org/team-jorge-disinformation/ [Accessed 21 November 2024].

Angwin, J. (2009) *Stealing MySpace: The Battle to Control the Most Popular Website in America*. New York: Random House, p 371.

Angwin, J. (2014) *Dragnet Nation: A Quest for Privacy, Security, and Freedom in a World of Relentless Surveillance*. New York: St. Martin's Press.

Angwin, J. (2024) 'Your driving app is leading you astray'. *The New York Times*, 10 July. Available from: https://www.nytimes.com/2024/07/10/opinion/google-maps-driving-apps-flaws.html [Accessed 28 December 2024].

Arendt, H. (1958) *The Human Condition*. Chicago: University of Chicago Press.

Arias, R., Lueth, K.L. and Rastogi, A. (2018) 'The effect of the Internet of Things on sustainability', World Economic Forum, [online]. Available from: https://www.weforum.org/agenda/2018/01/effect-technology-sustainability-sdgs-internet-things-iot/ [Accessed 29 November 2024].

Asprem, E. and Dyrendal, A. (2015) 'Conspirituality reconsidered: how surprising and how new is the confluence of spirituality and conspiracy theory?' *Journal of Contemporary Religion*, 30(3): 367–82.

Awaludin, A., Rusito, R. and Supriyo, D.A. (2023) 'Preventing illegal online loan crimes', *Proceedings of the International Conference on Law, Economics, and Health (ICLE)*, pp 182–9. Available from: https://doi.org/10.2991/978-2-38476-024-4_21

Baker, P. (2017) 'Trump calls meeting with military leaders: 'the calm before the storm', *The New York Times*, 6 October. Available from: https://www.nytimes.com/2017/10/06/us/politics/trump-calls-meeting-with-military-leaders-the-calm-before-the-storm.html [Accessed 18 March 2025].

Ball, J. (2023) *The Other Pandemic: How QAnon Contaminated the World*. London: Bloomsbury.

Bancroft, A. (2020) *The Darknet and Smarter Crime*. London: Palgrave Macmillan.

Barlow, J.P. (1996) 'A Declaration of the Independence of Cyberspace', Electronic Frontier Foundation. Available from: https://www.eff.org/cyberspace-independence [Accessed 11 March 2025].

Barratt, M., Maddox, A., Smith, N., Davis, J., Goold, L., Winstock, A. and Ferris, J. (2022) 'Who uses digital drugs? An international survey of "binaural beat" consumers', *Drug and Alcohol Review*, 41(5): 1126–30.

Barron, C.M. (2014) ' "I had no credit to ring you back": children's strategies of negotiation and resistance to parental surveillance via mobile phones', *Surveillance & Society*, 12(3): 401–13.

Barros, S.R. and Sandlin, J.A. (2024) 'Galactic transmissions from tantra bros, pu$$y priestesses, red-pilled starseeds, and ayahuasca girls: decoding the pedagogies of conspiritual life coaching', *Review of Education, Pedagogy, and Cultural Studies*: 1–27. Available from: https://doi.org/10.1080/10714413.2024.2388371

Bauman, Z. (2000) *Liquid Modernity*. Cambridge: Polity Press, p 228.

BBC News (2013) 'City of London calls halt to smartphone tracking bins', BBC News, August 12. Available from: https://www.bbc.co.uk/news/technology-23665490 [Accessed 9 December 2024].

BBC News (2016) 'US election 2016: Donald Trump wins presidency'. Available from: https://www.bbc.co.uk/news/world-us-canada-37639370 [Accessed 3 January 2025].

BBC News (2019) 'Christchurch shootings: 49 dead in New Zealand mosque attacks', BBC News, 15 March. Available from: https://www.bbc.com/news/world-asia-47578798 [Accessed 20 December 2024].

BBC News (2021) 'AI emotion-detection software tested on Uyghurs', BBC News, 26 May. Available from: https://www.bbc.co.uk/news/technology-57101248 [Accessed 11 November 2024].

BBC News (2022) 'Deepfake presidents used in Russia–Ukraine war', BBC News, 18 March. Available from: https://www.bbc.co.uk/news/technology-60780142 [Accessed 11 November 2024].

BBC News (2023) 'Controversial clothes hook spy cameras for sale on Amazon', BBC News. Available from: https://www.bbc.com/news/technology-67652317 [Accessed 11 November 2024].

BBC News (2025) 'Mark Zuckerberg takes stand to defend Meta against antitrust suit', BBC News, 14 April. Available from: https://www.bbc.co.uk/news/articles/c4g2z80e2kjo [Accessed 14 April 2025].

Beck, U. (2000) *The Brave New World of Work*. Cambridge: Polity Press.

Beer, D. (2016) *Metric Power*. London: Palgrave Macmillan.

Beer, D. (2019a) *The Data Gaze: Capitalism, Power and Perception*. London: SAGE Publications.

Beer, D. (2019b) *The Quirks of Digital Culture*. Bingley: Emerald Publishing Limited.

Beer, D. (2022) 'Why the metaverse will never happen', *The Fragment*. Available from: https://davidbeer.substack.com/p/why-the-metaverse-will-never-happen [Accessed 12 March 2025].

Belanger, A. (2022) 'Amazon finally admits giving cops Ring doorbell data without user consent', *Ars Technica*, July 14. Available from: https://arstechnica.com/tech-policy/2022/07/amazon-finally-admits-giving-cops-ring-doorbell-data-without-user-consent/ [Accessed 9 December 2024].

Belcher, D. (2022) 'A new city, built upon data, takes shape in South Korea', *The New York Times*, March 28. Available from: https://www.nytimes.com/2022/03/28/technology/eco-delta-smart-village-busan-south-korea.html [Accessed 28 March 2022].

Bell, G. (2022) 'The metaverse has always been a dystopian idea. The metaverse is a new word for an old idea: to understand what we are – and should be – building, we need to look beyond Snow Crash', *MIT Technology Review*, 8 February. Available from: https://www.technologyreview.com/2022/02/08/1044732/metaverse-history-snow-crash/ [Accessed 6 December 2024].

Berger, J. (1995) 'Democracy for sale', *The Observer*, 17 December, p 4.

Bhalla, N. and Harrisberg, K. (2023) 'The rise of surveillance tech in Africa: what you need to know', *Context News*, [online]. Available from: https://www.context.news/surveillance/the-rise-of-surveillance-tech-in-africa-what-you-need-to-know [Accessed 21 November 2024].

Bhuiyan, J. (2022) 'China's SenseTime facial recognition used in Uyghur surveillance, US sanctions claim', *The Guardian*, 7 January. Available from: https://www.theguardian.com/world/2022/jan/06/china-sensetime-facial-recognition-uyghur-surveillance-us-sanctions [Accessed 11 November 2024].

Bigo, D. (2006) 'Security, exception, ban and surveillance', in D. Lyon (ed) *Theorizing Surveillance: The Panopticon and Beyond*. London: Willan, pp 46–68.

Bigo, D. (2008) 'Globalised (in)security: the field and the ban-opticon', in D. Bigo and A. Tsoukala (eds) *Terror, Insecurity and Liberty*. London: Routledge.

Black, E. (2001) *IBM and the Holocaust: The Strategic Alliance between Nazi Germany and America's Most Powerful Corporation*, London: Little, Brown and Company.

Boellstorff, T. (2008) *Coming of Age in Second Life: An Anthropologist Explores the Virtually Human*. Princeton, NJ: Princeton University Press.

boyd, D.M. and Ellison, N.B. (2007) 'Social network sites: definition, history, and scholarship', *Journal of Computer-Mediated Communication*, 13(1): 210–30.

Breland, A. (2020) 'NY attorney general orders Alex Jones to stop selling coronavirus cures', CNBC, 12 March. Available from: https://www.cnbc.com/2020/03/12/ny-attorney-general-orders-alex-jones-to-stop-selling-coronavirus-cures.html [Accessed 19 March 2025].

Broadbent, S. and Lobet-Maris, C. (2015) 'Towards a grey ecology', in L. Floridi (ed) *The Onlife Manifesto*. Cham: Springer, pp 111–24.

Brown, D.W. (2023) 'A security camera for the planet', *The New Yorker*. Available from: https://www.newyorker.com/news/annals-of-climate-action/a-security-camera-for-the-planet [Accessed 13 March 2025].

Browne, S. (2015) *Dark Matters*. Durham, NC: Duke University Press.

Browne, S., Klauser, F. and Wood, D.M. (2022) 'Conversation: surveillance/environment/nature/sustainability', *Surveillance & Society*, 20(4): 462–76.

Brunton, F. and Nissenbaum, H.F. (2015) *Obfuscation: A User's Guide for Privacy and Protest*. Cambridge, MA: MIT Press.

Burke Winkelman, S., Ooman Early, J., Walker, A.D., Chu, L. and Yick, A. (2015) 'Exploring cyber harassment among women who use social media', *Universal Journal of Public Health*, 3(5): 194–201.

Burnett, D. (2016) 'Why the Earth is actually 100% flat', *The Guardian*, [online] 26 January. Available from: https://www.theguardian.com/science/brain-flapping/2016/jan/26/earth-totally-flat-conspiracy-bob [Accessed 19 March 2025].

Burt, A. and Geer, D. (2017) 'The end of privacy', *The New York Times*, 5 October.

Butler, B. (2015) 'The face everyone dreams about', *Vice*, [online] 15 January. Available from: https://www.vice.com/en/article/znw9d3/have-you-ever-dreamed-of-this-man-111 [Accessed 20 December 2024].

Butz, A., Beshers, C. and Feiner, S. (1998) 'Of vampire mirrors and privacy lamps: privacy management in multi-user augmented environments', *Proceedings of the 11th Annual ACM Symposium on User Interface Software and Technology*, pp 171–2. Available from: http://www.cs.columbia.edu/ [Accessed 26 March 2024].

Calasso, R. (2017) *L'innominabile attuale*. Milan: Adelphi.

Calechman, S. (2019) 10,000 steps a day – or fewer? *Harvard Health Publishing*, July 11. Available from: https://www.health.harvard.edu/blog/10000-steps-a-day-or-fewer-2019071117305 [Accessed 11 July 2019].

Caled, D. and Silva, M.J. (2022) 'Digital media and misinformation: an outlook on multidisciplinary strategies against manipulation', *Journal of Computational Social Science*, 5: 123–59.

Calma, J. (2022) 'Amazon's carbon emissions are worse than ever, report says', *The Verge*, 1 August. Available from: https://www.theverge.com/2022/8/1/23287351/amazon-climate-change-carbon-emissions-worse-2021 [Accessed 18 April 2025].

Carnemolla, P. (2018) 'Ageing in place and the internet of things – how smart home technologies, the built environment and caregiving intersect', *Visualization in Engineering*, 6(7): 1–16.

Carr, D. (2009) 'Sundance toasts an early online life', *The New York Times*, 26 January. Available from: https://www.nytimes.com/2009/01/26/movies/26josh.html [Accessed 18 November 2024].

Carr, N.G. (2014) *The Glass Cage: How Our Computers Are Changing Us*. New York: W.W. Norton & Company.

Casey, R. (2021) 'Left to their own devices: a technosocial ethnography of penal electronic monitoring in Scotland', PhD thesis, University of Glasgow.

Caulfield, M. and Wineburg, S.S. (2023) *Verified: How to Think Straight, Get Duped Less, and Make Better Decisions about What to Believe Online*. Chicago: University of Chicago Press.

CBS News (2024) 'Mark Zuckerberg apologizes to families of social media victims at Senate hearing', [Video]. CBS News, January 31. Available from: https://www.cbsnews.com/video/mark-zuckerberg-apologizes-to-families-of-social-media-victims-at-senate-hearing/

Ceccagno, A. (2015) 'The mobile emplacement: Chinese migrants in Italian industrial districts', *Journal of Ethnic and Migration Studies*, 41(7): 1111–30.

Ceccagno A. and Thunø M. (2022) 'Digitized diaspora governance during the COVID-19 pandemic: China's diaspora mobilization and Chinese migrant responses in Italy', *Global Networks*, 23(1): 90–105.

Cep, C. (2014) 'The pointlessness of unplugging', *The New Yorker,* March 19. Available from: https://www.newyorker.com/culture/culture-desk/the-pointlessness-of-unplugging [Accessed 9 December 2024].

Chalmers, D. (2017) 'The mind bleeds into the world', *Edge*, 24 January. Available from: https://www.edge.org/conversation/david_chalmers-the-mind-bleeds-into-the-world [Accessed 17 March 2025].

Chalmers, D. (2022) *Reality: Virtual Worlds and the Problems of Philosophy*. London: Allen Lane.

Chan, C. (2016) 'When one app rules them all: the case of WeChat and Mobile in China', a16z, November 15. Available from: https://a16z.com/when-one-app-rules-them-all-the-case-of-wechat-and-mobile-in-china/ [Accessed 15 November 2016].

Chan, J. (2022) 'Online astroturfing: a problem beyond disinformation', *Philosophy & Social Criticism*, 50(3): 507–28.

Chippindale, C. (2000) 'Capta and data: on the true nature of archaeological information', *American Antiquity*, 64(5): 605–12.

Chokshi, M., Carter, C., Gupta, D., Martin, T. and Allen, R. (1995) *Computers and Apartheid: The Role of Technology in South Africa's Oppression*, CS201 Final Project, Stanford University. Available from: http://www-cs-students.stanford.edu/~cale/cs201/apartheid.comp.html [Accessed 9 December 2024].

Chowdhury, N.S., Livesy, E.J., Blaszczynski, A. et al (2017) 'Pathological gambling and motor impulsivity: a systematic review with meta-analysis', *Journal of Gambling Studies*, 33(4): 1213–39.

Christl, W. and Spiekermann, S. (2016) *Network of Control*. Vienna: Facultas Verlags.

Chung, J.W., Fu, X.J., Deocadiz-Smith, Z., Jung, M. and Huang, J. (2023) 'Negotiating dyadic interactions through the lens of augmented reality glasses', Proceedings of the 2023 ACM Designing Interactive Systems Conference, pp 493–508. Available from: https://doi.org/10.1145/3563657.3595967

Citron, D.K. (2009) 'Law's expressive value in combating cyber gender harassment', *Michigan Law Review*, 108(3).

Cohen, L. and Felson, M. (1979) 'Social change and crime rates: a routine activity approach', *American Sociological Review*, 44: 508–68.

Cole, M. (2023a) 'Unionising Amazon', *Tribune Magazine*, [online] 13 May. Available from: https://tribunemag.co.uk/2023/05/unionising-amazon [Accessed 29 November 2024].

Cole, M. (2023b) '(Infra)structural discontinuity: capital, labour, and technological change', *Antipode*, 55(2): 348–72.

Collier, B. (2023) 'The UK uses targeted Facebook ads to deter migrants. Now Meta is releasing the data'. *New Lines Magazine*. Available from: https://newlinesmag.com/reportage/the-uk-uses-targeted-facebook-ads-to-deter-migrants-now-meta-is-releasing-the-data/ [Accessed 26 December 2023].

Collier, B. (2024) *Tor: From the Dark Web to the Future of Privacy*. Cambridge, MA: The MIT Press.

Conger, K. and Hirsch, L. (2022) 'Elon Musk completes $44 billion deal to own Twitter', *The New York Times*, October 27. Available from: https://www.nytimes.com/2022/10/27/technology/elon-musk-twitter-deal-complete.html [Accessed 8 December 2024].

Couldry, N. and Mejias, U.A. (2019) *The Costs of Connection: How Data Is Colonizing Human Life and Appropriating It for Capitalism*, Stanford, CA: Stanford University Press.

Craker, N. and March, E. (2016) 'The dark side of Facebook®: the Dark Tetrad, negative social potency, and trolling behaviours', *Personality and Individual Differences*, 102: 79–84.

Cugurullo, F. (2023) 'Good and evil in the autonomous city', in D. MacKinnon, R. Burns and V. Fast (eds) *Digital (In)justice in the Smart City*. Toronto: University of Toronto Press, pp 183–94.

Curtis, A. (Director) (2016) *HyperNormalisation*. BBC Documentary.

Curtis, A. (Director) (2021) *Can't Get You Out of My Head*. BBC Film.

Dal Dosso, S. (2023) 'The future ahead will be weird AF (the ultimate AI corecore experience)', YouTube [online]. Available from: https://www.youtube.com/watch?v=RhZ058-lI6g [Accessed 21 November 2024].

Dataverse (2023) 'What is a data wallet and why does it matter?' Available from: https://medium.com/@DataverseOS/what-is-a-data-wallet-and-why-does-it-matter-738fd47138f0 [Accessed 26 December 2024].

Davis, M. and Monk, D.B. (2007) *Evil Paradises: Dreamworlds of Neoliberalism*. New York: The New Press.

Deleuze, G. (1992) *Postscript on the Societies of Control*. Cambridge, MA: MIT Press.

Deleuze, G. and Guattari, F. (1987) *A Thousand Plateaus: Capitalism and Schizophrenia*. London: Athlone Press.

Del Valle, L. (2022) 'Sandy Hook parent recounts years of harassment after Alex Jones called him a crisis actor', CNN, [online] 29 September. Available from: https://edition.cnn.com/2022/09/29/tech/sandy-hook-parent-harassment/index.html [Accessed 24 November 2024].

Descalsota, M. (2022) 'Inside Forest City, a $100 billion "dream paradise" turned ghost town', *Business Insider*, 20 June. Available from: https://www.businessinsider.com/ghost-town-malaysia-forest-city-china-developer-estate-photos-2022-6?international=true&r=US&IR=T [Accessed 11 November 2024].

Dewandre, N. (2015) 'Rethinking the human condition in a hyperconnected era: why freedom is not about sovereignty but about beginnings', in L. Floridi (ed) *The Onlife Manifesto*. Cham: Springer, pp 195–215.

Dignam, P.A. and Rohlinger, D.A. (2019) 'Misogynistic men online: how the red pill helped elect trump', *Signs*, 44(3): 589–612.

Dilanian, K., Seidman, J. and Sanchez, G. (2021) 'Project "El Salvador" shows how China is exerting growing power in America's backyard', NBC News, [online]. Available from: https://www.nbcnews.com/politics/national-security/project-el-salvador-shows-how-china-exerting-growing-power-america-n1278464 [Accessed 29 November 2024].

Doctorow, C. (2023) 'The 'enshittification' of TikTok', *Wired,* 23 January. Available from: https://www.wired.com/story/tiktok-platforms-cory-doctorow/ [Accessed 28 December 2024].

Dodd, V. (2023) 'Metropolitan police to use live facial recognition in crowds at King Charles's coronation', *The Guardian*, 3 May. Available from: https://www.theguardian.com/uk-news/2023/may/03/metropolitan-police-live-facial-recognition-in-crowds-at-king-charles-coronation [Accessed 11 November 2024].

Douglas M. (1990 [1950]) 'No free gifts', in M. Mauss (ed) *The Gift: The Form and Reason for Exchange in Archaic Societies*. New York: Routledge, pp ix–xxi.

Dragiewicz, M., Burgess, J., Matamoros-Fernández, A. et al (2018) 'Technology facilitated coercive control: domestic violence and the competing roles of digital media platforms', *Feminist Media Studies*, 18(4): 609–25.

Dreher, R. (2017) *The Benedict Option: A Strategy for Christians in a Post-Christian Nation*. New York: Sentinel.

Drolet, J.F. and Williams, M.C. (2020) 'America first: paleoconservatism and the ideological struggle for the American right', *Journal of Political Ideologies*, 25(1): 28–50.

Eco, U. (2015) 'Umberto Eco – internet, social media e giornalismo', YouTube. Available from: https://www.youtube.com/watch?v=u10XGPuO3C4 [Accessed 11 November 2024].

Eggers, D. (2013) *The Circle*. New York: Knopf.

Eggers, D. (2021) *The Every*. New York: Knopf.

Eghtebas, C., Klinker, G., Boll, S. and Koelle, M. (2023) 'Co-speculating on dark scenarios and unintended consequences of a ubiquitous(ly) augmented reality', Proceedings of the 2023 ACM Designing Interactive Systems Conference, pp 2392–407. Available from: https://doi.org/10.1145/3563657.3596073

Eikren, E. and Ingram-Waters, M. (2016) 'Dismantling "you get what you deserve": towards a feminist sociology of revenge porn', *Ada New Media*, 10.

European Commission (2024) 'Data Act explained', *Digital Strategy*, [online] 6 September. Available from: https://digital-strategy.ec.europa.eu/en/factpages/data-act-explained [Accessed 18 December 2024].

European Parliament (2024) 'Right to repair: making repair easier and more appealing to consumers', *European Parliament News*, 19 April. Available from: https://www.europarl.europa.eu/news/en/press-room/20240419IPR20590/right-to-repair-making-repair-easier-and-more-appealing-to-consumers [Accessed 14 March 2025].

Fallon-O'Leary, D. (2023) 'One-click purchasing: how click to buy is revolutionizing e-commerce', *Business.com*, [online]. Available from: https://www.business.com/articles/one-click-purchasing-how-click-to-buy-is-revolutionizing-ecommerce/ [Accessed 29 November 2024].

Faulkner, W. (2003) *Privacy*. Milan: Adelphi.

Ferrer-Conill, R. (2018) 'Playbour and the gamification of work: empowerment, exploitation and fun as labour dynamics', in P. Bilić, J. Primorac and B. Valtysson (eds) *Technologies of Labour and the Politics of Contradiction*. Cham: Springer, pp 193–210.

Ferrigine, G. and Saha, J. (2023) 'Taylor Swift dispels "gaylor" rumors to the dismay of many fans who feel queerbaited', *Salon*, October 27. Available from: https://www.salon.com/2023/10/27/taylor-swift-gaylor-rumors-queerbaited/ [Accessed 19 March 2025].

Festinger, L., Riecken, H.W. and Schachter, S. (1956) *When Prophecy Fails*. Minneapolis: University of Minnesota Press.

Fincher, D. (Director) (2010) *The Social Network*. Columbia Pictures.

Finlayson, A. (2021) 'Neoliberalism, the alt-right and the intellectual Dark Web', *Theory, Culture & Society*, 38(6): 167–90.

Fisher, M. (2009) *Capitalist Realism: Is There No Alternative?* Ropley, Hants: Zero Books.

Floridi, L. (ed) (2015) *The Onlife Manifesto: Being Human in a Hyperconnected Era*. Cham: Springer.

Floridi, L. (2020) 'The green and the blue: a new political ontology for a mature information society', *SSRN Electronic Journal*. Available from: https://doi.org/10.2139/SSRN.3831094

Floridi, L. (2023) 'On good and evil, the mistaken idea that technology is ever neutral, and the importance of the double-charge thesis', *Philosophy and Technology*, 36(3): 1–5.

Floridi, L. (2024) 'Hypersuasion – on AI's persuasive power and how to deal with it', *Philosophy and Technology*, 37(2): 1–10.

Floridi, L. and Sotgiu, S. (2021) 'Green pass e hacker, l'Italia onlife di Draghi vista da Floridi'. Available from: https://formiche.net/2021/08/green-pass-e-hacker-litalia-onlife-di-draghi-vista-da-floridi/ [Accessed 17 March 2025].

Fludernik, M. (2017) 'Panopticisms: from fantasy to metaphor to reality', *Textual Practice*, 31(1): 1–26.

Forestal, J. (2023) 'Social media, social control, and the politics of public shaming', *American Political Science Review*, 118(4): 1–15.

Forssell, R. (2016) 'Exploring cyberbullying and face-to-face bullying in working life – prevalence, targets and expressions', *Computers in Human Behavior*, 58: 454–60.

Foucault, M. (1978) *Security, Territory, Population* (2009 edn). London: Picador.

Foucault, M. (1979) *Discipline and Punish: The Birth of the Prison*, London: Penguin.

Foucault, M. (2014) *On the Government of the Living*. London: Palgrave Macmillan.

Foucault, M. and Hurley, R. (2012) *The Care of the Self: Volume 3 of The History of Sexuality*. New York: Knopf Doubleday.

France 24 (2025) 'US Pizzagate conspiracy theory gunman killed by police'. Available from: https://www.france24.com/en/live-news/20250110-us-pizzagate-conspiracy-theory-gunman-killed-by-police-media [Accessed 16 March 2025].

Franko, K. (2020) *The Crimmigrant Other: Migration and Penal Power*. London: Routledge.

Franzen, C. (2015) 'It's the end of Google Glass, and Glassholes are taking it hard', *Vice*, January 19. Available from: https://www.vice.com/en/article/wnj7gw/how-glassholes-are-handling-the-end-of-google-glass [Accessed 6 December 2024].

Fraser, A. (2019) 'Land grab/data grab: precision agriculture and its new horizons', *The Journal of Peasant Studies*, 46(5): 893–912.

Freeman, W. and Perelló, L. (2024) 'The drop in crime in El Salvador is stunning, but it has a dark side', *The New York Times*, 8 February. Available from: https://www.nytimes.com/2024/02/08/opinion/el-salvador-bukele-election.html [Accessed 11 March 2025].

Freude, L. and Waites, M. (2023) 'Analysing homophobia, xenophobia and sexual nationalisms in Africa: comparing quantitative attitudes data to reveal societal differences', *Current Sociology*, 71(1): 173–95.

Fuller, R. Buckminster (1973) *Nine Chains to the Moon*. London: Jonathan Cape.

Furedi, F. (2001) *Paranoid Parenting: Abandon Your Anxieties and Be a Good Parent*. London: Allen Lane.

Furedi, F. (2020) *Democracy Under Siege: Don't Let Them Lock it Down!* Winchester: John Hunt Publishing.

Gamio, L. (2024) 'CrowdStrike outage explained', *The New York Times*, 19 July. Available from: https://www.nytimes.com/interactive/2024/07/19/technology/crowdstrike-outage-explained.html [Accessed 11 November 2024].

Gasser, U., Ienca, M., Scheibner, J., Sleigh, J., and Vayena, E. (2020) 'Digital tools against COVID-19: taxonomy, ethical challenges, and navigation aid', *Lancet Digital Health*, 2(8): e425–34.

Gassmann, O., Böhm, J., and Palmié, M. (2019) *Smart Cities: Introducing Digital Innovation to Cities*. UK: Leeds: Emerald Publishing.

Gates, B. (1995) *The Road Ahead*. New York: Viking Books.

Gearty, C. (2013) *Liberty and Security*. Cambridge: Polity Press.

Geoghegan, P. (2022) *Democracy for Sale: Dark Money and Dirty Politics*. New York: Apollo.

George, J.J., Yan, J., and Leidner, D.E. (2020) 'Data philanthropy: corporate responsibility with strategic value?', *Information Systems Management*, 37(3): 186–97.

Gerbner, G. and Gross, L. (1976) 'Living with television: the violence profile', *Journal of Communication*, 26(2): 172–99.

Gibson, W. (2016 [1984]) *Neuromancer*. London: Gollancz.

Giglioli, M.F. (2019) *I Labirinti della Sorveglianza Informatica*. Milan: Mulino.

Gillespie, A.A. (2006) 'Cyber-bullying and harassment of teenagers: the legal response', *Journal of Social Welfare and Family Law*, 28(2): 123–36.

Ging, D. (2019) 'Alphas, betas, and incels: theorizing the masculinities of the manosphere', *Men and Masculinities*, 22(4): 638–57.

Ginsburg, R. (2022) 'What is the metaverse? A complete guide to our Web3 future', *NFT Now*, August 10. Available from: https://nftnow.com/guides/what-is-the-metaverse-a-complete-guide-to-our-web3-future/ [Accessed 6 December 2024].

Globalist.it (2021) 'Chi sono i "mattoncini fascio-negazionisti", la nuova piaga della destra sui social'. Available from: https://www.globalist.it/news/2021/03/02/chi-sono-i-mattoncini-fascio-negazionisti-la-nuova-piaga-della-destra-sui-social/ [Accessed 21 November 2024].

Glotz, P., Bertschi, S., and Locke, C. (2005) *Thumb Culture: The Meaning of Mobile Phones for Society*. Bielefeld: Verlag.

Goffman, E. (1956) *Presentation of the Self in Everyday Life* (1971 edn). London: Pelican Press.

Goodin, T. (2021) *My Brain Has too Many Tabs Open: How to Untangle Our Relationship with Tech*. London: White Lion Publishing.

Gould, S.J.J. (2024) 'Stochastic machine witnesses at work: today's critiques of Taylorism are inadequate for workplace surveillance epistemologies of the future', *Conference on Human Factors in Computing Systems – Proceedings*, p 12. Available from: https://doi.org/10.1145/3613904.3642206/SUPPL_FILE/3613904.3642206-TALK-VIDEO.VTT

Graham, M. and Dittus, M. (2022) *Geographies of Digital Exclusion: Data Power and Inequality*, London: Pluto Press.

Greenwald, G. (2014) *Nothing to Hide*, London: Penguin Random House.

Grišinas, A. (2024) The *Western Crisis of Truth in the Early 21st Century: As the Enlightenment Dims*. Abingdon: Routledge.

Gross, J. (2023) 'He drove into a creek and died. His family blames Google Maps', *The New York Times*, 21 September. Available from: https://www.nytimes.com/2023/09/21/us/google-maps-lawsuit-collapsed-bridge.html [Accessed 25 December 2024].

The Guardian (2023) 'Team Jorge unmasked: the secret disinformation team who distort reality', [video], [online]. Available from: https://www.theguardian.com/world/video/2023/feb/15/team-jorge-unmasked-the-secret-disinformation-team-who-distort-reality-video [Accessed 21 November 2024].

Guest, P. (2022) 'China's troll army is "swatting" its critics', *Business Insider*, August. Available from: https://www.businessinsider.com/chinese-troll-attacks-against-activists-2022-8 [Accessed 10 December 2024].

Haggerty, K.D. and Ericson, R.V. (2000) 'The surveillant assemblage', *The British Journal of Sociology*, 51(4): 605–22.

Haggerty, K.D. (2005)'Visible war: surveillance, speed, and information war', in K. Haggerty and R. Ericson (eds) *The New Politics of Surveillance and Visibility*. Toronto: University of Toronto Press, pp 250–68.

Hale, K. (2022) *Slenderman: Online Obsession, Mental Illness, and the Violent Crime of Two Midwestern Girls*. New York: Grove Press.

Han, B.-C. (2015) *The Burnout Society*. Stanford, CA: Stanford University Press.

Hao, K. (2021) 'Facebook's responsible AI team has a problem: it keeps sidestepping the real issues', *Technology Review*, [online] 11 March. Available from: https://www.technologyreview.com/2021/03/11/1020600/facebook-responsible-ai-misinformation/ [Accessed 24 November 2024].

Harari, Y.N. (2015) *Homo Deus: A Brief History of Tomorrow*. London: Harper Collins.

Haraway, D.J. (2016) *Staying with the Trouble: Making Kin in the Chthulucene*. Durham, NC: Duke University Press.

Harbisch, A. (2023) 'Children or productive adults? Infantilisation and exploitation of refugees in Germany and Austria', *Journal of Ethnic and Migration Studies* [Preprint]. Available from: https://doi.org/10.1080/1369183X.2023.2166908

Harcourt, B.E. (2017) 'Exposed: desire and disobedience in the digital age', *Surveillance & Society*, 15(2): 354–56. Available from: https://www.hup.harvard.edu/books/9780674504578 [Accessed 19 July 2024].

Hari, J. (2023) *Stolen Focus*. London: Bloomsbury.

Harwell, D. (2018) 'Scarlett Johansson on fake AI-generated sex videos: 'Nothing can stop someone from cutting and pasting my image', *Washington Post*, [online] 31 December. Available from: https://www.washingtonpost.com/technology/2018/12/31/scarlett-johansson-fake-ai-generated-sex-videos-nothing-can-stop-someone-cutting-pasting-my-image/?noredirect=on [Accessed 21 November 2024].

Hawley, G. (2017) *Making Sense of the Alt-Right*. New York: Columbia University Press.

Hayles, N.K. (2005) *My Mother Was a Computer: Digital Subjects and Literary Texts*. Chicago: University of Chicago Press.

Hayward, K. (2020) 'Five smart city futures: a criminological analysis of urban intelligence', in *The Algorithmic Society*, Abingdon: Routledge, pp 172–92.

Hector, H. (2024) 'Samsung XR/VR headset – everything we know so far and what we want to see', *TechRadar*, November 11. Available from: https://www.techradar.com/computing/virtual-reality-augmented-reality/samsung-xr-vr-headset [Accessed 6 December 2024].

Henry, N., Flynn, A. and Powell, A. (2020a) 'Technology-facilitated domestic and sexual violence: a review', *Violence Against Women*, 26(15–16): 1828–54.

Henry, N., McGlynn, C., Flynn, A., Johnson, K., Powell, A. and Scott, A.J. (2020b) *Image-based Sexual Abuse: A Study on the Causes and Consequences of Non-consensual Nude or Sexual Imagery*. London: Routledge.

Hern, A. (2018a) 'Apple removes Infowars podcasts from iTunes and podcast apps', *The Guardian*, 6 August. Available from: https://www.theguardian.com/technology/2018/aug/06/apple-removes-podcasts-infowars-alex-jones [Accessed 17 March 2025].

Hern, A. (2018b) 'AI face-swap pornography is a new threat to women's privacy', *The Guardian*, 25 January. Available fom: https://www.theguardian.com/technology/2018/jan/25/ai-face-swap-pornography-emma-watson-scarlett-johansson-taylor-swift-daisy-ridley-sophie-turner-maisie-williams?google_editors_picks=true [Accessed 11 December 2024].

Hess, A. (2020) 'The social-distancing shamers are watching', *The New York Times*, [online] 11 May. Available from: https://www.nytimes.com/2020/05/11/arts/social-distance-shaming.html

Hildebrandt, M. (2015) *Smart Technologies and the End(s) of Law.* Northampton, MA: Elgar Publishing.

Hildebrandt, M. (2020) 'Smart technologies', *Internet Policy Review*, 9(4): 1–16.

Hill, K. (2020) 'Wrongfully accused by an algorithm', *The New York Times*, 24 June. Available from: https://www.nytimes.com/2020/06/24/technology/facial-recognition-arrest.html [Accessed 26 December 2024].

Hill, K. and Mattu, S. (2018) 'Facebook knows how to track you using the dust on your camera lens', *Gizmodo*, [online] 11 January. Available from: https://gizmodo.com/facebook-knows-how-to-track-you-using-the-dust-on-your-1821030620#:~:text=We%20can't%20know%20when,thinks%20these%20things%20are%20possible [Accessed 17 March 2025].

Hillyard, P., Pantazis, C., Tombs, S. and Gordon, D. (2004) *Beyond Criminology: Taking Harm Seriously.* London: Pluto Press.

Hjorth, L., Ohashi, K., Sinanan, J., Horst, H., Pink, S., Kato, F. et al (2020) 'Friendly social surveillance', in L. Hjorth et al (eds) *Digital Media Practices in Households: Kinship through Data.* Amsterdam: Amsterdam University Press, pp 61–76.

Hoel, E. (2024) 'Here lies the internet, murdered by generative AI', *The Intrinsic Perspective*, [online] 27 February. Available from: https://www.theintrinsicperspective.com/p/here-lies-the-internet-murdered-by [Accessed 21 November 2024].

Hoffman, B., Ware, J. and Shapiro, E. (2020) 'Assessing the threat of incel violence', *Studies in Conflict & Terrorism*, 43(7): 565–87.

Holt, A.G. and Udroiu, C. (2022) 'Financing terrorism through cryptocurrencies', *Serie Litere şi Ştiinţe Sociale*, 1(Supp): 29–34.

Home Office news team (2023) 'Police use of facial recognition: factsheet', Home Office, 29 October. Available from: https://homeofficemedia.blog.gov.uk/2023/10/29/police-use-of-facial-recognition-factsheet/ [Accessed 25 December 2024].

Hoskins, A. (2024) 'AI and memory', *Memory, Mind & Media,* 3: e18.

Hoskins, A. and Tulloch, J. (2016) *Risk and Hyperconnectivity: Media and Memories of Neoliberalism*. Oxford: Oxford University Press.

Howe, D.C. and Nissenbaum, H. (2009) 'TrackMeNot: resisting surveillance in web search 1', in I. Kerr, I.R. Kerr, V.M. Steeves and C. Lucock (eds) *Lessons from the Identity Trail: Anonymity, Privacy and Identity in a Networked Society*. Oxford: Oxford University Press.

Hsu, T. and Myers, S.L. (2024) 'Russia's RT is banned in Europe, but its disinformation lives on', *The New York Times*, [online], 30 May. Available from: https://www.nytimes.com/2024/05/30/business/media/russia-rt-disinformation-europe-ban.html [Accessed 19 December 2024].

Huang, E. (2018) 'China's social media giants want their users to help out with the crushing burden of censorship', *Quartz*. Available from: https://qz.com/1172536/chinas-social-media-giants-tencent-toutiao-weibo-want-their-users-to-help-out-with-censorship [Accessed 10 December 2024].

Huang, G. and Wang, S. (2023) 'Is artificial intelligence more persuasive than humans? A meta-analysis', *Journal of Communication*, 73(6): 552–62.

Huang, Q. (2021) 'The mediated and mediatised justice-seeking: Chinese digital vigilantism from 2006 to 2018', *Internet Histories*, 5(3–4): 304–22.

Humphries, M. (2017) 'Elon Musk buys back X.com from PayPal', *PCMag*, 11 July. Available from: https://www.pcmag.com/news/elon-musk-buys-back-xcom-from-paypal [Accessed 8 December 2024].

Huxley, A. (1932) *Brave New World*. London: Chatto & Windus.

Huxley, A. (1958) *Brave New World Revisited*. New York: Rosetta Books.

Hynes, M. (2021) *The Social, Cultural and Environmental Costs of Hyper-Connectivity: Sleeping Through the Revolution*. Leeds: Esmerald Publishing

Hyzen, A. and Van Den Bulck, H. (2021) 'Conspiracies, ideological entrepreneurs, and digital popular culture', *Media and Communication*, 9(3): 179–88.

Illich, I. (1974) *Energy and Equity*. New York: Harper & Row.

Innis, H. (1951) *The Bias of Communication*. Toronto: University of Toronto Press.

Ishiguro, K. (2015) *The Buried Giant*. London: Faber & Faber.

Jackman, A., Richardson, M., and Veber, M. (2024) 'Where are the pandemic drones? On the 'failure' of automated aerial solutionism', *New Media & Society*, 26(3): 1183–203.

Jacob, E. (2021) 'How much does Spotify pay per stream?', *Business Insider*, [online] 24 Febuary. Available from: https://www.businessinsider.com/guides/streaming/how-much-does-spotify-pay-per-stream?international=true&r=US&IR=T [Accessed 29 November 2024].

Jacobs, J. (1961) *The Death and Life of Great American Cities*. New York: Random House.

Jaishankar, K. (2007) 'Cyber criminology: evolving a novel discipline with a new journal', *International Journal of Cyber Criminology*, 1(1): 1–6.

Jewell, T. (2023) 'Jelqing: does it work? Medically reviewed by J. Keith Fisher, MD', Healthline, 26 February. Available from: www.healthline.com/health/jelqing [Accessed 6 December 2024].

Johanssen, J. and Kay, J. B. (2024) 'From femcels to "femcelcore": women's involuntary celibacy and the rise of heteronihilism', *European Journal of Cultural Studies*. Available from: https://doi.org/10.1177/13675494241293731

Johnson, B. (2010) 'Privacy no longer a social norm, says Facebook founder' *The Guardian*, [online] 11 January. Available from: https://www.theguardian.com/technology/2010/jan/11/facebook-Privacy [Accessed 22 February 2020].

Johnson, B., Co, S., Sun, T., Lim, C.C.W., Stjepanovic, D., Leung, J. et al (2023) 'Cryptocurrency trading and its associations with gambling and mental health: a scoping review', *Addictive Behaviors*, 136: 107504.

Jones, A. and Angelini, G. (2024) *The Antisocial Network: Memes to Mayhem* [Documentary]. Fandango Media.

Jones, R. and Brown, E. (2024) 'CEO of Saudi Arabia's futuristic city project leaves abruptly', *Wall Street Journal*, 12 November. Available from: https://www.wsj.com/world/middle-east/ceo-of-saudi-arabias-futuristic-city-project-leaves-abruptly-43489eb4 [Accessed 9 December 2024].

Jordan, M. and Pfarr, N. (2014) 'Forget the Quantified Self, we need to build the Quantified Us', *Wired*, 4 April. Available from: https://www.wired.com/2014/04/forget-the-quantified-self-we-need-to-build-the-quantified-us/ [Accessed 9 December 2024].

Just, S.N., Storm, K. and Haru, S.L. (2023) 'Onlife intersectionalities as flows of playbour: the case of women in gaming', *Media, Culture & Society*, 45(5): 899–915. Available from: https://doi.org/10.1177/01634437231155345

Kapaló, J. (2020) *Faith – Trust – Secrecy: Religion Through the Lenses of the Secret Police*. Budapest: Vera and Donald Blinken Open Society.

Kapoor, S. and Narayanan, A. (2023) 'How to prepare for the deluge of generative AI on social media', Knight First Amendment Institute at Columbia University, 16 June. Available from: https://knightcolumbia.org/content/how-to-prepare-for-the-deluge-of-generative-ai-on-social-media [Accessed 6 December 2024].

Kassem, S. (2024) *Work and Alienation in the Platform Economy*. Bristol: Bristol University Press.

Kaufmann, M., (2021) 'This is a secret: learning from children's engagement with surveillance and secrecy', *Cultural Studies Critical Methodologies*, 21(5): 424–37.

Kennedy, L. and Madelaine C. (2022) 'Security, suspicion, and surveillance? There's an app for that', *Surveillance & Society*, 20(2): 127–41.

Kirk, J. (2011) 'Europe rejects one-click-to-buy Amazon patent application', *PC World*, 7 July. Available from: https://www.pcworld.com/article/487010/article-1139.html [Accessed 14 November 2024].

Kirkpatrick, R. (2019) 'The power of data philanthropy', Milken Institute, 10 May. Available from: https://milkeninstitute.org/article/power-data-philanthropy [Accessed 9 December 2024].

Klein, J. (2021) 'The darkly soothing compulsion of doomscrolling', *BBC Worklife*. Available from: https://www.bbc.com/worklife/article/20210226-the-darkly-soothing-compulsion-of-doomscrolling [Accessed 3 January 2025].

Klein, N. (2008) *The Shock Doctrine: The Rise of Disaster Capitalism*. London: Penguin.

Klein, N. (2020) 'Andrew Cuomo, Eric Schmidt, and the coronavirus tech shock doctrine', *The Intercept*, 8 May. Available from: https://theintercept.com/2020/05/08/andrew-cuomo-eric-schmidt-coronavirus-tech-shock-doctrine/ [Accessed 11 November 2024].

Klein, N. (2023) *Doppelganger: A Trip into the Mirror World,* London: Allen Lane.

Kleinman, Z. (2025) 'Apple pulls data protection tool after UK government security row', BBC News, 22 February. Available from: https://www.bbc.com/news/technology-62819873 [Accessed 19 April 2025].

Klinenberg, D. (2024) 'Does deplatforming work?', *The Journal of Conflict Resolution,* 68(6): 1199–225.

Knapp, A. (2023) 'This asteroid mining startup is ready to launch the first-ever commercial deep space mission', *Forbes*, [online]. Available from: https://www.forbes.com/sites/alexknapp/2023/10/18/this-asteroid-mining-startup-is-ready-to-launch-the-first-ever-commercial-deep-space-mission/ [Accessed 29 November 2024].

Knight, A. and Saxby, S. (2014) 'Identity crisis: global challenges of identity protection in a networked world', *Computer Law & Security Review*, 30(6): 617–32.

Knight, P. (2000) *Conspiracy Culture: American Paranoia from the Kennedy Assassination to the X-Files,* London: Routledge.

Knights, R. and Morris, E. (2015) 'Move to intelligence-driven security', *Network Security*, 2015(8): 15–18.

Kriner, M., Barbarossa, E. and Bernardo, I. (2022) 'The Buffalo terrorist attack: situating the lone actor threat', Center on Terrorism, Extremism, and Counterterrorism, Middlebury Institute of International Studies, 19 July. Available from: https://www.middlebury.edu/institute/academics/centers-initiatives/ctec/ctec-publications/buffalo-terrorist-attack-situating-lone-actor [Accessed 18 November 2024].

LaFrance, A. (2017) 'The internet is mostly bots', *The Atlantic*, [online] 31 January. Available from: https://www.theatlantic.com/technology/archive/2017/01/bots-bots-bots/515043 [Accessed 20 December 2024].

Langa, V. (2024) 'Rise of Chinese surveillance tech in Africa:dDevelopment or espionage? *The Africa Report*, [online]. Available from: https://www.theafricareport.com/354469/rise-of-chinese-surveillance-tech-in-africa-development-or-espionage/ [Accessed 21 November 2024].

Lanier, J. (2006) 'Digital Maoism: the hazards of the new online collectivism', *Edge*, 29 May. Available from: https://www.edge.org/conversation/jaron_lanier-digital-maoism-the-hazards-of-the-new-online-collectivism [Accessed 17 March 2025].

Lanier, J. (2010) *You Are Not a Gadget: A Manifesto.* London: Allen Lane.

Lanier, J. (2018) *Dawn of the New Everything: A Journey Through Virtual Reality*, London: Penguin, pp 1–5.

Lanigan, R. (1994) *Capta versus Data: Method and Evidence in Communicology.* Cham: Springer.

Latour, B. (1990) 'Technology is society made durable', *The Sociological Review*, 38(1): 103–31.

Latour, B. (2005) *Reassembling the Social: An Introduction to Actor-Network-Theory,* Oxford and New York: Oxford University Press.

Lauckner, C., Truszczynski, N., Lambert, D., Kottarmasu, V., Meherelly, A. and Schipani-McLaughlin, A.M. (2019) '"Catfishing," cyberbullying, and coercion: An exploration of the risks associated with dating app use among rural sexual minority males', *Journal of Gay & Lesbian Mental Health*, 23(3): 289–306.

Lauder, C. and March, E. (2023) 'Catching the catfish: exploring gender and the Dark Tetrad of personality as predictors of catfishing perpetration', *Computers in Human Behavior*, 140: 107599.

Lauer, D. (2021) 'Facebook's ethical failures are not accidental; they are part of the business model', *AI and Ethics*, 1(4): 395.

Lavorgna, A., Tartari, M. and Ugwudike, P. (2022) 'Criminogenic and harm-enabling features of social media platforms: the case of sharenting practices', *European Journal of Criminology*, 20(3): 1037–60.

Lebeck, K., Ruth, K., Kohno, T. and Roesner, F. (2018) 'Towards security and privacy for multi-user augmented reality: foundations with end users', *Proceedings – IEEE Symposium on Security and Privacy*, May, pp 392–408. Available from: https://doi.org/10.1109/SP.2018.00051

Le Conte, M. (2022) *Escape: How a Generation Shaped, Destroyed and Survived the Internet.* London: Bonnier Books.

Leloup, D. and Reynaud, F. (2023) 'Storykillers: a deep dive into Team Jorge, the disinformation mercenaries operating worldwide', *Le Monde*, [online] 15 February. Available from: https://www.lemonde.fr/en/pixels/article/2023/02/15/storykillers-a-deep-dive-into-team-jorge-the-disinformation-mercenaries-operating-worldwide_6015839_13.html [Accessed 21 November 2024].

Le Monde (2025) 'An AI scam targeting a cabinet minister heats up Italy's political climate'. Available from: https://www.lemonde.fr/en/international/article/2025/02/14/an-ai-scam-targeting-a-cabinet-minister-heats-up-italy-s-political-climate_6738143_4.html [Accessed 17 March 2025].

Lenton, P. (2024) 'A wild investigation of transvestigators: the people who think celebs are all trans', *Vice*, 8 February. Available from: https://www.vice.com/en/article/jg54kd/a-wild-investigation-of-transvestigators-the-people-who-think-celebs-are-all-trans [Accessed 17 March 2025].

Lessing, L. (1999) *Code and Other Laws of Cyberspace*. New York: Harper Collins.

Leukfeldt, E.R. and Yar, M. (2016) 'Applying routine activity theory to cybercrime: a theoretical and empirical analysis', *Deviant Behavior*, 37(3): 263–80.

Levinovitz, A. (2024) '*We are all Big Brother now', The Boston Globe*, 20 June. Available from: https://www.bostonglobe.com/2024/06/20/opinion/nextdoor-ring-nest-grassroots-surveillance/ [Accessed 11 November 2024].

Levinson, B. (Director) (1997) *Wag the Dog*. New Line Cinema.

Levinson, P. (2001) *Digital McLuhan: A Guide to the Information Millennium*. Abingdon: Routledge.

Liang, F. (2020) 'COVID-19 and health code: how digital platforms tackle the pandemic in China', *Social Media and Society*, 6(3). Available from: https://doi.org/10.1177/2056305120947657

Lianos, M. and Douglas, M. (2000) 'Dangerization and the end of deviance: the institutional environment', *British Journal of Criminology*, 40(2): 261–78.

Lim, L. (2014) *The People's Republic of Amnesia*, Oxford: Oxford University Press.

Lingel, J. (2019) *The Gentrification of the Internet*. Oakland: University of California Press.

Lingel, J. (2021) *The Gentrification of the Internet: How to Reclaim Our Digital Freedom*. Oakland, CA: University of California Press.

Liu, C. (2015 [2008]) *The Dark Forest*. London: Head of Zeus.

Livingstone, S. (2002) *Young People and New Media: Childhood and the Changing Media Environment*. Thousand Oaks, CA: Sage.

Lloyd, T. (2021) 'Facebook's Metaverse heralds a brave new underworld of metacrime', *The New Republic*. Available from: https://newrepublic.com/article/164497/facebook-metaverse-cybercrime-marc-zuckerberg [Accessed 12 March 2025].

Lopatto, E. (2024) 'The moral bankruptcy of Marc Andreessen and Ben Horowitz', *The Verge*, 24 July. Available from: https://www.theverge.com/2024/7/24/24204706/marc-andreessen-ben-horowitz-a16z-trump-donations [Accessed 9 December 2024].

Lorenz, T. (2024) '"BlueAnon" conspiracy theories flood social media after Trump rally shooting', *The Washington Post*, [online] 14 July. Available from: https://www.washingtonpost.com/technology/2024/07/14/blueanon-conspiracy-theories-trump-rally-shooting/ [Accessed 24 November 2024].

Lovink, G. (2019) *Sad by Design*. London: Pluto Press.

Lovink, G. (2022a) *Stuck on the Platform: Reclaiming the Internet*. Amsterdam: Valiz.

Lovink, G. (2022b) *Geert Lovink: Extinction Internet*. Amsterdam: Institute of Network Cultures. Available from: https://networkcultures.org/blog/publication/extinction-internet/ [Accessed 17 July 2024].

Lowry, P.B., Zhang, J., Wang, C. and Siponen, M. (2016) 'Why do adults engage in cyberbullying on social media? An integration of online disinhibition and deindividuation effects with the social structure and social learning (SSSL) model', *Information Systems Research*, 27(4): 962–86.

Lumet, S. (Director) (1986) *Power*. Columbia Pictures.

Lupton, D. (2016) *The Quantified Self*. Cambridge: Polity Press.

Lupton, D. and Thomas, G.M. (2015) 'Playing pregnancy: the ludification and gamification of expectant motherhood in smartphone apps', *M/C Journal*, 18(5). Available from: http://journal.media-culture.org.au/index.php/mcjournal/rt/printerFriendly/1012/0 [Accessed 21 February 2024].

Lyon, D. (1994) *Electronic Eye: Rise of the Surveillance Society*. Cambridge: Polity Press.

Lyon, D. (2003) *Surveillance as Social Sorting: Privacy, Risk, and Digital Discrimination*. London: Routledge.

Lyon, D. (2009) 'Surveillance, power and everyday life', in C. Avgerou, R. Mansell, D. Quah and R. Silverstone (eds) *Oxford Handbook of Information and Communication Technologies*. Oxford: Oxford University Press.

Lyon, D. (2018) *The Culture of Surveillance: Watching as a Way of Life*. London: Polity Press.

Lyon, D (2022) *Pandemic Surveillance*. Cambridge: Polity Press.

Lyon, D. and Bauman, Z. (2013) *Liquid Surveillance*. Cambridge: Polity Press.

Maalsen, S. (2024) 'Home in cybersymbiosis: making home with digital oddkin', *Information, Communication & Society* [Preprint]. Available from: https://doi.org/10.1080/1369118X.2024.2311243

Maalsen, S. and Sadowski, J. (2019) 'The smart home on FIRE: amplifying and accelerating domestic surveillance', *Surveillance & Society*, 17(2): 118–24.

Mackey, D. (2024) 'Soiled gold: gold mining in El Salvador', *The Dial*, [online] 12 March. Available from: https://www.thedial.world/issue-14/gold-mining-el-salvador [Accessed 29 November 2024].

MacKinnon R. (2011) 'China's "networked authoritarianism"', *Journal of Democracy*, 22(2): 32–46.

Malleret, C., Milmo, D. and Hern, A. (2023) 'Pro-Bolsonaro violence highlights the role of social media platforms', *The Guardian*, 9 January. Available from: https://www.theguardian.com/world/2023/jan/09/pro-bolsonaro-violence-social-media-platforms?CMP=Share_iOSApp_Other [Accessed 11 November 2024].

Mangmeechai, A. (2022) 'The life-cycle assessment of greenhouse gas emissions and life-cycle costs of e-waste management in Thailand', *Sustainable Environment Research*, 32(1): 1–13.

Mann, S. (2016) 'Surveillance (oversight), sousveillance (undersight), and metaveillance (seeing sight itself)', IEEE Conference on Computer Vision and Pattern Recognition Workshops.

Maras, M.H., Miranda, M.D. and Wandt, A.S. (2023) 'The use of COVID-19 contact tracing app data as evidence of a crime', *Science & Justice*, 63(2): 158–63.

Marcum, C.D., Higgins, G.E., Freiburger, T.L. and Ricketts, M.L. (2017) 'Exploration of sexting behaviors among middle and high school students in a midwestern county', *International Journal of Cyber Criminology*, 11(2): 174–91.

Marcuse, H. (2006) 'Some implications of modern technology,' in A. Arato and E. Gebhardt (eds) *The Essential Frankfurt School Reader*. New York: Continuum.

Marganski, A and Melander, L (2021) 'Technology-facilitated violence against women and girls in public and private spheres: moving from enemy to ally', in J. Bailey, A. Flynn, and N. Henry (eds) *The Emerald International Handbook of Technology-Facilitated Violence and Abuse*. Leeds: Emerald Publishing, pp 623–41.

De Martin, J.C. (2023) *Contro lo smartphone. Per una tecnologia più democratica*. Turin: ADD Editore.

Marx, G.T. (1998) 'Ethics for the new surveillance', *The Information Society*, 14(3): 171–85.

Marx, G.T. (2017) *Windows Into the Soul: Surveillance and Society in an Age of High Technology*. Chicago: University of Chicago Press.

Marx, G.T. and Steeves, V. (2010) 'From the beginning: children as subjects and agents of surveillance', *Surveillance & Society*, 7(3/4): 192–230.

Mason, P. (2016) *PostCapitalism: A Guide to Our Future*. New York: Farrar, Straus and Giroux.

Masri, L. (2023) 'Special Report: Russia's detentions of Ukrainians', *Reuters*. Available from: https://www.reuters.com/investigates/special-report/ukraine-crisis-russia-detentions/ [Accessed 11 November 2024].

Massanari, A. (2017) '#Gamergate and The Fappening: how Reddit's algorithm, governance, and culture support toxic technocultures', *New Media & Society*, 19(3): 329–46.

Mathiesen, T. (1997) 'The viewer society: Michel Foucault's "Panopticon" revisited', *Theoretical Criminology*, 1(2): 215–34.

Mayer-Schönberger, V. (2009) *Delete: The Virtue of Forgetting in the Digital Age*. Princeton, NJ, and Oxford: Princeton University Press.

Mbembe, A.J. (2021) *Out of the Dark Night: Essays on Decolonisation*. New York: Columbia University Press.

McCarthy, P.A. (1984) 'Zamyatin and the nightmare of technology (Zamyatine et le cauchemar de la technologie)', *Science Fiction Studies*, 11(2): 122–9.

McIndoe, P. (2023) 'Birds aren't real? How a conspiracy takes flight', *TED* [video]. Available from: https://www.youtube.com/watch?v=3VEkzweBJPM [Accessed 11 November 2024].

McNeill, F. (2019) 'Mass supervision, misrecognition and the "Malopticon"', *Punishment & Society*, 21(2): 207–30.

Meacham, T. (2019) 'I, Pastafari: we all have something to learn from the Church of the Flying Spaghetti Monster', *The Conversation*, 18 October. Available from: https://theconversation.com/i-pastafari-we-all-have-something-to-learn-from-the-church-of-the-flying-spaghetti-monster-124035 [Accessed 11 November 2024].

Mehta, D., Siddiqui, M.F.H. and Javaid, A.Y. (2018) 'Facial emotion recognition: a survey and real-world user experiences in mixed reality', *Sensors*, 18(2): 416.

Mejias, U.A. and Couldry, N. (2024) *Data Grab: The New Colonialism of Big Tech and How to Fight Back*. Chicago: University of Chicago Press.

Melossi, D. (2003) '"In a peaceful life": migration and the crime of modernity in Europe/Italy', *Punishment & Society*, 5(4): 371–97.

Melossi, D. (2008) *Controlling Crime, Controlling Society*. Cambridge: Polity Press.

Merchant, B. (2017) *The One Device: The Secret History of the iPhone*. Boston, MA: Little Brown.

Merrin, W. and Hoskins, A. (2024) 'Sharded war: seeing, not sharing', *Digi War*, 5: 115–18.

Metz, R. and Thorbecke, C. (2022) 'What we learned from Mark Zuckerberg's 3-hour chat with Joe Rogan', CNN, 26 August. Available from: https://edition.cnn.com/2022/08/26/tech/mark-zuckerberg-joe-rogan-interview/index.html [Accessed 6 December 2024].

Mihailidis, P. and Viotty, S. (2017) 'Spreadable spectacle in digital culture: civic expression, fake news, and the role of media literacies in "post-fact" society', *American Behavioral Scientist*, 61(4): 441–54.

Milivojevic, S. (2021) *Crime and Punishment in the Future Internet: Digital Frontier Technologies and Criminology in the Twenty-First Century*, Abingdon: Routledge, pp 1–135.

Miller, M.E. (2021) 'The Pizzagate gunman is out of prison: conspiracy theories are out of control', *The Seattle Times*, [online] 16 February. Available from: https://www.seattletimes.com/nation-world/the-pizzagate-gunman-is-out-of-prison-conspiracy-theories-are-out-of-control/ [Accessed 17 March 2025].

Miller, M.E. (2022) 'The "Pizzagate" gunman is out of prison: conspiracy theories are out of control', *The Seattle Times*, [online] 7 January. Available from: https://www.seattletimes.com/nation-world/the-pizzagate-gunman-is-out-of-prison-conspiracy-theories-are-out-of-control/ [Accessed 24 November 2024].

Milmo, D. (2024) '"Godfather of AI" shortens odds of the technology wiping out humanity over next 30 years', *The Guardian*, 27 December. Available from: https://www.theguardian.com/technology/2024/dec/27/godfather-of-ai-raises-odds-of-the-technology-wiping-out-humanity-over-next-30-years?utm_term=676fb12fcf3e898217716816d54426a0&utm_campaign=SaturdayEdition&utm_source=esp&utm_medium=Email&CMP=saturdayedition_email [Accessed 27 December 2024].

Mir, A. (2023) 'Malinformation and the wrong truth', *Discourse Magazine*, [online] 16 March. Available from: https://www.discoursemagazine.com/p/malinformation-and-the-wrong-truth [Accessed 13 March 2025].

Montgomery, B. (2024) 'Zuckerberg Augustus: Meta's emperor rebrands in new clothes', *The Guardian*, 28 September. Available from: https://www.theguardian.com/technology/2024/sep/28/mark-zuckeberg-revamps-public-image-style [Accessed 10 December 2024].

Morelock, J. and Narita, FZ (2021) 'A dialectical constellation of authoritarian populism in the United States and Brazil', in J. Morelock (ed) *How to Critique Authoritarian Populism: Methodologies of the Frankfurt School*. Leiden: Brill, pp 85–107.

Morelock, J. and Narita, F.Z. (2022) 'The nexus of QAnon and COVID-19: legitimation crisis and epistemic crisis', *Critical Sociology*, 2022(6): 1005–24.

Morrison, S. (2022) 'Amazon's Ring privacy problem is back', *Vox*, 14 July. Available from: https://www.vox.com/recode/23207072/amazon-ring-privacy-police-footage [Accessed 9 December 2024].

de Nadal, L. (2024) 'Climate change: bad news for populism? How the rassemblement national used COVID-19 to promote its environmental agenda', *Nationalities Papers*, 52(2): 414–29.

Nadel, L. and Wiener, H. (1977) 'Would you sell a computer to Hitler?', *Computer Decisions*, 9(2): 22–6.

Nagle, A. (2017) *Kill All Normies: The Online Culture Wars from Tumblr and 4chan to the Alt-Right and Trump*. Winchester: Zero Books.

Najibi, A. (2020) 'Racial discrimination in face recognition technology', *Harvard Science Policy Blog*. Available from: https://projects.iq.harvard.edu/sciencepolicy/blog/racial-discrimination-face-recognition-technology [Accessed 13 March 2025].

Nasywa, N. (2023) 'The psychology of scrolling: why we can't stop and its effect on mental health', *Medium*, 21 July. Available from: https://medium.com/@namiranasywa/the-psychology-of-scrolling-why-we-cant-stop-and-its-effect-on-mental-health-80b88287f621 [Accessed 10 December 2024].

Naughton, J. (2013) 'Jaron Lanier: the digital pioneer who became a web rebel – interview', *The Guardian*, 17 March. Available from: https://www.theguardian.com/technology/2013/mar/17/jaron-lanier-digital-pioneer-rebel [Accessed 10 December 2024].

Negro, G. and Hu, L. (2022) 'WeChat as a digital bridge for the Chinese community in Italy? The use of social media during the first wave of COVID-19', in *WeChat and the Chinese Diaspora: Digital Transnationalism in the Era of China's Rise*, Abingdon: Routledge, pp 79–94.

Nellis, M. (2013) 'Surveillance-based compliance using electronic monitoring', in P. Ugwudike and P. Raynor (eds) *What Works in Offender Compliance*. Cham: Springer, pp 143–64.

Nellis, S. and Chmielewski, D. (2024) 'Vision Pro headset is Apple's next Mac and TV combined', Reuters, 3 February. Available from: https://www.reuters.com/technology/vision-pro-headset-is-apples-next-mac-tv-combined-2024-02-03/ [Accessed 10 December 2024].

Nelson, M.K. and Garey, A.I. (2009) *Who's Watching? Daily Practices of Surveillance among Contemporary Families*. Nashville: Vanderbilt University Press.

Nevett, J. (2023) 'Prevent: rise in climate activists referred to anti-terror scheme', BBC News. Available from: https://www.bbc.co.uk/news/uk-67665218 [Accessed 12 March 2025].

Nguyen, M.H. (2021) 'Managing social media use in an "always-on" society: exploring digital wellbeing strategies that people use to disconnect', *Mass Communication and Society*, 24(6): 795–817.

Nietzsche, F. (2007) *On the Genealogy of Morality*. Ed. K. Ansell-Pearson, trans. C. Diethe. Cambridge: Cambridge University Press.

Nissenbaum, H. (2009) *Privacy in Context: Technology, Policy, and the Integrity of Social Life*. Stanford, CA: Stanford University Press.

Nolan, H. (2023) 'A world in which your boss spies on your brainwaves? That future is near', *The Guardian*, 9 February. Available from: https://www.theguardian.com/commentisfree/2023/feb/09/boss-spies-brainwaves-dystopian-future [Accessed 24 November 2024].

Novak, M. (2017) 'Elon Musk launches mystery website, X.com', *Gizmodo*, 14 July. Available from: https://gizmodo.com/elon-musk-launches-mystery-website-x-com-1796911047 [Accessed 8 December 2024].

Nyce, C.M. (2024) 'Google wins the gold medal for worst Olympic ad', *The Atlantic*, 30 July. Available from: https://www.theatlantic.com/technology/archive/2024/07/google-dear-sydney-olympic-ad/679292/ [Accessed 28 December 2024].

Nyrhinen, J., Lonka, K., Sirola, A., Ranta, M. and Wilska, T.-A. (2023) 'Young adults' online shopping addiction: the role of self-regulation and smartphone use', *International Journal of Consumer Studies*, 47(5): 1871–84.

Odgen, L.E. (2020) 'Training facial recognition on some new furry friends: bears'. *The New York Times*, 11 November. Available from: https://www.nytimes.com/2020/11/11/science/bears-facial-recognition.html [Accessed 25 December 2024].

Ofcom (2024) 'Tech firms must tame toxic algorithms to protect children online', Ofcom, 8 May. Available from: https://www.ofcom.org.uk/online-safety/protecting-children/tech-firms-must-tame-toxic-algorithms-to-protect-children-online [Accessed 28 November 2024].

Ogawa, Y. (2020) *The Memory Police*. London: Harvill Secker.

O'Hagan, J., Gugenheimer, J., Mathis, F., Bonner, J., Jones, R. and McGill, M. (2024) 'A viewpoint on the societal impact of everyday augmented reality and the need for perceptual human rights', *IEEE Security and Privacy*, 22(1): 64–8.

Olumhense, E. (2023) 'Axon's ethics board resigned over taser-armed drones. then the company bought a military drone maker'. *The Markup*, 8 September. Available from: https://themarkup.org/2023/09/08/axons-ethics-board-resigned-over-taser-armed-drones-then-the-company-bought-a-military-drone-maker [Accessed 25 December 2024].

O'Neill, S. (2023) 'Sizing down to scale up: how Amazon reworked its fulfillment network to meet customer demand', *Amazon Science*, [online]. Available from: https://www.amazon.science/news-and-features/how-amazon-reworked-its-fulfillment-network-to-meet-customer-demand [Accessed 29 November 2024].

Ong, R. (2012) 'Online vigilante justice Chinese style and privacy in China', *Information & Communications Technology Law*, 21(2): 127–45.

Orlowski, J. (Director) (2020) *The Social Dilemma*. Netflix.

O'Sullivan, F. and Bliss, L. (2020) 'Paris's 15-minute city could be coming to an urban area near you', *Bloomberg*, 12 November. Available from: https://www.bloomberg.com/news/features/2020-11-12/paris-s-15-minute-city-could-be-coming-to-an-urban-area-near-you [Accessed 24 November 2024].

Packard, V.O. (1957) *The Hidden Persuaders*. London: Longmans, Green.

Pagallo, U. (2015) 'Good Onlife governance: on law, spontaneous orders, and design', in L. Floridi (ed) *The Onlife Manifesto*. Cham: Springer.

Pali, B. and Schuilenburg, M. (2020) 'Fear and fantasy in the smart city', *Crit Crim,* 28: 775–88.

Paris, B. and Donovan, J. (2019) 'Deepfakes and cheap fakes', Data & Society Research Institute. Available from: https://datasociety.net/library/deepfakes-and-cheap-fakes/ [Accessed 16 July 2024].

Pariser, E. (2011) *The Filter Bubble: What the Internet Is Hiding from You*, New York: Penguin Press.

Parmigiani, G. (2021) 'Magic and politics: conspirituality and COVID-19', *Journal of the American Academy of Religion*, 89(2): 506–29.

Partington, R. (2023) 'Tackling the 15-minute cities conspiracy means fixing inequality', *The Guardian*, [online]. Available from: https://www.theguardian.com/business/2023/feb/26/uk-economic-uncertainty-adds-fuel-to-fire-for-conspiracy-theorists [Accessed 20 December 2024].

Pasquale, F. (2015) *The Black Box Society: The Secret Algorithms That Control Money and Information*, Cambridge, MA: Harvard University Press.

Pearson, J. (2024) 'A crowd attacked a Waymo self-driving car and set it on fire', *Vice*, 12 February. Available from: https://www.vice.com/en/article/3akeev/a-crowd-attacked-a-waymo-self-driving-car-and-set-it-on-fire [Accessed 11 November 2024].

Pemberton, S. (2015) *Harmful Societies: Understanding Social Harm*. Bristol: Policy Press.

Perlroth, N. (2021) *This Is How They Tell Me the World Ends: The Cyberweapons Arms Race*. London: Bloomsbury.

Phelan, S. (2019) 'Neoliberalism, the far right, and the disparaging of "social justice warriors"', *Communication, Culture and Critique*, 12(4): 455–75.

Pizzorno, A. (2005) 'Saggio sulla maschera', *Studi culturali, Rivista quadrimestrale*, 1: 85–110.

Plantin, J.-C. and de Seta, G. (2019) 'WeChat as infrastructure: the techno-nationalist shaping of Chinese digital platforms', *Chinese Journal of Communication*, 12(3): 257–73.

Poon, L. (2024) 'Paris to replace parking with trees in new climate plan', Bloomberg, 18 November. https://www.bloomberg.com/news/newsletters/2024-11-18/paris-to-replace-parking-with-trees-in-new-climate-plan-citylab-daily [Accessed 9 December 2024].

Postman, A. (2017) 'My dad predicted Trump in 1985 – it's not Orwell, he warned, it's Brave New World', *The Guardian*. Available from: https://www.theguardian.com/media/2017/feb/02/amusing-ourselves-to-death-neil-postman-trump-orwell-huxley [Accessed 11 November 2024].

Qiu, J.L. (2016) *Goodbye iSlave: A Manifesto for Digital Abolition*. Urbana-Champaign: University of Illinois Press.

Rabinow, P. (1996) 'Artificiality and englightenment: from sociobiology to biosociality', in *Essays on the Anthropology of Reason*. Princeton, NJ: Princeton University Press, pp 91–111.

Rabinow, P. (2017) 'Artificiality and enlightenment: from sociobiology to biosociality', in *The Ethics of Biotechnology*, Abingdon: Routledge, pp 101–22.

Rauda Zablah, N. (2022) 'The inside story of how El Salvador's official crypto wallet crashed and failed', *El Faro*, [online] 15 December. Available from: https://elfaro.net/en/202212/el_salvador/26601/The-Inside-Story-of-How-El-Salvador%E2%80%99s-Official-Crypto-Wallet-Crashed-and-Failed.htm [Accessed 29 November 2024].

Redden, J. (2018) 'The harm that data do', *Scientific American*, 319(5): 76.

Redstone, I. (2020) 'Many people don't care about what's true anymore. That's dangerous', *Forbes*, 20 July. Available from: https://www.forbes.com/sites/ilanaredstone/2020/07/20/many-people-dont-care-about-whats-true-anymore-thats-dangerous/ [Accessed 11 November 2024].

Reid, L. (2021) 'Home as riskscape: Exploring technology enabled care', *Geographical Journal*, 187: 85–97.

Renshaw, D. (2013) 'Thom Yorke labels Spotify "The last desperate fart of a dying corpse"', *NME*, [online] 4 October. Available from: https://www.nme.com/news/music/radiohead-154-1246066 [Accessed 29 November 2024].

Renteria, N. (2020) 'China signs on for gigantic investment in El Salvador infrastructure', Reuters, [online]. Available from: https://www.reuters.com/article/markets/china-signs-on-for-gigantic-investment-in-el-salvador-infrastructure-idUSL1N28E00J/ [Accessed 29 November 2024].

Reuters (2016) 'Italian tourist shot dead after entering Rio slum on motorcycle', Reuters, 19 December. Available from: https://www.reuters.com/article/world/italian-tourist-shot-dead-after-entering-rio-slum-on-motorcycle-idUSKBN13X2KH/ [Accessed 6 December 2024].

Reuters (2023) 'Crypto's role in terrorist financing'. Reuters, [online] 23 October. Available from: https://www.reuters.com/technology/cryptos-role-terrorist-financing-2023-10-23/ [Accessed 29 November 2024].

Reuters (2024) 'Musk's SpaceX is building spy satellite network for US intelligence agency – sources', *Reuters,* 16 March. Available from: https://www.reuters.com/technology/space/musks-spacex-is-building-spy-satellite-network-us-intelligence-agency-sources-2024-03-16/ [Accessed 11 November 2024].

Rigotti, A. (2024) 'Nine Inch Nails' Trent Reznor says streaming has "mortally wounded" many artists: "It's great if you're Drake, it's not great if you're Grizzly Bear"', *NME*, 7 April. Available from: https://www.nme.com/news/music/nine-inch-nails-trent-reznor-says-streaming-has-mortally-wounded-many-artists-its-great-if-youre-drake-its-not-great-if-youre-3614437 [Accessed 10 December 2024].

Ritzer, G. (1983) 'The "McDonaldization" of society', *Journal of American Culture*, 6(1): 100–7.

Rodotà, S. (2014) *Il mondo nella rete. Quali i diritti, quali i vincoli*. Rome: Laterza.

Rooney, T. (2010) 'Trusting children: how do you surveillance technology is alter a child experience of trust, risk and responsibility', *Surveillance and Society,* 7(3/4): 344–55.

Roose, K. (2019) 'Maybe only Tim Cook can fix Facebook's privacy problem', *The New York Times,* 30 January. Available from: https://www.nytimes.com/2019/01/30/technology/facebook-privacy-apple-tim-cook.html [Accessed 6 December 2024].

Rose, N. (2000) 'The biology of culpability: pathological identity and crime control in a biological culture', *Theoretical Criminology*, 4(1): 5–34.

Rotman, D. (2013) 'How technology is destroying jobs', *MIT Technology Review*, [online]. Available from: https://www.technologyreview.com/2013/06/12/178008/how-technology-is-destroying-jobs/ [Accessed 29 November 2024].

Rotman, E. (2000) 'The globalization of criminal violence', *Cornell Journal of Law and Public Policy*, 10(1): 1–43.

Salanti, A., Malighetti, P. and Redondi, R. (2012) 'Low-cost pricing strategies in leisure markets', *Tourism Management*, 33(2): 249–56.

Salkin, A. (2009) 'For him, the web was no safety net', *The New York Times*, 28 August. Available from: https://www.nytimes.com/2009/08/30/fashion/30harris.html [Accessed 9 December 2024].

Salter M. (2016) 'Privates in the online public: sex(ting) and reputation on social media', *New Media & Society*, 18(11): 2723–39.

Salter, M. (2018) 'From geek masculinity to Gamergate: the technological rationality of online abuse', *Crime, Media, Culture*, 14(2): 247–64.

Sampson, F. (2021) 'If you've done nothing wrong: 5 reasons why this is no defence for surveillance', Video Surveillance Blog, [online]. Available from: https://videosurveillance.blog.gov.uk/2021/05/27/if-youve-done-nothing-wrong-5-reasons-why-this-is-no-defence-for-surveillance/ [Accessed 21 November 2024].

Sánchez, C.M. (2000) 'Motives for corporate philanthropy in El Salvador: altruism and political legitimacy', *Journal of Business Ethics*, 27(4): 363–75.

Sankin, A., Mehrotra, D., Mattu, S. and Gilbertson, A. (2021) 'Crime prediction software promised to be free of biases. new data shows it perpetuates them', *The Markup*, 2 December. Available from: https://themarkup.org/prediction-bias/2021/12/02/crime-prediction-software-promised-to-be-free-of-biases-new-data-shows-it-perpetuates-them [Accessed 11 November 2024].

Schick, N. (2020) *Deep Fakes and the Infocalypse: What You Urgently Need to Know*. London: Hachette.

Schill, D. (2014) 'Astroturfing', in K. Harvey (ed) *Encyclopedia of Social Media and Politics*. Thousand Oaks, CA: Sage Publications, pp 383–5.

Schuilenburg, M. and Peeters, R. (2018) 'Smart cities and the architecture of security: pastoral power and the scripted design of public space', *City, Territory and Architecture*, 5(1): 1–9.

Schuster, D. (2014) 'The revolt against Google "Glassholes"', *New York Post*, 14 July. Available from: https://nypost.com/2014/07/14/is-google-glass-cool-or-just-plain-creepy/ [Accessed 17 March 2025].

Seddon, M. (2023) 'Gleb Pavlovsky, Russian spin doctor, 1951–2023', *Financial Times*, 11 March, [online]. Available from: https://www.ft.com/content/9a101862-7f39-4894-9bf6-ac0636f2e08f [Accessed 18 December 2024].

Selyukh, A. and Domonoske, C. (2016) 'Apple, the FBI, and iPhone encryption: a look at what's at stake', *NPR*, 17 February. Available from: https://www.npr.org/sections/thetwo-way/2016/02/17/467096705/apple-the-fbi-and-iphone-encryption-a-look-at-whats-at-stake [Accessed 9 December 2024].

Serres, M. (2012) *Thumbelina* (2015 edn). Lanham, MD: Rowman & Littlefield.

Serres, M. (2018) *Contro i bei tempi andati*. Turin: Bollati Boringhieri.

Shariff, S. (2014) *Sexting and Cyberbullying*. Cambridge: Cambridge University Press.

Shearing, C. and Stenning, P. (1985) 'From the Panopticon to Disneyworld: the development of discipline', in A. Doob and E. Greenspan (eds) *Perspectives in Criminal Law: Essays in Honour of John Ll. J. Edwards*. Ontario: Aurora, pp 335–49.

Shen, L. (2017) 'The truth about whether airlines jack up prices if you keep searching the same flight', *Time*, 18 September, [online]. Available from: https://time.com/4899508/flight-search-history-price/ [Accessed 29 November 2024].

Silverman, M. (2019) 'Review of P.W. Singer and Emerson T. Brooking's *LikeWar: The Weaponization of Social Media*', *International Review of the Red Cross*, 101(910): 383–7.

Simmel, G. (2012) 'The fragmentary character of life', *Theory, Culture & Society*, 29(7–8): 237–48.

Simon, F.M., Altay, S. and Mercier, H. (2023) 'Misinformation reloaded: fears about the impact of generative AI on misinformation are overblown', *Misinformation Review*, 18 October. Available from: https://misinforeview.hks.harvard.edu/article/misinformation-reloaded-fears-about-the-impact-of-generative-ai-on-misinformation-are-overblown/ [Accessed 11 November 2024].

Simon, J. and Ess, C. (2015) 'The ONLIFE initiative – a concept reengineering exercise', *Philosophy and Technology*, 28(1): 157–62.

Singer, P.W. and Brooking, E.T. (2018) *LikeWar: The Weaponization of Social Media*. New York: Mariner Books.

Skinner, B.F. (1948) *Walden Two*. New York: Macmillan.

Skinner B.F. (1983) *A Matter of Consequences*. New York: Alfred A. Knopf, Inc.

Smith, G.J.D. (2015) *Opening the Black Box: The Work of Watching*. London: Routledge.

Snyder, C. (2022) 'AirTag stalking concerns raised around Baylor campus', *Baylor Lariat*, 17 March.

Solzhenitsyn, A.I. (2009) *In the First Circle: A Novel, the Restored Text*. New York: Harper Perennial.

Sommerlad, J. (2024) 'Taylor Swift conspiracy theory claims her support for Biden was a "psyop"', *The Independent*, [online]. Available from: https://www.independent.co.uk/news/world/americas/us-politics/taylor-swift-biden-psyop-conspiracy-b2489364.html [Accessed 2 February 2024].

Sonavane, N. (2023) 'Deconstructing police discretion as Brahminism', *Socio-Legal Review*, 19(1): 52.

Søraa, R.A. and Vik, J. (2021) 'Boundaryless boundary-objects: digital fencing of the CyborGoat in rural Norway', *Journal of Rural Studies*, 87: 23–31.

Sorkin, A. (Director) (2017) *Molly's Game*. STX Entertainment.

Southall, A. (2019) 'Alleged mob boss killer believed he was aiding Trump, lawyer says', *The New York Times*, 17 March. Available from: https://www.nytimes.com/2019/03/17/nyregion/anthony-comello-frank-cali.html [Accessed 17 March 2025].

Sprenger, P. (1999) 'Sun on privacy: 'Get over it', *Wired*, 28 January. Available from: http://www.wired.com/politics/law/news/1999/01/17538 [Accessed 17 March 2025].

Srinivasan, R. and IlamParithi, V. (2018) 'A study on interpersonal surveillance on social media using WhatsApp', *International Journal of Research in Engineering, IT and Social Sciences*, 8(5): 58.

Stavola, F. De (2020) 'Potere, controllo e soggettività nelle piattaforme digitali di food delivery: un'analisi foucaultiana dell'app latinoamericana Rappi', *Sociologia Del Lavoro*, 158: 178–98.

Steeves, V. and Jones, O. (2010) 'Editorial: surveillance and children', *Surveillance & Society*, 7(3): 187–91.

Stephenson, N. (1992) *Snow Crash*. New York: Bantam.

Stevenson, R.L. (2014 [1886]) *Dr Jekyll and Mr Hyde*. New York: Simon and Schuster.

Stille, Alexander (2006) *The Sack of Rome: Media + Money + Celebrity = Power = Silvio Berlusconi*. London: Penguin.

Stone, B. (2014) *The Everything Store: Jeff Bezos and the Age of Amazon*. New York: Back Bay Books.

Stratton, G., Powell, A. and Cameron, R. (2017) 'Crime and justice in digital society: towards a "digital criminology"?', *International Journal for Crime, Justice and Social Democracy*, 6(2): 17–33.

Strittmatter, K., (2020) *We Have Been Harmonized: Life in China's Surveillance State*. New York: Custom House.

Summers, T.C. (2018) 'Facebook is killing democracy with its personality profiling data', *The Conversation*, 21 March. Available from: https://theconversation.com/facebook-is-killing-democracy-with-its-personality-profiling-data-93611 [Accessed 6 December 2024].

Sumsion, A., Torrie, S., Lee, D. and Sun, Z. (2024) 'Surveying racial bias in facial recognition: balancing datasets and algorithmic enhancements', *Electronics*, 13(12): 2317.

Sunderland, M. (2016) 'Can't shake it off: how Taylor Swift became a Nazi idol', *Vice*, May 23. Available from: https://www.vice.com/en/article/cant-shake-it-off-how-taylor-swift-became-a-nazi-idol [Accessed 9 December 2024].

Surowiecki, J. (2004) *The Wisdom of Crowds: Why the Many Are Smarter than the Few and How Collective Wisdom Shapes Business, Economies, Societies, and Nations*, London: Abacus, p 296.

Sweeny, J. (2018) 'Incitement in the era of Trump and Unite the Right', *SSRN Electronic Journal* [Preprint]. Available from: https://doi.org/10.2139/SSRN.3254500

Szakolczai, J.M. (2021) '"What have you caught?" Nannycams and hidden cameras as normalised surveillance of the intimate', in P. O'Connor and M.I. Bența (eds) *The Technologisation of the Social*. Abingdon: Routledge, pp 139–52.

Szakolczai, J.M. (2023) 'Exiting the captaverse: digital resistance and its limits pre and post the Covid-19 pandemic', *Criminology & Criminal Justice*, July.

Taffel, S. (2022) 'AirPods and the earth: digital technologies, planned obsolescence and the Capitalocene', *Environment and Planning E: Nature and Space*, 6(1): 433–54.

Táíwò, O.O. (2022) *Elite Capture: How the Powerful Took Over Identity Politics (and Everything Else)*. London: Pluto Press.

Talesnik D. (2021) 'Privacy in a pandemic: Oxford professor explores ethics of contact tracing', *NIH Record*, 5 February, LXXII(3). Available from: https://nihrecord.nih.gov/2021/02/05/oxford-professor-explores-ethics-contact-tracing [Accessed 11 March 2025].

Tanczer, L.M. (2023) 'Technology-facilitated abuse and the Internet of Things (IoT): the implication of the smart, internet-connected devices on domestic violence and abuse', in B. Harris and D. Woodlock (eds) *Technology and Domestic and Family Violence: Victimisation, Perpetration and Responses*. Abingdon: Routledge, pp 76–87.

Taplin, J.T. (2017) *Move Fast and Break Things: How Facebook, Google, and Amazon Cornered Culture and Undermined Democracy*. London: Little Brown.

Tarkovsky, A. (Director) (1979) *Stalker*. Film. Soviet Union: Mosfilm.

Taylor, A. (2024a) 'Jelqing: the latest in a long history of attempts to enlarge the male member', *The Conversation*, 15 February. Available from: https://theconversation.com/jelqing-the-latest-in-a-long-history-of-attempts-to-enlarge-the-male-member-222634 [Accessed 6 December 2024].

Taylor, E. (2024b) 'A timeline of the conspiracy theories surrounding Kate Middleton', *Vogue*, [online]. Available from: https://www.vogue.co.uk/article/kate-middleton-conspiracy-theories-timeline [Accessed 21 November 2024].

Teachout, Z. (2024) 'Ending Big Tech's child exploitation', *Compact Magazine*, 7 June. Available from: https://www.compactmag.com/article/ending-big-techs-child-exploitation/ [Accessed 11 November 2024].

Thomas, J. (2024) 'No, Iran has not started attacking Tel Aviv', Euronews, 11 April. https://www.euronews.com/my-europe/2024/04/11/no-iran-has-not-started-attacking-tel-aviv [Accessed 17 March 2025].

Threadgold, S. (2019) 'Figures of youth: on the very object of Youth Studies', *Journal of Youth Studies*, 23(6): 686–701.

Tokunaga, R.S. (2011) 'Social networking site or social surveillance site? Understanding the use of interpersonal electronic surveillance in romantic relationships', *Computers in Human Behavior*, 27(2): 705–13.

Tolliver, C. (1999) 'X.com opens its virtual doors: new wave for financial services?', CBS MarketWatch, [online] 10 December. Available from: https://www.marketwatch.com/story/xcom-opens-its-virtual-doors [Accessed 29 November 2024].

Torpey, J. (2020) 'A sociological agenda for the tech age', *Theory and Society*, 49: 749–69.

Trottier, S. (2015) *Social Media as Surveillance*. New York: Taylor & Francis.

Tsai, W.T. (2020) 'Recycling Waste Electrical and Electronic Equipment (WEEE) and the management of its toxic substances in Taiwan: a case study', *Toxics*, 8(3): 48.

Turkle, S. (2005) *The Second Self: Computers and the Human Spirit* (20th anniversary, 1st MIT Press edn). Cambridge, MA: MIT Press.

Turkle, S. (2011) *Alone Together: Why We Expect More from Technology and Less from Each Other*. New York: Basic Books.

Turkle, S. (2023) 'Always-on/always-on-you: the tethered self', in W. Longhofer and D. Windchester (eds) *Social Theory Re-Wired*. Abingdon: Routledge, pp 485–5.

Turnbull, A. (2022) 'Onlife harms: Uber and sexual violence', *Canadian Journal of Law & Technology*, 19(2). Available from: https://papers.ssrn.com/abstract=4013857 [Accessed 18 July 2024].

United Nations (2022) 'China Responsible for 'Serious Human Rights Violations' in Xinjiang Province', UN Human Rights Report. *United Nations News*, [online] 31 August. Available from: https://news.un.org/en/story/2022/08/1125932 [Accessed 13 November 2024].

Vaidhyanathan, S. (2008) 'Naked in the "Nonopticon"', *The Chronicle of Higher Education*, [online] 15 February. Available from: https://www.chronicle.com/article/naked-in-the- nonopticon/?cid2=gen_login_refresh&cid=gen_sign_in [Accessed 17 March 2025].

Vaidhyanathan, S. (2018) *Antisocial Media: How Facebook Disconnects Us and Undermines Democracy*. Oxford: Oxford University Press.

Valentini, D., Lorusso, A.M. and Stephan, A. (2020) 'Onlife extremism: dynamic integration of digital and physical spaces in radicalization', *Frontiers in Psychology*, 11: 524.

Van Brakel, R. and Govaerts, L. (2024) 'Exploring the impact of algorithmic policing on social justice: developing a framework for rhizomatic harm in the pre-crime society', *Theoretical Criminology*, 29(1): 91–109.

Van Den Bulck, H. and Hyzen, A. (2020) 'Of lizards and ideological entrepreneurs: Alex Jones and Infowars in the relationship between populist nationalism and the post-global media ecology', *International Communication Gazette*, 82(1): 42–59.

van Dijck, J. (2014) 'Datafication, dataism and dataveillance: Big Data between scientific paradigm and ideology', *Surveillance & Society*, 12(2): 197–208.

Veltman, C. (2023) 'Worried about AI hijacking your voice for a deepfake? This tool could help', *NPR*, 13 November. Available from: https://www.npr.org/2023/11/13/1211679937/ai-deepfake [Accessed 6 December 2024].

Verdery, K. (2014) *Police, Secrets and Truth: Ethnography in the Archive of Romania's Secret*. Budapest: Central European University Press.

Vervaet, F.J. (2019) 'Mark Zuckerberg's admiration for Emperor Augustus is misplaced – here's why', *The Conversation*, 2 January. Available from: https://theconversation.com/mark-zuckerbergs-admiration-for-emperor-augustus-is-misplaced-heres-why-108172 [Accessed 10 December 2024].

Virilio, P. (1998) *The Information Bomb*. London: Verso.

Virilio, P. (2000) *Polar Inertia*. London: Sage.

Waddell, K. (2021) 'When Amazon expands, these communities pay the price', *The Guardian*, 9 December. Available from: https://www.theguardian.com/us-news/2021/dec/09/when-amazon-expands-these-communities-pay-the-price [Accessed 18 April 2025].

Wagner, J.A. (2023) *Making a Metaverse That Matters: From Snow Crash & Second Life to A Virtual World Worth Fighting For*. Chichester: Wiley.

Waite, S. (2020) 'We Live in Public: the story of Josh Harris, a delusional visionary', *Medium*, 15 March. Available from: https://medium.com/im310-sp20-social-media/we-live-in-public-the-story-of-josh-harris-a-delusional-visionary-df659d6b1f5e [Accessed 18 November 2024].

Wall, D.S. (2008) 'Cybercrime and the culture of fear', *Information, Communication & Society*, 11(6): 861–84.

Wang, Y. (2020) 'In China, the "Great Firewall" is changing a generation', *Politico*, 1 September. Available from: https://www.hrw.org/news/2020/09/01/china-great-firewall-changing-generation [Accessed 10 December 2024].

Wardle, C. (2019) 'Misinformation has created a new world disorder', *Scientific American*, [online] 1 September. Available from: https://www.scientificamerican.com/article/misinformation-has-created-a-new-world-disorder/ [Accessed 19 December 2024].

Wardle, C. and Derakhshan, H. (2017) *Information Disorder: Toward an Interdisciplinary Framework for Research and Policy Making*. Strasbourg: Council of Europe

Warofka, A. (2018) 'An independent assessment of the human rights impact of Facebook in Myanmar', Facebook Newsroom, 5 November. Available from: https://about.fb.com/news/2018/11/myanmar-hria/ [Accessed 6 December 2024].

Warzel, C. (2023) 'The rise of AI photo editing is making it harder to trust smartphone images', *The Atlantic*, 3 October. Available from: https://www.theatlantic.com/technology/archive/2023/10/smartphone-camera-ai-photo-editing-fakery/675710/ [Accessed 11 March 2025].

Warzel, C. (2024a) 'I'm running out of ways to explain how bad this is: what's happening in America today is something darker than a misinformation crisis', *The Atlantic*, 10 October. Available from: https://www.theatlantic.com/technology/archive/2024/10/hurricane-milton-conspiracies-misinformation/680221/?utm_source=chatgpt.com [Accessed 30 July 2024].

Warzel, C. (2024b) 'Evidence maximalism' is how the internet argues now', *The Atlantic,* 9 February. Available from: https://www.theatlantic.com/technology/archive/2024/02/evidence-maximalism-conspiracy-theories-taylor-swift/677390/ [Accessed 17 March 2025].

Waters, J. (2021) 'Constant craving: how digital media turned us all into dopamine addicts', *The Guardian*, 22 August. Available from: https://www.theguardian.com/global/2021/aug/22/how-digital-media-turned-us-all-into-dopamine-addicts-and-what-we-can-do-to-break-the-cycle [Accessed 10 December 2024].

Whelan, E., Laato, S. and Najmul Islam, A.K.M. and Billieux, J. (2021) 'A casino in my pocket: gratifications associated with obsessive and harmonious passion for mobile gambling', *PLoS ONE*, 16(2): e0246432.

Whitehead, A.N. (1929) *The Function of Reason*. Princeton, NJ: Princeton University Press.

Wiens, K. (2011) 'Apple's diabolical plan to screw your iPhone', iFixit, [online] 20 January. Available from: https://www.ifixit.com/News/14279/apples-diabolical-plan-to-screw-your-iphone [Accessed 29 November 2024].

Wikhamn, B.R. and Knights, D. (2016) 'Associations for disruptiveness: The Pirate Bay vs. Spotify', *Journal of Technology Management & Innovation*, 11(3): 40–9.

Williams, S.N. and Dienes, K. (2021) 'Public attitudes to COVID-19 vaccines: a qualitative study'. Available from: https://www.medrxiv.org/content/10.1101/2021.05.17.21257092v1

Wilson, E. (2012) 'Crimes against reality: parapolitics, simulation, power crime', in S. Hall and S. Winlow (eds) *New Directions in Criminological Theory*. Abingdon: Routledge.

Witley, S. (2023) 'Amazon, Microsoft deals on kids' data send warning to Big Tech', *Bloomberg Law*, 8 June. Available from: https://news.bloomberglaw.com/privacy-and-data-security/amazon-microsoft-deals-on-kids-data-enforce-ftcs-privacy-vow [Accessed 9 June 2023].

Wolchover, N. (2011) 'Ingenious 'flat earth' theory revealed in old map', *Live Science*, June 23. Available from: https://www.livescience.com/14754-ingenious-flat-earth-theory-revealed-map.html [Accessed 6 December 2024].

Wong, A. and Zheng, S. (2024) 'Top US envoy in Hong Kong warns of creeping internet curbs', *Bloomberg*, 1 March. Available from: https://www.bloomberg.com/news/articles/2024-03-01/us-envoy-warns-hong-kong-is-moving-to-china-style-internet-curbs [Accessed 10 December 2024].

Wong, V. (2024) 'E' il momento di costruire', Google Blog, [online] 26 January. Available from: https://blog.google/intl/it-it/e-il-momento-di-costruire/ [Accessed 18 December 2024].

Wood, M.A. (2018) *Antisocial Media: Crime-watching in the Internet Age*. London: Palgrave Macmillan.

Wood, M.A. (2022) 'Mapping technology-harm relations: from ambient harms to zemiosis', *Crime, Media, Culture*, 18(4): 509–26.

Wood, A.J., Graham, M., Lehdonvirta, V., and Hjorth, I. (2018) 'Good gig, bad gig: autonomy and algorithmic control in the global gig economy', *Work, Employment and Society*, 33(1), 56–75.

Woodcock, J. (2020) 'The algorithmic panopticon at Deliveroo: measurement, precarity, and the illusion of control', *Ephemera*, 20(3): 67–95.

Woodlock, D., Salter, M., Dragiewicz, M. and Harris, B. (2022) '"Living in the darkness": technology-facilitated coercive control, disenfranchised grief, and institutional betrayal', *Violence Against Women*, 29(5): 987–1004.

Woolley, S. (2023) *Manufacturing Consensus: Understanding Propaganda In The Era Of Automation And Anonymity*. Ne Haven, CT: Yale University Press. Available from: https://yalebooks.yale.edu/9780300251234/manufacturing-consensus [Accessed 16 July 2024].

Wrethed, J. (2022) 'Cancel culture and the trope of the scapegoat: a Girardian defense of the importance of contemplative reading', *Contagion: Journal of Violence Mimesis and Culture*, 29: 15–37.

Wu Ming 1 (2021) *Q for Qonspiracy: How Conspiracy Theories Defend the System* [*La Q di Qomplotto. QAnon e dintorni. Come le fantasie di complotto difendono il Sistema*]. Rome: Edizioni Alegre.

Yar, M. (2012) 'Critical criminology, critical theory and social harm', in S. Hall and S. Winlow (eds) *New Directions in Criminological Theory*. London: Routledge.

Yar, M. (2014) *The Cultural Imaginary of the Internet: Virtual Utopias and Dystopias*. London: Palgrave Macmillan.

Yarow, J. (2012) 'The bottom line: Apple really is going to try to kill Google', *Business Insider*, 11 June. Available from: https://www.businessinsider.com/apple-really-is-going-to-try-to-kill-google-2012-6 [Accessed 12 March 2025].

Youkee, M. (2021) 'El Salvador's bitcoin experiment goes live – as president offers tech support', *The Guardian*, [online] 7 September. Available from: https://www.theguardian.com/world/2021/sep/07/el-salvador-bitcoin-experiment-nayib-bukele [Accessed 29 November 2024].

Yu, H. (2022) 'Living in the era of codes: a reflection on China's health code system', *Biosocieties*, 19(1): 1–18.

Zhai, K., Zhu, J. and Leng, C. (2020) 'How billionaire Jack Ma fell to earth and took Ant's mega IPO with him', Reuters, [online] 5 November. Available from: https://www.reuters.com/article/idUSKBN27L2GW/ [Accessed 29 November 2024].

Ziccardi, G. (2015) '*Internet, Controllo e Libertà*'. Milan: Raffaello Cortina.

Ziccardi, G. (2019) '*Tecnologie per il Potere*'. Milan: Raffaele Cortina.

Žižek, S. (2022) 'Warum ich bei Russia Today veröffentlicht habe', *Berliner Zeitung*, [online] 8 May. Available from: https://www.berliner-zeitung.de/politik-gesellschaft/slavoj-zizek-warum-ich-weiterhin-bei-russia-today-veroeffentliche-li.226691 [Accessed 12 December 2024].

Zuboff, S. (2015) 'Big other: surveillance capitalism and the prospects of an information civilization', *Journal of Information Technology*, 30(1): 75–89.

Zuboff, S. (2019) *The Age of Surveillance Capitalism: The Fight for a Human Future at the New Frontier of Power*. London: Profile Books.

# Index